The Ethics of Doping and Anti-Doping

With every positive drugs test the credibility and veracity of modern elite sport are diminished. In this radical and provocative critique of current anti-doping policy and practice, Verner Møller argues that the fight against doping – promoted as an initiative to cleanse sport of cheats – is at heart nothing less than a battle to save sport from itself, located on the fault-line between the will to purity and the will to win.

Drawing on extensive and detailed case studies of doping in sport, and using a highly original blend of conceptual ideas from philosophy and sociology, Møller strongly criticises current anti-doping regimes and challenges our commonly held ideas about the nature of sport and the risks posed by drugs to health and fair play. He argues forcefully that we must understand the precarious position of the athlete and that only by containing coaches, doctors and drug companies within the anti-doping regime can we hope to ever make progress on this critical issue.

Written in a lively and engaging style, and skilfully blending empirical case studies with cutting-edge theory, *The Ethics of Doping and Anti-Doping* represents an important statement on the nature of sport, morality and modernity. It is essential reading for all serious students and scholars of the ethics, sociology and politics of sport.

Verner Møller is Professor of Sports Science at Aarhus University, Denmark. He is the co-ordinator of the International Network of Humanistic Doping Research (INHDR) and a leading expert on the cultural and philosophical aspects of doping.

Ethics and Sport

Series editors
Mike McNamee
University of Wales Swansea
Jim Parry
University of Leeds
Heather Reid
Morningside College

The Ethics and Sport series aims to encourage critical reflection on the practice of sport, and to stimulate professional evaluation and development. Each volume explores new work relating to philosophical ethics and the social and cultural study of ethical issues. Each is different in scope, appeal, focus and treatment but a balance is sought between local and international focus, perennial and contemporary issues, level of audience, teaching and research application, and variety of practical concerns.

Also available in this series:

Ethics and Sport
Edited by Mike McNamee and Jim Parry

Values in Sport
Elitism, nationalism, gender equality and the scientific manufacture of winners
Edited by Torbjörn Tännsjö and Claudio Tamburrini

Spoilsports
Understanding and preventing sexual exploitation in sport
Celia Brackenridge

Fair Play in Sport
A moral norm system
Sigmund Loland

Sport, Rules and Values
Philosophical investigations into the nature of sport
Graham McFee

Sport, Professionalism and Pain
Ethnographies of injury and risk
David Howe

Genetically Modified Athletes
Biomedical ethics, gene doping and sport
Andy Miah

Human Rights in Youth Sport
A critical review of children's rights in competitive sports
Paulo David

Genetic Technology and Sport
Ethical questions
Edited by Claudio Tamburrini and Torbjörn Tännsjö

Pain and Injury in Sport
Social and ethical analysis
Edited by Sigmund Loland, Berit Skirstad and Ivan Waddington

Ethics, Money and Sport
This sporting Mammon
Adrian Walsh and Richard Giulianotti

Ethics, Dis/Ability and Sports
Edited by Ejgil Jespersen and Michael McNamee

The Ethics of Doping and Anti-Doping
Redeeming the soul of sport?
Verner Møller

The Ethics of Doping and Anti-Doping

Redeeming the soul of sport?

Verner Møller

Routledge
Taylor & Francis Group

LONDON AND NEW YORK

First published 2010
by Routledge
2 Park Square, Milton Park, Abingdon, Oxon, OX14 4RN

Simultaneously published in the USA and Canada
by Routledge
270 Madison Avenue, New York, NY 10016

Routledge is an imprint of the Taylor & Francis Group, an informa business

© 2010 Verner Møller

Typeset in Goudy by Taylor & Francis Books
Printed and bound in Great Britain by TJ International Ltd, Padstow,
Cornwall

British Library Cataloguing in Publication Data
A catalogue record for this book is available from the British Library

Library of Congress Cataloging in Publication Data
A catalog record for this book has been requested

ISBN10: 0-415-48465-0 (hbk)
ISBN10: 0-415-48466-9 (pbk)
ISBN10: 0-203-87701-2 (ebk)

ISBN13: 978-0-415-48465-7 (hbk)
ISBN13: 978-0-415-48466-4 (pbk)
ISBN13: 978-0-203-87701-2 (ebk)

$39.95

Contents

	Acknowledgements	viii
	Introduction	1
1	What is doping?	4
2	What is sport?	13
3	Unchristian sport	22
4	Doping history: fact or fiction?	32
5	The law of silence	49
6	When good intentions turn bad	69
7	The fear of modernity	90
8	Legalisation of doping	107
9	The athletes' viewpoint	123
10	The need for a fresh start	136
	Appendix: Pro-Tour Teams' Code of Ethics	145
	Notes	148
	Bibliography	153
	Index	160

Acknowledgements

This book owes a debt of gratitude to a small number of important people. I owe my thanks to John Bale for a long, stimulating friendship and for prompting me to write this book; to John Hoberman, whom it has been my pleasure to have as a working and sparring partner during his many years as visiting professor to Denmark; to Mike McNamee and Jim Parry whose encouragement and support to make this book materialise have been invaluable; to PhD student Lise Joern, reader Carwyn Jones, and to my day-to-day fellow-researcher, Ask Vest Christiansen, who have been generous in their suggestions and critical comments on the manuscript; to my translator John Mason, whom I got to know and value in earnest during some intense working days at a writers' retreat in Skagen; to Claire Neesham for her scrupulous effort at the final stage of the preparation of the manuscript to make it a better read; and finally to commissioning editor, Simon Whitmore, who did not shy away from publishing a manuscript that deals with a rather controversial and inflammatory issue.

Finally, I owe a debt of thanks to the Ministry of Culture's Sports Research Committee, which provided financial support for the translation of the manuscript.

Verner Møller
Aarhus, 2009

Introduction

During the course of the twentieth century, science made huge strides in the field of medicine. The consumption of medicine increased immensely during the same period, and nothing points to any alteration in that trend in the twenty-first century. Quite the contrary, on top of the steady increase in the number of prescription drugs available and their potential users, there are also increasing numbers of people who look to medication as a means to overcome some physiological weakness or shortcoming. While doping as a modern phenomenon – in other words, since the mid-nineteenth century – has been narrowly related to sporting competition, it has today taken on an additional meaning. Body-builders who train solely with a view to becoming larger and stronger use anabolic steroids to promote muscle growth. Ever larger numbers of students suffering from exam anxiety have begun to use Betablockers to calm their nerves. Others take stimulants to fight jetlag or to enable them to study for longer periods without sinking into the arms of sleep (Sahakian and Morein-Zamir 2007).

Such forms of 'doping', although now widely discussed, are outside the scope of this book, which focuses on the use of doping in elite sport. Examples from cycling will take a prominent place, since cases of doping have been most frequent among athletes in this field – or at least most frequently reported – and where the pressure to put an end to the problem has been at its most extreme. Examples of the sport's determination to tackle doping include proposals for DNA sampling and – in advance of the Tour de France 2007 – the demand that riders should sign up to accepting a fine of one year's salary for a doping infringement, in addition to the two-year quarantine penalty already in place (*Associated Press* 2007). Although, cycling offers many examples that are relevant to this book's line of discussion, the book is not exclusively dedicated to the analysis of the use of doping in cycling. Its aim is, rather, to pave the way for a greater understanding of the mechanisms at work behind the use of doping in elite sport in general and in so doing to reveal problems in the way the issue has so far been tackled.

My working hypothesis is that the fight against doping – promoted as an initiative to cleanse sport of cheats – is at heart an attempt to redeem sport from itself. At the heart of this book runs a fault-line between the will to purity and the will to win. I have been fortunate both as a PhD supervisor and as the head of a research project funded by the Danish Ministry for Culture on athletes' attitudes to the doping issue, to be able to generate a wealth of interview material with top athletes from home and abroad. This material provides the sounding board for my analysis and discussion explicitly in the final chapters of the book.

Overall, this book aims to analyse and discuss the philosophical, social and political issues raised in equal measure by the use of and the fight against doping. My aim is to develop a coherent understanding of the complex problem by drawing on a variety of disciplines and sources. The idea has not been to write a textbook. Therefore, references to other scholars' works have been kept to a minimum. In the few instances where I address specific arguments, the purpose is not to counter certain authors but to show by concrete examples the problems and shortcomings of the various common and not so common arguments presented.

With these aims in mind, Chapter 1 leads with the question of 'What is doping?'. The discussion that follows shows that finding an answer to this question is not as easy as the everyday use of the term might lead us to believe. Consideration is then given to the advantages and disadvantages of having a lexical definition of doping as a basis for anti-doping work. From this opening discussion on the meaning of doping, Chapter 2 attempts to address the question of 'what is sport?' and goes on to develop a perception of the nature of sport that lays the foundation for the book. Drawing on the philosophy of Friedrich Nietzsche, Chapter 3 examines more closely the motives for engaging in sport as defined in the previous chapter. Accordingly, this chapter provides the background for a deeper understanding of athletes' incentives to use doping. Chapter 4 shows how the doping problem has been constructed as a form of narrative blurring fact and fiction, and discusses the way in which the outlawing of performance-enhancing measures has resulted in athletes constructing their doping use as taboo. Although it has become an issue athletes are now frequently confronted with, the norm is to express a strong anti-doping attitude. Only in very rare cases have athletes questioned the wisdom inherent in the actual anti-doping policy, and when it has happened they have been strongly opposed by sports' leaders and fellow-athletes. Chapter 5 analyses new methods employed by athletes for managing truth since doping revelations have become so widespread that it is no longer possible for them to keep their counsel and retain credibility if they come under suspicion of doping or indeed test positive for doping. In Chapter 6, the focus is on the 'fight against doping'. Here the discussion turns to how the well-intentioned, for all their enthusiasm, sacrifice law and logic and make anti-doping work resemble a modern crusade, whose moral base is undermined by a fixation on ends. That is, in the pursuit of clean sport, *ad hoc* alterations and proscriptions are presented about which athletes have no prior knowledge. Chapter 7 continues this line of argument, showing how the fight against doping has its roots in a more general scepticism of modernity. This prepares the way for a discussion of the rationale behind the prohibition of doping. Intellectual adherents of modernity have increasingly spoken in favour of the deregulation of doping. Examples of these arguments are analysed in Chapter 8, and this is followed by a presentation of athletes' viewpoints in Chapter 9. In the concluding chapter of the book, I sketch an alternative strategy for combating doping that would be at least as effective as that which is currently being pursued, and which shows greater respect for the situation and viewpoints of athletes.

1   What is doping?

In view of the increased priority given to the fight against doping since 1999 both by governments and sporting authorities, one might be forgiven for believing that there exists a clear definition of what doping is. This is not, however, the case, as can be seen from the evident pragmatism of the (circular) definition used by the World Anti-Doping Agency (WADA): 'Doping is defined as the occurrence of one or more of the anti-doping rule violations set out in Article 2.1 through Article 2.8 of the Code' (WADA 2003: 8). Doping is simply defined as infringement of WADA's doping regulations. In other words, doping is whatever WADA at any moment assesses it to be.

On the basis of a definition that is void of content, the rules of doping risk taking on an entirely random character. This WADA has accepted, presumably driven by the concern that any attempt to be more specific as regards the content of their definition of doping would either render it too narrow or too broad. If, for example, doping was defined as 'the use of artificially produced performance-enhancing substances', anabolic steroids, EPO and suchlike would be prohibited but not doping by using the performer's own blood or by chewing the coca leaf. If, on the other hand, it was defined broadly as 'all performance-enhancing substances', then the definition would include blood-doping and coca leaf chewing – but to them would have to be added hitherto accepted energy boosters such as chocolate, cola and energy bars, which athletes consume to prevent them collapsing during long-term physical exertion.

There are perhaps those who will claim that an energy bar is not a performance-enhancing substance, since it simply contributes to the maintenance of blood sugar levels, or in other words keeps the body in balance. But the same argument could be used to defend giving athletes testosterone. For example, it could be argued that a sporting event such as the Tour de France is an activity that causes physical degeneration, and since strenuous branches of sport are not prohibited, the least those in charge can do is to keep an eye on the athlete's health and if, for example, their testosterone level falls, offer them a compensatory dose that carries no risk.

WADA avoids having to take issue with this kind of reasoning by choosing a vacuous definition of doping. In so doing, they have forearmed themselves against such difficulties as the Council of Europe created for itself in its 1963 ruling that doping was:

> the administration to or the use by, a competing athlete of any substance foreign to the body or any physiological substance taken in abnormal quantity or by an abnormal route of entry into the body, with the sole intention of increasing in an artificial and unfair manner his performance in competition.
>
> (Houlihan 1999: 130)

This formulation contains glaring difficulties. It could, for example, never be proved that a substance was consumed with the sole purpose of increasing a level of performance; and it would take lengthy disputes to reach agreement as to how much of a substance could be consumed before it constituted an abnormal quantity. That the wording takes no account of this kind of objection is probably due to the fact that the author relied on common sense and trusted that the reader, whether it be policy-makers, administrators or athletes, would approach the text with the intention of understanding it. Read in the spirit in which it was intended, the wording is clear enough. Experience tells us, however, that if athletes can gain advantage by turning a blind eye to the spirit of the law and clinging to its letter, they will be inclined to do so. Nor was it many years before the council recognised the shortcomings of this wording. In 1967, there was an attempt to make it more precise. Some of the glaring ambiguities were removed, but others remained and new ones arose. For example, doping was now said to be 'administration to or use by a healthy person, in any matter whatsoever, of agents foreign to the organism' (ibid.: 130f). But what does it actually mean for a substance to be foreign to the organism? And is it acceptable for people who are *not* healthy to consume performance-enhancing substances? In that case many athletes will be 'home safe', if the WHO's authoritative definition of health is used as the basis for a judgement, since it presents health as a state of complete physical, psychological and social well-being and not as simply absence of sickness (WHO [1946] 1948). On this basis, athletes unable to take part in competitions without medical aids would be able to invoke the right to take medication simply because they felt hard-done-by.

It looks as though Charles Dubin, who headed the Canadian investigation into doping in sport launched after the Ben Johnson case, was right when in his report he quoted Sir Arthur Porritt, chairman of the British Association of Sports Medicine for saying that 'to define doping is, if not impossible, at best extremely difficult' (Dubin 1990: 77f). Nevertheless, it is questionable whether he was right in quoting the rest of the sentence and the next: 'and yet, everyone who takes part in competitive sport or who administers it knows exactly what it means. The definition lies not in words but in integrity of character' (ibid.: 78).

There is presumably agreement among practitioners of sport that athletes' use of potent substances such as amphetamine, anabolic steroids, growth hormones and EPO are to be regarded as doping. But in the absence of a definitive doping list as a reference point, there can scarcely be unanimous agreement as to the range of substances and methods that should constitute doping. The use of creatine has been debated for a long time, but has not been included in the doping list despite several studies indicating that it has a performance-enhancing effect (Jäger *et al.* 2008). Some will also continue to believe that caffeine is a doping substance, since it, too, has been proved to be performance-enhancing (Paluska 2003). The fact that it has been removed from the doping list can, however, only mean that other people must have provided sufficiently convincing arguments for it not being a doping substance. Perhaps it has been argued that although it can improve athletic performance, it has no harmful side-effects so long as the substance is not consumed in larger quantities than required to produce the desired effect. At first glance, this argument may appear convincing but it brings with it the problem that this goes for many of the substances on the prohibited list. A number of debatable substances and methods could be mentioned. There is no consensus, for example, as to whether the use of hypobaric chambers is an acceptable performance-enhancing practice. At the WADA Congress in Montreal in 2006, it was decided that their use should continue to be accepted but it is not obvious why. And nothing in the minutes of the executive committee meeting advances our understanding. On the contrary, at the meeting it was confirmed that the hypoxic devices are performance-enhancing. It was also stated 'that such devices might be dangerous in the hands of unqualified people'. It is true, it was determined that 'properly used under proper supervision', there was no basis for saying that they induced health risks. But the same could also be said about the medicine, erythropoietin (EPO), which is used for the same purpose as hypobaric chambers. Furthermore, the matter had gone to WADA's Ethical Issues Review Panel, which, it held, 'had determined that these devices were against the spirit of sport' (WADA 2006: 38). Despite this, WADA approved their use. This example is yet further evidence that Dubin's claim that there exists unanimity on the subject of the concept of doping does not hold. But this is of no consequence, since the way WADA has chosen to address the question means that the organisation can adjust its rules at will.

WADA does have, however, a moral obligation to ensure that doping rules are reasonable. If the reasonableness of the organisation's measures and methods is called into question, there is the danger that the support of athletes and the authorities will be eroded with serious consequences for the fight against doping. It makes sense then to consider whether WADA should operate with a more substantial definition than that presented in the anti-doping code, so that the fight against doping can be carried out more in accordance with good sense.

If, however, an adequate definition of doping cannot be formulated as an official basis for anti-doping work, there will not be much likelihood of providing a definition stringent enough to consolidate the efforts of those working within the sport. It is more probable that new initiatives will be coordinated according to the particular form of reasoning prevailing in the narrow community of anti-doping officialdom, reasoning that cannot avoid being coloured by the task that that particular community centres on and regards as being of importance or relevance. In other words, those working in the field of anti-doping develop a structure of relevance that is at variance with everyday common sense. It can be assumed that this has contributed to the fact that the offspring of the IOC, WADA, which in its infancy was the darling of all the forces for good, has found itself running into a number of 'unfortunate' cases (see Chapter 5).

The root of the difficulties that the anti-doping campaign has to wrestle with remains precisely because the concept of doping has not been sufficiently clarified. This becomes further apparent as soon as the concept is studied more closely.

Doping, medicine and health

Doping substances are primarily forms of medicine taken for their potential performance-enhancing effect. Athletes can legitimately take doping drugs without being guilty of a doping offence. Several, for example – especially in the field of endurance sports – suffer from exertion-induced asthma.[1] They can be given dispensation to use medicine on the doping list. It is true that WADA tightened up the rules in 2005 so that the old medical certificate can no longer be used. Today a Therapeutic Use Exemption (TUE) certificate is needed. The stiffer rules mean that permission does not give *carte blanche* to use any medicine needed if it appears on the doping list. On the application form the athlete has to declare the dose of administration, the route of administration, the frequency of administration as well as the length of time the treatment is expected to continue. If an athlete with a TUE certificate tests positive for medicine that he or she has a dispensation to use, then tests are carried out to see whether the content of active substances in the blood corresponds to the dose required by the treatment. If the athlete has taken more than prescribed, then this is regarded as a contravention of the doping rules and is treated as such. Behind such decisions lies, of course, WADA's desire not to discriminate against individuals who do suffer from an illness. Necessary medication is regarded as a means to compensate for a physical handicap in order that the ill person can compete on an equal footing. On the other hand, it should not be possible for athletes to exploit their legitimate need for treatment to acquire a competitive advantage. For that reason the quantity of active substances contained in the body is regulated. This appears to be logical. Nevertheless the very fact that an opportunity for dispensation exists raises at least one significant question.

One of the central pillars of anti-doping work is consideration for the health of the athlete, and one reason for prohibiting the intake of performance-enhancing substances (and of substances that can mask their use) is to protect the athletes. Nevertheless, it is a feature of much sporting activity that it involves a relatively high risk for its practitioners. Torn ligaments, damage to muscles and menisci, broken fingers, arms, legs and backs, concussion and death are regular occurrences in the sporting arena. The only way to eliminate this risk would be to prohibit the great majority of sports, and that is not realistic. On the other hand, it is possible to tighten up the safety requirements. This has been done in a number of areas. Restrictions have been introduced in boxing over the course of time such as limits on the length of the fight, requirements to use gloves, gum-shields, and in amateur circles the obligatory use of a helmet – a precaution that, by the way, no evidence suggests has remedied the risk of brain damage (Zetterberg *et al.* 2007). Cyclists have also been required to wear helmets, and footballers have had to get used to playing with shin-guards. Rules of this kind have been introduced to limit the risk of athletes being subjected to physical damage. The prohibition of doping can be seen as yet one more rule added to the list of those whose purpose is to protect the health of the athlete. It is just not, however, quite that simple. For while it is easy enough to argue for the expediency of shin-guards, helmets, gum-shields and gloves as measures promoting health even though the outcome may be debatable, the same cannot be said to be true of the prohibition against doping. Anyone wanting to argue for doping prohibition on the grounds of health alone is only on firm ground as long as the premise holds that doping damages health. And this is not always the case. As a rule, the substances that athletes dope themselves with are forms of medicine developed to *improve* human health.

Athletes are, of course, gambling with health if they take courses of EPO that raise their haematocrit level to around 60 per cent, at which point their blood becomes so thick that they have to take supplementary anti-coagulant medicine to reduce the risk of blood clotting. It is less obvious why ephedrine should appear on the doping list. Ephedrine can be found in cough mixtures that doctors have been prescribing for runny-nosed children for years. It is hard to see the rationale on health grounds for allowing athletes to feed ephedrine to their children but not allowing them to take it themselves if they catch the same cold. The argument that ephedrine in exceptionally high doses can damage health immediately falls apart in the face of the fact that the same is true for permitted substances such as painkillers. And just as relatively few of them are needed to achieve the desired effect, so the doses of ephedrine needed to cause a positive doping test are not such that they constitute a significant danger to health (Ros *et al.* 1999). On the other hand and rather ironically, it seems that larger doses of ephedrine do not have a positive effect on exercise performance (Dekhuijzen *et al.* 1999).

Nor can the health argument be used to counter viewpoints along the lines that it is precisely in the interest of their health that athletes should be allowed to take supplements of those substances that sporting competitions have drained out of them. The argument that, faced with such a deficit, athletes should give up their competition and go home to recover in a natural manner is somewhat divorced from reality and is no real defence in terms of health-related counteractions. Ambitious sportspeople do not give up competing because they feel themselves to be drained physically. If they are law-abiding citizens, they try to recharge their batteries through legal means, by using energy bars, vitamin supplements, and so on. If that does not work, they keep on going anyway as long as they can. In the past, countless athletes have entered competitions despite physical discomfort or sickness. If there was a serious consensus that those who are not physically on top form should be excluded, then the necessary consequence would be to carry out obligatory health checks at regular intervals on all participants in tournaments and races of longer duration as a supplement to doping tests. Proposals for preventative health checks on a regular basis have, however, never been presented by sports organisations. The international cycling union (UCI) undertakes a health test prior to a major race, but in reality this is an indirect doping test, whose purpose is to check that every cyclist's hematocrit is below 50 per cent. If it is not, then the cyclist involved is regarded as being ill and, as a means of protecting his or her health, is grounded for 15 days (UCI Cycling Regulations, Part 13, Sporting Safety and Conditions, {§}4, no. 13.1.086). As a rule, it is up to the individual athlete to assess whether they are in a fit state to take part in a competition or whether to continue if they have fallen, have been hit or are in crisis. One of the most grotesque examples seen in recent years of the degree to which the athlete's 'right to self-determination' is respected was when the Swiss runner Gabriela Anderson-Schiess in a state of almost lethal dehydration teetered unconscious and crippled by exhaustion across the finishing line during the marathon at the Olympic Games in Los Angeles in 1984. Yet no one stepped in to stop this internationally televised madness.

A boxer in an equivalent state would not have been allowed to continue, though otherwise the individual boxer is also regarded to a considerable extent as responsible for his own health. If the referee steps in and stops the fight, it is on the basis of an assessment that the boxer who has been hit is punch-drunk, has momentarily lost his power of judgement and is therefore no longer in a position to take care of his own health. If, on the other hand, the boxer is only shaken, it is up to him to decide whether he wishes to continue regardless of the fact that experience indicates that this is a situation in which the risk of being knocked out is imminent, and his ability to decide what is best for him is disturbed.

Consideration for the health of athletes is compromised in any number of sports. It applies, for example, when athletes take a knock and let themselves be given a superficial treatment with pain-killing ice spray, so they can quickly get on with the game; or when because of an injury they are not entirely match-ready but agree to play an important game with the aid of a pain-killing injection; or when they reduce a high temperature by taking Paracetamol and so get to play a match, when other people would go to bed or take things easy. It cannot be denied that the use of ice spray, injections and Paracetamol in these contexts is intended to improve the athlete's performance ability *in situ*. Nor that it overrides concerns about health. But it is nevertheless not regarded as doping.

Nor is it seen as such when an athlete suffers torments to lose weight, whether it be by sweating it out in a sauna or by following a strict diet, possibly using slimming medication not on the doping list. It is particularly true of endurance sports that athletes are often extremely concerned with getting their weight down as far as possible without it affecting their performance level, because every superfluous kilo that has to be carried reduces the chance of success. In his autobiography, the Danish cyclist, Brian Holm, writes that from having weighed 80 kg during his first years as a professional in the 1980s he ended up weighing 67 kg in the 1990s when he earned his way as a valued support rider and among other things contributed to the Tour de France victory of his countryman, Bjarne Riis, on Team Deutsche Telekom in 1996. With hindsight, Holm can see that his weight was too low during the final years of his career, but, as he writes:

> Unfortunately I followed the trend in becoming extremely thin because I simply believed that that made me into a better cyclist. It became natural for me to go to bed hungry every evening and to wake in the night because my stomach rumbled with hunger. I got up and ate cornflakes without milk in order to get some more sleep. It almost became an obsession to be thin. When people told me that I looked like a concentration camp victim, I took it as a compliment and was almost proud of it. At one point I even had veins on my buttocks. But my body could not really function without a little layer of fat, and it began to deteriorate because its immune system was no longer on top form.
>
> (Holm 2002: 98)

A body that has virtually no fat has less resistance than it would have with a normal weight. But being as lean as a racing greyhound gives a competitive advantage. Abnormal thinness, therefore, places an indirect pressure on competitors. If they do not want to take part with a handicap, then it is equally incumbent on them to reduce their amount of body fat to a competitive level.

If considerations of health were just as important for the integrity of sport as defenders of doping prohibitions like to maintain, we might expect the campaign against slimming to excess to have the same priority as the campaign against doping. In relation to WADA's definition of doping, there is nothing to stop methods used for losing weight being included in anti-doping regulation. What is more, unhealthy forms of extreme dieting would be easier to put a stop to than other doping methods, since one could simply introduce a weight limit in the same way as we now operate with a blood density limit.

If, for instance, a Tour de France cyclist presents himself below a certain specified weight at the start of the race,[2] he could be subject to a penalty weight, which would in one fell swoop eliminate any advantage accrued through unhealthy low weight. In spite of the fact that it is well known that extreme dieting leads in some cases to athletes developing anorexia, the practice remains unregulated. This is just another example of the fact that, although one of the mainstays of doping work is concern for health, it is not possible to formulate a consistent definition of doping by focusing on a phenomenon's risk to health. On the one hand, to attempt to do so would create considerable problems in isolating the methods and substances that should be regarded as being harmful to health and therefore prohibited. On the other, it would pave the way for a whole range of marginal cases and disputes with athletes who had their doctor's certification that their particular use of medication was in the interests of their health.

We can, then, conclude that a doping prohibition is not necessarily the result of a basic concern for athletes' health in sport. We can further conclude that prohibition cannot possibly be grounded in a justification relating to methods or measures that are artificial or foreign to the body, or to any performance-enhancing effect, since it is not possible to define methods or measures that are artificial or foreign to the body in any meaningful way. For instance, it seems to be artificial to use video footage to interpret and prepare for the opponent's technique and tactics; to use ball machines, rowing machines, and so on to maximise the effect of training; to put on synthetic clothing as a way of getting a better footing, to grip, or to slice through water with the least resistance possible. There are innumerable examples of artificial performance-enhancing measures that are approved.

And the dividing line is not, as might be expected, whether the artificial measure in question is extraneous in relation to the athlete (i.e., does not work inside the body). In that case athletes would be forbidden from eating vitamin pills, which like EPO are artificially produced and just as foreign to the body. The rationale behind WADA's apparent decision in effect to give up the attempt to define the concept of doping becomes apparent. At the same time, however, it is clear that the doping rules are without foundation in logic and reason. Strictly speaking, they are simply a result of an arbitrary taste – or rather distaste – for certain performance-enhancing practices, and for that reason the anti-doping campaign has at best to be understood as being based upon an intuitive sense that there are 'wrong' ways to improve an athlete's sporting performance.

The premises of inclusion on the doping list

The fact that WADA has not wanted to let its doping work be hamstrung by a strict definition of the concept of doping does not, of course, mean that the agency's doping list has been determined without any criteria at all. The conditions governing whether a substance should be considered for addition to the doping list are that it fulfils two of the following three criteria:

1 It must be performance-enhancing.
2 It must be harmful to health.
3 It must run counter to the spirit of sport.

(WADA 2003)

On the surface, it might seem as though these criteria limit the arbitrary nature of the doping list. If we scrutinise them more carefully, however, then it becomes clear that in reality they contribute to its arbitrariness. The fact that a substance or method, which fulfils two of the three criteria, is not automatically placed on the list is one thing. Another and more significant objection is that these criteria lack any form of specificity. If a dentist were to join the governing body of WADA, he would be able to use these criteria to argue convincingly for including sweets in the doping list. Sweets (candy in the USA) may have a performance-enhancing effect, in that they provide a source of rapid new energy – and one that is also artificially produced. They contribute to the world-wide epidemic of obesity and are therefore harmful to health. If someone else objected that this is not a problem that confronts top athletes in real life, the dentist would at least be able to argue that sweets are bad for the teeth, and that athletes who eat sweets set a bad example – not least at a time when the numbers of obese children and young adults are growing at an alarming rate.

In addition, the notion of 'the spirit of sport', one could argue, is completely meaningless and therefore utterly impossible to argue for or against. So, returning to the dentist scenario for a moment, when WADA maintains that health is an element of the spirit of sport, and there is a consensus among professionals that sweets are unhealthy, then the dentist can invoke support for his point of view by saying that sweets are against the spirit of sport.

A careful examination of the concept of doping shows that doping is a foe without a face. The anti-doping campaign can find words to back their actions – but no backing for their words. In other words, they are fighting the fog. There is no doubt that their motives are good. Unfortunately, though, experience tells us that the road to Hell is paved with good intentions. And the anti-doping campaign appears to be no exception, as this book will illustrate.

2 What is sport?

Judging from the reactions caused by the massive drugs haul of the 1998 Tour de France, it seems to have come as a complete surprise to the authorities that doping was a widespread phenomenon in top professional sport. While this may be a cause for wonderment, it can in all likelihood be linked to the fact that since Pierre de Coubertin hit upon the idea of creating the Olympic Games, sport has been over-promoted as character-building; as a public or social good. It is not surprising, therefore, that time and again it manages to arouse the indignation of politicians, the media and the broader public.

It is certainly true that Coubertin had a picture of the nature of sport and honoured the innate human will to excel and strive for perfection, a view reflected, for example, in the Olympic motto, 'citius, altius, fortius'. However, in order to gain backing for his idea, he often promoted sport in words that were in direct opposition to its true nature. He described it as healthy and character-building, and when, during the Olympic Games of 1908 he heard Bishop Talbot in St. Paul's Cathedral say the now famous words, 'In these Olympiads, the important thing is not winning, but taking part' (Coubertin 2000: 587), he evidently recognised that no maxim could better promote the Olympic idea, and he immediately made it his own, adding: 'The important thing in life is not victory, but struggle: the essential is not to conquer, but to fight well' (ibid.: 587). In doing so, however, he set out on a pedagogical quest and placed a burden on sport which it cannot bear. This pedagogical aspect has to a large extent become the basis for sport's legitimisation, and this is echoed in WADA's idealistic notion of the values of sport:

> Often referred to as 'the spirit of sport'; it is the essence of Olympism, it is how we play true. The spirit of sport is the celebration of the human spirit, body and mind, and is characterised by the following values:

> Ethics, fair play and honesty.
> Health.
> Excellence in performance.
> Character and education.
> Fun and joy.

Teamwork.
Dedication and commitment.
Respect for rules and laws.
Respect for self and other participants.
Courage.
Community and solidarity.   (WADA 2003)

Whereupon the agency asserts: 'Doping is fundamentally contrary to the spirit of sport' (ibid.: 3).

However, it is not self-evident that doping should be incompatible with values such as courage, dedication and commitment, and exceptional performance, all of which are unmistakable aspects of the practice of sport. And if it is incompatible with the remainder of the values mentioned, then it might be argued that these in turn are not characteristic features of sport. Where, for example, do we find community and solidarity in sport nowadays? Professionalism means that athletes now switch clubs (franchises) and sometimes even nationality, if that is what pays best. But even prior to professionalisation, athletes were already inclined to have an eye to better clubs in order to realise their ambitions without paying much attention to either community or solidarity. It is also difficult to see where respect for rules comes in, if what is meant is that athletes make a virtue of upholding them. And in reality, instead of 'respect for', it is more a question of 'acceptance of' a competitor, whose primary role is to be beaten. Finally ethics, fair play and honour are concepts that mean no more in sport than they do in the world outside sport. In fact, it is tempting to say that the ideal of 'fair play' arose out of the experience that sport itself encourages the opposite, 'foul play'. To talk of the spirit of sport is, in other words, to talk of a notion that apparently has no foothold in reality, one that describes what idealists might wish it to be – if not one actually cultivated through sheer opportunism and the fear that a recognition of the real nature of sport would result in politicians and others who finance these activities rushing off in horror to put a stopper on the cash flow.

If we want to go beyond this simplistic condemnation and arrive at an actual understanding of the doping problem, we have to shift our focus and give up any idea of there being evil spirits outside sport – club management, doctors, sponsors, and so on – who are the root *cause* of the mess. It must be said that this line of thinking is attractive in that it makes it possible to retain the notion of sport as being the harmless victim of destructive financial interests. Unfortunately, it is a distorting image which inhibits an understanding of the doping problem being generated by the inner dynamics of sport itself. This becomes visible when we clarify for ourselves what sport is.

A definition of sport

The first difficulty we come across here is that there is no consensus as to what the activity we call sport comprises. There are those who think that taking exercise – even having sex – is a form of sport.[1] A more precise, a narrower definition is required, however, and in looking for that we do not get far by differentiating between different activities. The same activity can easily be practised both as sport and as a recreational activity.[2] Sport here is, therefore, defined as those activities in which the following four criteria are satisfied:

1   The activity is played out as a competition,[3] which is taken seriously even though it serves no external purpose and in that sense can be regarded as not serious.
2   The aim is to win and to move upwards within the activity's hierarchical structure.
3   The activity is organised and functions in an institutionalised framework, in which results are recorded and are ascribed significance.
4   The activity is governed by a written set of rules, which are administered by a judge who ideally is impartial.[4]

These criteria immediately cover the entire range of sporting activities on the Olympic programme but are still narrow enough to eliminate a number of instances that, if they were included, would make a consistent analysis impossible. A run or a bicycle ride, therefore, even if it is on a racing bike and at speed, alone or with good friends, falls outside the category of sport. These activities come under the category of exercise. The same is true of non-organised badminton or squash. A wrestling match on the lawn or a race to see who can get to the garden gate first can easily be called competitive play, but is not sport according to the definition proposed here.

With its tournament systems, championships, divisions and rankings, sport is hierarchical in structure and that implies an aspiration upwards. This aspiration is the fundamental condition governing the functioning of sport. For anyone who has taken part in sport will know that it is more fun to win than to lose. If we did not know better, therefore, we could expect a second division team, faced with the chance of promotion, to lose the decisive games on purpose in order to be able to win more often the following year. But that does not happen. Nor will we find any players celebrating relegation, even though that promises well for the next season's chances of winning games. Practising sport implies a clear sense of purpose. Sportspersons do not merely want to succeed. They want to excel. To excel to the utmost. That is why sportspersons do not look for opponents they can beat easily, but those who are able to provide them with opposition that is worthy of them.

Opposition is the core element in sport; challenge, which set alongside sporting aspiration is also termed ambition, is its driving force. Opposition stimulates the athlete, creates tension and consolidates the hierarchical structure of sport. Yet opposition is only productive when competitors are on an equal footing. If competitors are too unevenly balanced, and if one player in reality has no chance of winning, then opposition is ineffective. This means that the competition is without tension, and is therefore regarded as being without interest. Equal opponents will, on the other hand, match themselves up against each other. Each of them will strive to gain the upper hand and press the opponent to give of his best. This is true of all levels of sport. The difference between elite sport and sport of the second rank is primarily the level of the athletes' abilities, but in addition there are differences in ambition and commitment – and, related to these, in the spirit of self-sacrifice – as decisive factors. If athletes are not willing to make a substantial contribution in the form of training, if they are not in a position to press themselves to the limit, they will never reach the highest levels, even though they might have the potential.[5] But since the difference between elite level and serious but sub-elite sport is not essential here, we would do well to restrict our focus in what follows to top level sport and for the rest confine ourselves to the observation that some sports practitioners do not have the talent to make it in top level sport, while others may have talent, but they lack the motivation needed to compete at the highest levels. So, what is left is a group of elite athletes who live and breathe for their sport and who are prepared to make substantial sacrifices to rise as far as possible in the sporting hierarchy. The question then arises: What makes sport so attractive?

One obvious reply, if we were solely referring to professional footballers or NBA basketball players, would be the astronomical sums of money they can earn. But if we are looking for an answer that also includes sports in which the elite still consists of amateurs or semi-professionals with modest incomes – swimming, rowing and volleyball, for instance – we have to look beyond financial factors and possibly ignore them completely, looking instead at the inner qualities of sport. Since it is, however, not so easy to distinguish inner motivational factors from outer ones, further clarification is needed here.

While a lucrative contract can immediately be identified as external motivation, the fantastic feeling derived from competing and giving one's all, from achieving the perfect shot, jump, kick, pull, throw or whatever, or from attaining a state in which all sense of time is lost and the player becomes one with the rhythm of the sport, can equally easily be understood as being aspects of sport's inner motivation. But there are also other factors that are not so easy to categorise. It is more difficult to know, for example, whether the 'sweet taste of victory' is an internal or external motivator.[6] The joy of victory is a motivational factor that extends beyond sport, and for that reason it seems reasonable to include it as an external motivation. As a rule it brings with it recognition, local or (inter)national fame, and at times victory takes on a material form as a financial prize. In addition, the will to win is not something that is inherent in sport but a factor that athletes bring with them into the sports arena. These considerations might serve to support the premise that winning is an external motivational factor. However, winning is generally reckoned to be among those factors that are internal to sport, since the chance of winning is an essential catalyst for the sporting activity. Without it, sport would be lifeless. It is of no significance that victory at times brings financial reward with it, since this does not follow of necessity and has no bearing on the athlete's activity. In contrast to the experiential qualities that are internal to sport, victory is a motivational factor that becomes visible to the eyes of the world outside in relation to the presentation of prizes, laps of honour, and so on. But the fact that victory is visible to the public and can bring the victor a prize-winner's cheque is not the same as saying that it is an external motivational factor. Sport has an attraction for people who are competitive. The will to win is a necessity but not a sufficient precondition for achieving sporting success. Aside from talent, the elite athlete usually exhibits a high level of self-sacrifice, personal aspiration and ambition. Considering these characteristics, it is perhaps not surprising that doping is a temptation to the sporting elite, although most choose not to follow this route.

Misguided notions about the nobility of sport

Ever since the storm about doping broke in 1998 there have been strenuous efforts to restore the sense that the problem was limited to a few black sheep within what was an otherwise noble flock. Ten years after the Canadian sprinter Ben Johnson was disgraced after a positive doping test, following his victory in the 100m dash, an entire team was thrown out of the Tour de France (see Chapter 4). There was no alternative, since it was not a matter of an individual or of a few particular cyclists who were caught, but of a soigneur,[7] who in an official Tour de France car was carrying illegal substances for the team. Since then, however, it has once again become common practice to focus on individual cases of doping. Athletes who get caught in the trap are sentenced like common cheats. Particularly within cycling, which has always been prone to the problem, this is extreme. As soon as a cyclist comes under suspicion, he is now immediately suspended. The explanation was that this was a result of the code of ethics which was introduced on the initiative of the Pro-Tour teams in January 2005 – an explanation which proved to be misleading (see Chapter 6). In doing so, the sport's directors, who even after 1998 had been put under pressure by a number of doping cases, attempted to retouch the dented image of cycling and to bolster the belief that it is at heart a healthy and positive activity, which a few undesirable elements were undermining with their over-exaggerated desire to win.

The positive view of sport can, if need be, be supported by a variety of sporting gestures, such as when footballers kick the ball into touch if an opponent is injured. Those who wish to believe in the good qualities of sport avert their eyes from the question of why the opponent is lying injured, because it threatens other values, that are commonly attributed to sport. If, like Coubertin, we value sport for its character-building qualities, such situations give us cause to speculate as to what traits of character it fosters.[8] It is, in fact, self-evident that those values and ideals that are associated with sport are the very values and ideals contravened time and again in the practice of sport. There seems, then, to be no tenable basis for linking that practice with the ancient adage, 'A healthy mind in a healthy body'.

It has been common for doping users to be compared to drug addicts, but at no time during the debate of recent years has anyone compared sport itself with a narcotic. This analogy belongs to the sports critique of the 1970s (Rigauer 1969; Vinnai 1970; Brohm 1978). As things have developed since, however, it might seem that that critique still has some substance if the stress is moved from the pacifying, enervating nature of the narcotic to its obsessive and addictive qualities.

Earlier sports critiques analysed sport on the basis of the exploitative mechanisms of industrial capitalism. Like capitalist work, sport was subject to the tyranny of abstract time and could be seen as a surreptitious means of socialising people into an acceptance of the rigid time-discipline of the factory. In the same way the maximisation of records that were a part of sport could be understood as corresponding to the maximisation of profits, and by extension as a glorification of an untenable and alienating ideology of growth.

Referring to the colossal training programmes on which legendary sporting stars such as the Czech runner Emil Zatopek and the American swimmer Mark Spitz built their performances, one of the most prominent representatives of the Marxist critique of sport, Jean-Marie Brohm, for example, provided the following justification for his reasons for opposing competitive sport: 'Sports training is thus structurally similar to production line work in a factory and involves the same inhuman work pace' (Brohm 1978: 68).

This analogy is typical of early sports sociological critique. But even though it is thought-provoking, the analogy lacks precision and is of limited value for extending our understanding of the attraction of sport. The analogy gives rise to an erroneous conclusion and has therefore no argumentative force. It runs: 'Sport *resembles* (in many ways) work, ergo sport *is the same as* work.' That is, of course, wrong.[9]

Having said that, it must be added that Marxist sports critique was not blind to the particular character of sport and to the logic that propelled it forward. Brohm, for example, makes an early break with the sense of sport as an appropriate pedagogical tool that promotes virtues such as *fair play* and *sportsmanship*. With a view to the developmental tendencies of sport he writes:

> The reality of sport is not as rosy as is often made out. In every field people are beginning to realise the price paid for success in the medals race. Everywhere people are wondering about the human, educational, cultural and political consequences of the hunt for new records, of the frantic drive for biological output and of nerve-racking physical challenges. The unease caused by this painful questioning of sport's perspectives

contributes to the crisis. 'Just how far can top-level competitive sport go? Will not the many deviations suffered by sport sooner or later lead to its complete degeneration?'

(ibid.: 14)

It is precisely the same concern that is being brought into the arena today, a quarter of a century later. The woman who was behind the doping revelations during the Tour de France in 1998, the French Minister for Youth and Sport, the communist Marie-George Buffet, justified her heavy-handed action in relation to the race by saying that it was necessary if they were to get to the bottom of the doping problem. As the politician responsible, she had no alternative. It was a necessary initiative to protect the cyclists.

In an interview with the Danish daily *Politiken*, she expressed her view of the cyclists. She saw the cycling stars as exploited workers. 'The majority of cyclists may be highly paid. But their career is short, they often remain without further qualifications throughout their lives, and they pay the price with their health', she says in the interview (Buffet 1998). On two stages of the notorious Tour de France in 1998, the cyclists showed their displeasure by downing the tools of their trade (i.e. their bikes and bodies) and 'striking'. To Buffet's surprise, they were not striking because of the pressure on them to use doping, but on the contrary because of the police and the press, who each in their own way supported her anti-doping initiative. The minister's statement sounds almost like an echo of Brohm. Her comment suggests a view of the cyclists as spiritually impoverished people, who are not in a fit state to understand what serves them best.

The interesting aspect here is not the minister's attitude – her *de facto* exclusion of the possibility that doping might be based on adult individuals' free choice – but the fact that in order to justify this intervention in sport it is apparently necessary to construct a narrative about sportspersons as helpless victims led astray by money-grabbing exploiters. The fact that the minister has a suspicion that this construction may not entirely hold water can be seen in her handling of the fact that these practitioners earn princely salaries. This indeed they do, but what she emphasises is the brevity of their careers, and she adds: 'the majority remain without qualifications for the remainder of their lives' (ibid.). In this way she consolidates her narrative about the exploitation of the athletes. Their brief passage across the starry firmament carries a heavy price. She implicitly attempts to persuade us that the athletes are impoverished in the longer term.

If we consider the sums of money that professional sportspersons are paid, then this idea that they are impoverished is hard to follow. Several of them have annual salaries that exceed the lifetime earnings of ordinary workers. We already touched on this precise problem when Brohm thinks in analogies in his critique of sport. Using ski sports as an example, he shows how sport runs out of control in its striving towards ever better per-formances. Much is invested in improvements to skiers' equipment, so that they become faster and faster, which naturally increases risks at the same time. At one point a skin-tight ski outfit with minimal wind resistance had been developed. It was so smooth that, if skiers fell, they would slide like a projectile without resistance across the snow. Only after a serious accident was the outfit banned, but this ban was certainly, as Brohm states, far from putting the brakes on further development.

> The maximum and average speeds reached in the down-hill events are steadily increasing: 75, 80, 90 m.p.h. At Cervina, in Italy, maximum speeds of up to 125 m.p.h. have been clocked up. So it should come as no surprise that the list of top-level skiers, seriously injured or killed on the 'field of battle' for a few dollars (or rather medals) more grows steadily longer.
>
> This absurd, inhuman obsession with winning is not limited to skiing.
>
> (Brohm 1978: 17)

Brohm's description brings immediately to mind memories of mineworkers, also exposed to significant risks in the depths of the earth in order to earn a few dollars. Skiers are, however, not driven by the same necessity as mineworkers. Their primary motivation is (as far as can be judged) extreme pleasure, and this is incomprehensible to Brohm. The particular attractions that drive sportspersons towards competition and high-risk activities never cross his mind. He simply sidesteps the challenge offered by their commitment, and allows it to remain incomprehensible and he contents himself with branding it an expression of an absurd obsession, whereupon he continues his collection of examples with a demonstration of the increased brutality of rugby. And there is no doubt that he has a point when he says:

> However, those who sing the praises of this noble sport can no longer conceal the fact that the risks of the game are on the increase and accidents are becoming alarmingly frequent – an awkward fact for a 'game' which is supposed to be 'educative'.
>
> (ibid.: 17)

Despite the fact, then, that Brohm gives up when it comes to the internal motivational factors that drive sport, he is precise when he places his finger on the weak point of conservative sports idealism. The notion of sport having character-building features that comply with the ideals so consistently lauded does not apparently hold. On the contrary there is substantial evidence for the opposite, that sport contains the germs of brutalisation.

Sporting behaviour is behaviour that goes against the grain. It is not the consequence of internal features of sports, but a consequence of an external disciplining strong enough to dam the feelings that the sporting encounter whips up (Grupe 1975). It is precisely because sport does *not* urge moderation but – as Coubertin could already see – encourages exaggeration that it can be used in the school situation for the training of self-control and self-limitation. But we cannot conclude from that that sports practice in every situation serves to promote those kinds of pedagogical values. On the contrary, the discrepancy between ideals and reality appears to be general. There is nothing new under the sun. The concerns that are being voiced today are by and large the same as those that people have had since sport became a popular spectator entertainment in the second half of the nineteenth century, which seems to support the notion that sport is not a moral business.[10]

When boxers fall upon each other's necks at the end of a fight, it is an example of what we habitually call sporting behaviour. It reminds us – in case we have forgotten it in the heat of the fight – that what has just been concluded is a sporting encounter not a battle. This gesture is nevertheless secondary. It is not what the whole affair is about. Passion for the sport, not love for their opponent is what attracts the boxers into the ring. It is therefore just as wrong to call their embrace 'sporting' as it would be to call the jubilation after a paralysing knockout unsporting.[11] The way we habitually use these terms is, however, an indication of how usual it is to regard sport through a pedagogical lens as a means to an end. Its actual attractions are pushed away into the background or removed from sight altogether, and we are therefore most inclined to understand the problems of sport as extraneous to the activity and forget that sport is a dangerous seducer.

3 Unchristian sport

Everyone in the modern world knows about sport. As a cultural phenomenon, it has become particularly ubiquitous. Its spread is promoted by media developments but is basically due to the fact that sport appeals to the masses. The masses allow themselves to be carried along, which is more surprising than it might appear at first glance.

Sports in many ways deviate from the prevailing norms and values of society and are occasionally offensive to them. The most obvious example is boxing. Normally we would find it completely unacceptable to hit each other. In boxing it is essential. It might be objected that this may not be the best of examples, since many ordinary sporting enthusiasts do, in fact, believe that the sport of boxing is so vicious that it should be banned. But if we take instead some of the most popular branches of sport – American and continental football, ice hockey or rugby – then even here we find plenty of examples of violent behaviour. One thing is the rocklike tackle that is mistimed once in a while so that the opponent gets hurt. That is part of the game. The knee, elbow or fist that deliberately hits and hurts the opponent is quite another thing. In the language of the sports commentator such actions are 'foul play'. In reality, this is 'just another part of the game'. By playing hard and by landing more or less well-judged body blows, a player can earn a form of respect; and if the opponent can be intimidated into giving ground, so much the better. This is why sports involving physical contact border on the edge of violence, sometimes crossing the line and ending in broken legs, bloody noses and smashed teeth. In youth sport, things do not get as violent as they do in senior sports at the elite levels. In other words, a gradual adaptation to brutality takes place, which is surely part of the explanation for elite sportspersons having the courage to walk onto the pitch at all, knowing full well that they are likely to receive some bruising treatment and that they risk even worse. From time to time we see games in which players have to stagger to their feet again after being knocked down. Once they have pulled themselves together, they get on with the game as though nothing had happened. Players' acceptance of opponents' hurtful rule-breaking fouls is manifest but not easily understood in the frame of ordinary codes of conduct.

Constructive and destructive violations

There is more to this, however, than simply athletes becoming accustomed over a number of years to a physical game that they have been equipped for through training. It can seem violent when we watch them crash together in their fight for the ball, but the crash arises because both parties have faith in their physique. And they know it. Tackles, kicks and blows that we as spectators experience as acts of violence are, as a rule, a calculated violation that is constructive in the sense that its purpose is to shake the other's self-confidence. Generally we are talking about violations that, metaphorically speaking, are written in the margins of the rulebook but remain within the confines of the cover. These blows hurt and are delivered in full awareness that they hurt but also in the certain knowledge that the opponent will not suffer serious injury. If injury does take place, it is as a rule unintentional, and this shows itself immediately in the violator's body language. If there is deliberate intent, then it is a destructive violation.[1]

The destructive violation is an act of frustration provoked by, for example, the inevitability of a stinging defeat or the desire to put a halt to the personal humiliation that a player feels at being wrong-footed on the ball time after time.[2] Destructive violations constitute a threat to sport and fortunately occur only rarely.

The self-limitation apparent in constructive violations alongside the evident lack of respect for destructive actions indicates that – despite the violence – there are moral standards in sport. They are simply different from the moral standards of society at large. In contact sports players are permitted to establish respect for themselves and to intimidate by using physical aggression. Those players who allow themselves to be intimidated do not rise in the hierarchy of these forms of sport, regardless of whether they are technically skilled at ball play or are blessed with the necessary physiological prerequisites such as a large lung capacity. Their chances for a sporting career lie in sticking to those sports in which physical confrontation is ruled out or plays a considerably less important role.

Not even here, however, is there a correlation between the norms and values of sport and those of society at large. If anyone thinks that sports such as cycling, rowing or athletics are non-violent, then they are mistaken. Here, too, it is a matter of forcing the opponent to buckle under. Here, too, violence is manifest, even though its manifestation is symbolic. When a cyclist forces the tempo to breaking point on a mountain climb, he is demonstrating his power and exposing the opponent's weakness. He pushes himself to the pain threshold to get his competitors to suffer and preferably to get them to collapse under their sufferings. The will to suffer in order to get your competitors to suffer even more is to be found in all endurance sports, and even in athletes' throwing disciplines, for example, something similar comes into play, although the suffering takes place in the gym away from the spectator's view. The aim is not to subject others to direct suffering, but to ensure that they suffer defeat.

Even in squash, the racquet sport which otherwise, as its rules stress, has a reputation for being the sport of gentlemen, violence is not hard to find. On the surface, it is true that it looks as though squash honours the virtues of society. Players are positioned side by side in the same space, where they take turns to hit the ball so that it strikes the front wall above a certain height. In the rules there is an emphasis on the players showing consideration, moving to give each other space so that the opponent has freedom to take their shot and a clear view of the ball. The rules also say that players are not allowed to behave in a destructive, intimidating or offensive manner, nor can they indulge in intentional physical contact, exaggerated swinging of the racquet or deliberate dangerous play. The explicit statements contained in the rules that players are to conduct themselves properly reflect the fact that sport is not by nature pedagogical but on the contrary promotes aggressive behaviour if it is not kept on a tight rein. And this is confirmed in practice by the rules being used as a weapon against the opponent. If an opponent stands in the least bit in the way and could be said to obstruct a player's shot, he leaves the ball and demands the point. That means that players constantly do their utmost to ensure that they do not obstruct the other. At the same time, they make their shots as unpleasant as possible. Each, of course, attempts to take advantage of the 'sporting gestures' of the other, stepping aside as they play the ball so that the opponent has maximum difficulty in returning it. No one is shy about hesitating to hit the ball, if by doing so they can get their opponent to be guilty of obstruction and so take the point when the opponent thought he or she was out of the way. In other words, even in the apparently noble game of squash, players make their opponents suffer as much as possible. If they can get away with it, players will force an opponent to chase around the court, just as there is nothing they like better than making an opponent suffer the humiliation of getting in the way. The objection that it is the very idea of the game to tire, catch, control and master the opponent only confirms that we have learnt to take violence for granted as an aspect of sport. Spectators have accustomed themselves to violence to such an extent that it only becomes visible the moment it shows itself as destructive violation.[3]

The evil of sport

Nevertheless it is hard to deny that most, if not all, sports nurture patterns of behaviour that differ from the central norms and values of society, for the simple reason that sport has victory as its pivotal point and its absolute value. Sport is a cultivation of the will to win taken to the threshold of evil. If this has gone almost unnoticed outside the sphere of Marxist sports criticism, the reason can be found in the fact that it takes place in the guise of innocent play, and furthermore that it has been possible to distort its truth and turn it into a healthy pedagogical project. It has gradually become common knowledge that elite sport is not characterised by being healthy, and it is beginning to dawn on people – not least because of the many doping scandals and television's exploitation of violent incidents – that while sport may have a pedagogical function, this is only at a fairly primitive pedagogical level. The concerns of reformist pedagogy as regards authoritarianism and discipline have no place here.

The same goes for the notion of the equal value of every human being. Sport ranks people in order, not only placing opponents in hierarchies, measured out in divisions and positions, but internally ranking members of the same club into first and second teams and possibly more. Even within a single team, there will be differences between stars, core players and reserves. Team mates are, in other words, also competitors, competing with each other for position and prestige. Everyone is fighting for their place in the team or the hierarchy. The 'ladder' pinned to the board is a physical mani-festation of this hierarchy. In team sports everyone is dependent on the performance of everyone else, but they are also threatened by it. The con-ditions that prevail here require self-confidence and promote aggression and social self-sufficiency. This is not to say that elite athletes turn into aggres-sive, self-sufficient members of society by dint of their socialisation in the world of sport. Far from it, the proposal here is that sportspersons live in two worlds with disparate norms and values, and that this plays a significant role in the development of the way they think. They can look at sport from both the inside and the outside but are unable to combine these viewpoints into a consistent idea of what is 'sporting'. *Outside* sport they will be inclined to assess foul play in accordance with the attitudes of society around them. The fact that foul play continues to happen bears witness to the way their attitudes change when, as players, they find themselves *inside* sport.

In practice, these two worlds are kept apart by means of rituals such as the change of clothing that signals the transition from member of society to athlete. Shaking hands after the match and thanking an opponent for the game is normally regarded as 'sporting'. Strictly speaking, however, this is not what it is, since it is precisely a demonstration of the acceptance that the sport is over and that players now return to being members of the wider society.

Despite the fact that these two worlds differ as far as morality, values and norms are concerned, they are not entirely separate. To some extent they exert an influence on each other. The public's idealisation of 'sporting' behaviour has, for example, left its marks in the form of symbolic actions within sport. An obvious example is to be found in football, where it has become common practice to throw the ball in to the opposing team if they have kicked the ball into touch in order to secure treatment for an injured player. This is now an unwritten rule symbolising fair play. But it just does not alter the overall system of values and norms in sport. As soon as the opponent has got the ball back again, it is no longer the extraneous ideals of fair play that prevail but the will to win, and the players go at each other again just as hard as before.

To maintain that the 'sporting' gesture has nothing to do with morality in sport is not, as I have said, the same as maintaining that sport is immoral.

Sport's appeal to the healthy

If we are to grasp the difference between the respective values and norms of sport and of society, it might be useful to consider what lies behind the different norms and values of society at large. Although the perception is widespread that Western societies are enlightened and secular, it remains a fact that they continue to be dominated by Christianity. In other words society bears the marks of a religion that to an unprecedented degree has nurtured the weak and in many contexts sees weakness as a quality. To nurture weakness as something fundamentally human is still second nature to the Christian culture, something we have to care for physically, psychologically and socially. Religious feeling has not surrendered to progress and reason (see Chapter 7).

Because sport gives our children rosy cheeks and strong limbs, the misplaced belief has arisen that it goes hand in glove with the predominant caring paradigm. Doping scandals, injuries and deaths have raised doubts about sport, but no one – not even the Marxists (though they did come close) – has dared to cast cultural Christian values aside, to take a proper look at those rosy cheeks and strong limbs and to provide a level-headed interpretation of the signs. Instead, the hideous things that happen in sport have been rationalised in terms of villainy beyond sports. Accusations have been thrown at doctors, sponsors, trainers and those athletes who, utterly unworthy of the name and altogether lacking morals, have crept into sport posing under the false name of sportsmen. This is how the ruin of sport is explained. In this way faith, hope and charity in sport can be retained without the inherited norms and values being compromised. A deeper understanding of the attraction of sport requires, however, that we take the body into consideration. Here Nietzsche comes to our aid with the following passage from his *Anti-christ*:

> No one is free to become a Christian or not to do so: one is not 'converted' to Christianity – one must be sufficiently sick for it ... we others, who have the *courage* for health *and* also for Contempt, what contempt *we* have for a religion which teaches Misunderstanding for the body!
>
> ... which makes a 'merit' of eating too little! which combats health as a kind of enemy, devil, temptation! which has persuaded itself that a 'perfect soul' could be carried about in a cadaver of a body and to do so needed to concoct a new conception of 'perfection', a pale, sickly, idiot-fanatic condition, so-called 'holiness' – holiness itself merely a symptom-syndrome of the impoverished, enervated, incurably corrupted body! ... Christianity has at its basis the *rancune* of the sick, the instinct directed *against* the healthy, *against* health. Everything well-constituted, proud,

high-spirited, beauty above all, is hurtful to its ears and eyes. I recall again the invaluable saying of Paul: 'God hath chosen the *weak* things of the world, the *foolish* things of the world, *base* things of the world and things which are *despised*': that was the formula, *in hoc signo, décadence* conquered. – God *on the Cross* – is the fearful hidden meaning behind this symbol still understood? Everything that suffers, everything that hangs on the Cross, is *divine* ... We all hang on the Cross, consequently *we* are divine ... We alone are divine ... Christianity was a victory, a *nobler* disposition perished by it.

(Nietzsche 1968: 168ff)

Nietzsche has given us a lens through which the unchristian element in sport can be viewed. Sport shares Nietzsche's contempt for the weak. The loser is relegated. There is no mercy. Once again boxing comes to mind as a clear-cut example. When the stunned boxer is on his way to the floor, the referee has to step in to avoid the risk of the groggy boxer being given the *coup de grâce* by the winner, whose thoughts are only on finishing off the match. That classic ethical rule, 'Do as you would be done by', is foreign to sport. Here the opposite counts, namely that we should do to the other what we wish them *not* to do to us.

If anyone still has difficulties in accepting that boxing might be representative of sport, we can take cycling instead and listen to Roland Barthes' description of Mount Ventoux, which in the context of the Tour de France towers up as the symbol of the demands of the sport: 'a god of Evil, to which sacrifice must be made. A veritable Moloch, despot of the cyclists, it never forgives the weak' (Barthes 1997: 82). In cycling, weak riders suffer much more than strong ones without that making them winners. If they cannot keep up the pace, they have to drop behind, and if they are not in a position to complete the race within the time limit, they are simply thrown out. In sport those who are mercilessly strong achieve the status of heroes. However strange it may sound, it looks as though a precondition for sporting success is a set of antichristian features modelled to a large extent on the deadly sins. It is certainly true that sportsmen do not get very far without *Greed*, the lust that breeds the player metaphorically hungry for success. *Anger* is, likewise, in many sports a performance-enhancing emotion, and where the emotion appears counterproductive, as, for example, in horse-jumping and gymnastics, its close relative, 'aggression', is often spoken of with approval.

Even though it is usual to speak of an opponent respectfully before the match and for players to say that they will approach the task with humility, they know all too well the importance of self-assurance, of an aura that speaks of victory, and as soon as one gets the upper hand what is demonstrated is not humility but *Pride*. The way in which athletes celebrate a goal or a victory speaks for itself. Rivalry means that players have difficulty dealing with the success of their opponent. The player who, metaphorically speaking, will not sell his soul to win by fair means or foul is unlikely to reach the top in sport. *Envy* is a common sporting feeling, and it is productive in the sense that it makes the envious player work to the utmost in order to win the laurels for himself. Envy is also common between 'club mates', where it functions as a driving force for internal competition. There are good reasons for not speaking openly about envy inside the club, but it can, for example, be felt in the unrest that often arises in clubs when a new star player arrives and unsettles the hierarchy.

To point out that sporting success demands unchristian characteristics is not to claim that sport creates bad people. It is important to understand that anti-Christianity is a manifestation of genuine human health. The will to win is the expression of the healthy body's will to power. In other words, the body is attracted to sport because it is healthy. Athletes have – as Nietzsche might have said – the courage to be healthy. They place their trust in it, take it for granted, put it on the line, and use it as the basis for a sublime joy in living.

Sport is attractive as a preserve in which the strong can deploy health to eliminate weakness with no sense of guilt. It is as a counter-image to the culture of weakness fostered by Christendom that sport exerts its fascination, its provocation. While athletes invest their health trusting in sport, weak people cultivate health as something delicate to be safeguarded. In this way the current cultivation of health is a secular reflection of Christianity. Or, as André Glucksmann has put it: 'The cultivation of health is post-religious and pre-scientific and arises neither from deception, hypocrisy or bad faith, but simply from faith' (Glucksmann 1997: 207).

Body and health

To cultivate health is a sign of weakness. It is stronger to take it for granted. The mismatch between, on the one hand, a defensive, careful approach to health and, on the other, that is offensive and willing to take risks is at the heart of the conflict of norms and values that exists between sport and society around it. A democratic society has difficulties in coming to terms with the Aristocratic tendencies of sport – its clear insistence on separating the sheep from the goats, on the differences between people and on celebrating the strong at the expense of the weak. At the same time it finds it hard not to admire the quality of greatness that this involves. Society attempts to overcome that ambivalence by imagining that sport is something that it is not. Fully aware of its aristocratic nature, the founder of modern Olympism, Pierre de Coubertin, recognised the strategic necessity of asserting a democratic approach in sport in order to secure backing for it. When we read his writings, we cannot but notice how he repeatedly tries to balance his insight into the aristocratic nature of sport with his knowledge of the power of democratic ideology. If, however, we cannot help being struck by his attempt to balance sport's will to excess with society's tendency to prudence, it is equally noticeable that it is when he speaks of the aristocratic side of sport that he expresses himself with the least obfuscation. 'The sporting instinct is', he writes without beating about the bush, 'above all a power instinct' (Coubertin 2000: 269). He regards the Greek cultivation of the body as a model and laments the low status given to the body in the Middle Ages. His explanation for the poverty of bodily culture during the Middle Ages sounds as though it were written with an eye to Nietzsche's writings:

> It is certain that the sporting spirit could easily have developed in Europe in the Middle Ages. But feudalism repressed it, and as soon as the Church became detached from Chivalry it returned to its distrust of physical culture, in which it appeared to descry a dangerous forerunner of free thought.
>
> (ibid.: 271)

Sport is no less dangerous now than it was then, though for different reasons. The project of modernism is constructed on a perception of the equal value of all people. Sport demonstrates that 'human equality' is an empty phrase. Women are not excluded, but they have to compete separately in the great majority of disciplines for otherwise they would be excluded in practice.[4] There is no equality between the sexes. Separation into divisions, or into first and second teams along with terms such as 'star' or 'workhorse' make it clear that there is no equality within the distinct male and female groupings either. It can be hard to accept it, and we might perhaps be tempted to claim that equality and equal status are not the same. However, a glance at differences between contracts in professional football, for example, provides hard-nosed proof of the difference in value accorded to players. Coubertin's way of making the inequality of sport harmonise with the ideals of equality represented by democratic society are striking:

> Inequality in sport is based on justice, because the individual owes what success he obtains only to his natural qualities multiplied by his will-power; it is moreover a very unstable inequality, because this ephemeral form of success exacts continuous effort if it is to endure even for a little.
>
> (ibid.: 273)

The reasoning is curious. Although it is natural for some people to be advantaged by being equipped with superior skills and a good physique, it is not self-evident that it is fair. Not even if the victor is invariably dethroned sooner or later. Those who are disadvantaged can just as easily argue that nature is unfair in that it has placed them in a worse position than others. For, when the king abdicates or falls, it is not they but some other first-rate athlete who takes his place on the throne.

In fact, the viewpoint of the disadvantaged would seem to be intrinsic to the development of civilisation. And we have been brought up with that point of view. Children are taught that they must not hit those who are smaller than them. Nor should they bully. The reason for it being necessary to teach children these things is that it is natural for them to bully and beat up smaller children.[5] As far as we can see, children know instinctively that it is important to get the hierarchy shaken into place and sort the wheat from the chaff. And the reason for the success of our own upbringing, training – or taming – us to respect the weak, may well have something to do with the fact that it started while we ourselves were weak.

It is, however, also clear that it is easier for people who experience frailty in their own physique to advocate the viewpoint of prudence than it is for people at the peak of their physical capacity. For we think through our bodies. In time, we become weak, and in our weakness we become more thoughtful, prudent, gentle. This experience may well have been behind Nietzsche's comment that we are not converted to Christianity, but have to be sufficiently ill to embrace it.

The Middle Ages revolved around the transience of the body as the fragile flesh was devalued and anathematised for the benefit of hope for life in the hereafter. The response of secular society has been to idealise the elasticity of the youthful body while at the same time doing everything in its power to prevent its decay, which is the modern counterpart to the Christian sanctification that Nietzsche castigates in the above quotation. The healthy, young, elastic body feels meanwhile no need for protection. On the contrary, it feels a will to power. But caged behind the bars of civilisation, the horizons of opportunity are beyond its reach. This has a two-fold consequence.

In the first place, 'All instincts that are not allowed free play turn inward. This is what I call man's interiorization', claims Nietzsche, and continues: 'Hostility, cruelty, the delight in persecution, raids, excitement, destruction all turned against their begetter' (Nietzsche 1990: 217ff). In his view, that is the origin of bad conscience. And that bad conscience embraces all members of society and creates the consensus that prevails as regards the norms and values of society.

Second, consensus is not the same thing as complete agreement, and it is self-evident that the physically strong chomp at the bit. The culture of youth is in many ways taking up arms against the ideology of prudence, which has in its own fashion become the *ersatz* religion of secularised society.[6] They feel themselves to be invulnerable and they show it when they smoke behind the bike-shed and later roar off on motorbikes, in cars, and so on. And it is no accident that the one thing most often promoted as a suitable means for seducing the young away from the street corner is sport. During the short span of years in which the body is strong, sport exerts an attraction as the preserve in which the body's will to power can legitimately be realised.

Willingness to sacrifice

The strong – in the case of the athlete – find themselves caught between two sets of values and norms. The demands of these two worlds are, strictly speaking, incompatible. One is play, the other is the real world. One is life in sport, the other in society. Rituals help athletes to move between them without becoming confused or disoriented. But this order falls to pieces the moment sport becomes everything and is prioritised over society. At the point when the athlete is fired by ambition and devotes himself in earnest to sport, he will to some extent unavoidably loosen the bonds that bind him to the norms of life in society. While society around him urges him to take care of his body, the athlete plunges it into his striving to attain his sporting ambitions. Athletes who live and breathe for their sport are prepared to barter their health for a gold medal. In a newspaper article dating from 2000, Dmitry Svatkovsky, the Olympic master in the pentathlon, describes in an interview this in telling terms:

> 'I have traded my health for the Olympic gold, but I have no regrets ... .' Svatkovsky, 29, battled against a number of serious injuries before the Olympics and ruptured his Achilles' tendon last month while playing tennis. 'Before the Olympics me and my doctor decided to go for broke – we killed the pain with (cortisone) shots and now I'm paying the price,' he said. 'That's why my Achilles didn't hold up and ruptured. I would love to remain an active sportsman but I'm tired of walking on crutches. I don't enjoy my life anymore,' he said ... But Svatkovsky said of his gold-medal performance in Sydney: 'It was the greatest day in my life.'
> (http://www.sportserver.com, 18 December 2000)

The spirit of self-sacrifice Svatkovsky expresses here is typical of the ambitious sportsman. There are no regrets at having paid for his success with his health. He is simply frustrated that his body has let him down. If he had been able to continue at the top levels, he would presumably have carried on regardless of the fact that the price would at the end of the day have been higher in the form of even more serious health problems. This is the stuff of which users of doping products are made.

4 Doping history

Fact or fiction?

For as long as human beings have competed with each other, they have used means designed to make the best of their capacity. Many books about doping start by talking about the ancient Greeks. Robert Voy, for instance, writes: 'The earliest accounts of doping among human athletes actually go far back to the ancient Olympic Games, whose documents reveal that athletes drank various brandy or wine concoctions or ingested mushrooms to enhance performance' (Voy 1991: 5). He then goes on to deal with some of the classical accounts from literature. We learn that 'Roman gladiators are said to have taken drugs to enhance performance in the arena and medieval knights frequently ingested stimulants to prepare them for their jousts' (ibid.: 5f). In the second half of the eighteenth century 'canal swimmers racing in Amsterdam were charged with taking *dop* as were a number of cyclists competing throughout Europe' (ibid.: 6). The measures taken were somewhat different from today. Among the substances used were strychnine, cocaine, ether, alcohol or pure oxygen. The purpose, however, was the same – to exploit potential and overcome fatigue and pain.

In the literature of doping, there are a number of stories that are frequently repeated, among them accounts of collapse and death, but they are used exclusively as a prelude to a subsequent analysis of the doping problem from the 1960s onwards. The *essential* information contained in the old narratives, of which some will be evaluated later in this chapter, has so far been overlooked.

In the first place, these narratives drive a stake through the heart of the widespread perception that the use of such measures is relatively new. This means that we can cast aside the thought that the use of doping is a perversion that has become prevalent due to the dizzying sums of money that have flowed into sports with the burgeoning interest shown by commercial television in the spectacle they provide. These stories puncture the notion that filthy lucre – or some other external force – has fundamentally altered noble sportspersons and turned them into monsters. As a result we can prepare to bury any idea that sport can be redeemed if only the forces of good stand together and drive out the evil that has possessed them. These old stories can instead open our eyes and allow us to understand that sport is not possessed by demons, but that it can itself become a demonic force capable of possessing others. A second and more noteworthy aspect of the history of the use of stimulants for competition before the anti-doping campaign is, however, that it contains astonishingly few examples of performance-enhancing substances having had fatal results, despite the fact that the use made by sportspersons of stimulants prior to the 1960s was completely unregulated.[1] This aspect is worth looking at in some detail.

Antiquity

The Greek athletes whom we have idealised in modern times were in reality a tough bunch. Stephen G. Miller gives examples of wrestlers who were strangled or boxers who were killed in the ring. He gives us, for example, a translation of Pausania's gruesome account of the victory of the boxer Kreugas during the Nemean Games. Kreugas was fighting against Damoxenos. The fight dragged on until darkness fell. The two bare-knuckled fighters agreed, therefore, in the presence of witnesses to decide the fight by each in turn giving the other a punch. Kreugas began in proper fashion with a punch to his opponent's head. Then it was Damoxenos' turn. He asked Kreugas to lift his arm and struck him a fearful blow below the ribs. He hit him with his fingers extended. There was such force to his blow that his fingers pierced the skin and penetrated Kreugas' belly, where he grabbed his opponent's intestines and drew them out. Kreugas died on the spot, but was accorded the victory by right, since Damoxenos had broken their agreement by striking with an open hand (Miller 1991: 37).

It was an unusual victory. But it was not unusual for a fight to be to the death. The athletes of ancient times apparently felt that their honour counted for more than their lives, which they willingly risked in order to win. Seen in this light, it is interesting that there are no accounts of athletes dying of the stimulants they took in preparation for these hard-fought combats. If there had been fatalities among athletes at that time due to performance-enhancing substances, one might have expected that they would have been recorded too by the sports critics of the day, who numbered among others the famous doctor Galen, who was never one to mince his words in his critical comment. He does not hesitate to point out, some athletes have their eyes torn out, others suffer repeated fractures to their limbs and end up as cripples at the close of their careers. And, taking as his starting point a quotation of that father of medical science, Hippocrates, he notes that:

> 'Excess is the enemy of nature.' But athletes pay no attention to these or others of his wonderful sayings which they transgress, and their practices are in direct opposition to his doctrines of good health. Furthermore, the extreme conditioning of athletes is treacherous and variable, for there is no room for improvement and it cannot remain constant, and so the only way which remains is downhill. Thus their bodies are in good shape while they are competing, but as soon as they retire from

competition degeneration sets in. Some soon die, some live longer but do not reach old age.

(ibid.: 175f)

Galen sees sport as a threat to good health, but says nothing about the fact that hallucinogenic mushrooms and other substances athletes consumed to give themselves strength had tragic consequences and should be avoided. Of all people Galen was presumably the one who would have known about the fatal consequences of such energising substances, however rare deaths might have been. And given the fact that he did whatever he could to discourage young people from seeking sporting honour and fame, there is no reason to believe that he would have kept his knowledge to himself.

Modern times

For all that, we have to wind the clock forward to modern times before we find the story of sport's first doping victim. This involved the English cyclist, Arthur Linton. The story is to be found in a variety of versions. In 1980, the cycling reporter, Les Woodland, wrote:

> The earliest recorded tragedy directly involving drugs concerned a racing cyclist, variously described as an Englishman called Linton, and as a Dutchman, who died in 1886 during the Bordeaux to Paris race. At around 560km, the event remains to this day the longest single-day cycle race in the world. Linton, according to reports, had been given an overdose of heroin or trimethyl by his trainer, who also manufactured the make of bicycle the hapless Linton was riding.
>
> (Woodland 1980: 13)

The factual uncertainty around this episode clearly bothered Woodland. At any rate he had looked into the case more closely by the time he published a second book on doping in 2003. Here we are told that Linton died ten years later, in 1896, after the Bordeaux–Paris race, which is credible in so far as Linton's name appears on the list of competitors for that year.[2] According to Woodland's new version, Linton is supposed to have been cycling badly and looked in poor shape until he was given a drink of an unknown substance by his manager, the infamous 'Choppy' Warburton. The drink had an amazing effect. Linton livened up to such a degree that – from having been apparently hopelessly behind – he managed to fight his way back into the race and win it. The surprising thing about Woodland's new account is that Linton does not now die immediately after the race but nine weeks afterwards at his home in Wales – and of a fever that also took the life of his brother (Woodland 2003: 20). In other words the account of the first doping fatality of modern sporting history appears to be a tall story, and this has to be said to alter the frame of resonance against which other classical doping dramas of the literature of doping have to be heard. Although they may sound pretty far-fetched, they (also) end without fatalities.

When, for example, the Englishman, Thomas Hicks, won the marathon in the Olympic Games in St Louis, he did so with the aid of a life-threatening dose of strychnine, which, according to Voy (1991), he ingested beaten into raw egg whites. In Woodland's account, it sounds, if possible, even more dramatic. With 16 kilometres to the finishing line, he was in the lead, a comfortable distance ahead of his nearest rivals, but was drained of resources. His assistants gave him yet another injection, whereupon he continued at a good speed for a further 3 kilometres. When he once again found he could go no further, his assistants gave him some brandy and more injections, and he ran on. Six kilometres before the finishing line, he was utterly exhausted and wanted to drop out. But his assistants urged him to keep going. He staggered the last stretch into the stadium and collapsed before he reached the line. Yet another injection and more brandy got him on his legs again and he managed to cross the line as the winner, at which point he fainted 'and in the flowery prose of the time "hung between life and death"' (Woodland 1980: 16). Fortunately he survived and some days later received his hard-earned gold medal.

Four years later, a similar drama was played out at the Olympic Games in London. This time it was the Italian, Dorando Pietri, who reached the stadium first in a wretched state. Completely disoriented, he set off the wrong way round the arena. Officials intervened and got him to turn around. On the point of collapse, he staggered on towards the line, falling several times and being helped to his feet again, as his assistants rushed to his aid. When his nearest rival, the American John Hayes, ran into the stadium looking as though he was going to take the lead from the incapacitated Italian, Pietri's fans took hold of him resolutely by the armpits and dragged him across the finishing line. This well-meant assistance led to Pietri being disqualified and Hayes being proclaimed the winner. The story tells us nothing about the way in which Hayes had got through the race, but Pietri, like Hicks four years earlier, had made use of the performance-enhancing substance, strychnine, which is often spoken of as the cause of his collapse.

Since the performance-enhancing qualities of strychnine were well known and since at that time no doping prohibitions or controls had been introduced, it would be odd if Hicks and Pietri were the only runners to make use of strychnine or other stimulants in the hope of getting through the ordeal at least with credit. If, however, the use of strychnine and other effective substances was – as we have to presume – widespread among long-distance runners and cyclists, we cannot but be struck by the thought that among the older stories that the literature of doping has to offer, there are only a small number of dramatic episodes and no fatalities, not least when we consider the lenient approach to stimulants which the story of Hicks' frequent injections illustrates. When we add to that the completely insane ordeals demanded by early cycling – first with its six-day races, which were exhausting in quite a different way from the moderated versions of our own time, and later with its murderously long road races – we might expect deaths to have been recorded *en masse*. But no. The human body is apparently exceptionally robust. Typical for the genre, Woodland's account of doping jumps from this story about Hicks to the 1930s with a remark that it was a period of experimentation, and he goes on to highlight the point with a curious story about Japanese swimmers who had reaped so many medals at the Olympic Games in Los Angeles in 1932 that suspicions had been aroused as to whether their habit of inhaling pure oxygen immediately before the race could have a performance-enhancing effect.

Of the intervening period Woodland has little to say. Nevertheless he does mention one thing that suggests that if everything were included in the record books there would have been more than enough to scandalise posterity. We are taken back in time to the Tour de France in 1923. The two French riders, brothers Henri and Francis Pélissier complained openly to the assembled press that the course had been so tough that they had been forced to take poison in the form of strychnine pills in order to survive. In the newspaper *Le Petit Parisien* the incident appears as follows:

> 'You have no idea what the Tour is like,' said Henri. 'It's a Calvary. But Christ had only 14 stations of the cross. We have 15. We suffer from start to finish. Do you want to see what we run on? Look.' From his bag he took out a phial: 'That's cocaine for the eyes; that's chloroform for the gums.' 'That,' said Ville, also emptying his *musette*, 'is a cream to warm up my knees.' 'And the pills, do you want to see the pills? Look, here are the pills.' They each took out three boxes. 'In short,' said Francis, 'we run on "dynamite".'
>
> (quoted from Mignon 2003: 230)

There can be no doubt that from the very first cycling was an extremely demanding and unhealthy way of life for professional riders. In the light of that, it appears the more remarkable that doping literature can only present one example of a death by doping prior to 1960, that of Linton – and even that one is highly questionable. This fact, however, seems to have been drowned out by the cries of outrage at the conditions athletes were subjected to and at the widespread use of performance-enhancing drugs long before sport became 'big business'. It can be assumed that doping has been used in all those branches of sport that could use it to procure some advantage. Woodland has even unearthed accounts of the use of doping in squash and football in the 1930s. Today it can be difficult to understand, but it helps to bear in mind that medicine at the time was seen in a more univocally positive light than it is now. Medicines were welcomed as scientific miracles. Side effects were not even a consideration. As late as 1957, the American Medical Association was reporting that: 'Clinical experience of more than twenty years has conclusively demonstrated that amphetamine sulphate is one of the safest drugs available to medical practice' (Woodland 1980: 18).

It is scarcely surprising that some people saw this as an assurance that there could be no problem in recommending amphetamines for performance-enhancing purposes. The use of doping rose dramatically during the course of the 1940s as professional sport began to be a lucrative business, but even here, as close to his own time as this, Woodland can scarcely find a single documented case of a doping fatality. This may be because media reporting and investigation were less intrusive and perhaps less interested in athletes' use of performance-enhancing stimulants at that time. The fact, however, is that in the literature there is often unsubstantiated mention of sports-persons dying as a result of stimulants in the period between Linton's death and 1960. Donahoe and Johnson (1986) even estimate that there were more than a thousand deaths from doping up until 1970. Woodland is more modest in his claims in his first book in 1980, mentioning a cyclist who is supposed to have died of amphetamine poisoning in the Italian town of Rapallo in 1949. Even this information, however, is provided without a reference and the victim's name is not recorded. That is not on the other hand true of the Danish cyclist who died during the Olympic Games in 1960. While in his second book in 2003, Woodland serves up again the myth of the death of Knud Enemark Jensen, he omits the account of the cyclist who was supposed to have died of amphetamine poisoning in Rapallo in 1949.

The death of Knud Enemark Jensen

There is general agreement that Jensen's tragic collapse during the 100 kilometre team event at the Olympic Games in Rome in 1960 was *the* event that placed the anti-doping campaign on the agenda of sports politics – and, indeed, of politics as a whole. WADA President, Dick Pound, writes for example:

> It was well known that stimulants, such as amphetamines, were widely used in cycling. The need to do something was underlined by the death of a Danish cyclist during the Rome Olympics ... the death being attributed at least in part to the use of stimulants. Momentum began to grow for a way to control such drugs and, by the time of the Grenoble Winter Olympics in 1968, the IOC had formed a medical commission for that purpose and had commenced drug testing.
>
> (Pound 2004: 55)

Pound expresses himself, we note, with care. He only links Jensen's death indirectly with use of amphetamines. This is not generally the case. As a rule, the link made is clear and unambiguous. The political scientist, Barrie Houlihan, expresses it, for example, as follows:

> In 1960 the Danish cyclist, Knut Jensen, collapsed and died at the Rome Olympic Games during the 175-kilometres team time-trials following his

use of amphetamines and nicotine acid. Jensen's two team-mates, who had taken the same mixture, also collapsed but later recovered in hospital.

(Houlihan 1999: 36)

That Jensen died as a result of his use of amphetamines is presented as a fact. If we ignore the facts that the name of the cyclist who died was not Knut, that the distance was not 175 kilometres and that Jensen did not have two but three team mates, namely Niels Baunsøe, Vagn Bangsborg and Jørgen B. Jørgensen, we can still take issue with two points. In the first place it is claimed that Jensen had taken amphetamines but no reference is given. In the second nowhere is there any evidence for the suggestion that other members of the team might (also) have taken amphetamines. That Houlihan writes with so little attention to the details is presumably because he has read the story of Knud Enemark Jensen's death so many times in the literature of doping that he has simply reworked it from memory. As far as I am aware, there is no researcher who has gone to the trouble of conducting an in-depth investigation into the circumstances surrounding Jensen's death. Instead a rumour has circulated, more or less unconsciously, and has gradually been elevated to the status of common knowledge. A Danish journalist, Lars Bøgeskov, has, however, studied the case, and his account is both exciting and provides a rich source of enlightenment. Since it raises questions about the deep-rooted myth, it deserves thorough scrutiny and evaluation.

Before the first half of the stage had been completed, one of the four riders on the team, Jørgen B. Jørgensen, had already given up trying to keep up to speed. He felt unwell in the heat and let himself drop out of the race. Since it was the third man's time that counted, it was therefore vital that Jensen – despite the fact that he, too, was complaining of feeling unwell during the race – made it to the finishing line with the others. In a photograph in the Danish tabloid *Ekstra Bladet* dated 27 August, the day after the tragedy, we can see the two remaining team-mates one on each side of Jensen, holding him up by his shirt, trying to support him to stop him keeling over. The caption on the photo reads: 'Team mates Baunsøe and Bangsborg try to keep Knud Enemark on his bike as he is hit by heat stroke.' Below it we see the famous picture where Jensen crashes to the ground, cracking his head and suffering concussion. The text continues: 'They did not manage to hold him up. Knud Enemark collapses on the road, as Niels Baunsøe looks on in horror.'

Despite this being part of the episode, it is never mentioned. Nor is it mentioned in the doping literature I am aware of that 31 other riders were struck by heat stroke during that famous race, which would seem to indicate that the heat was a significant factor. The literature of doping is also silent about what may be the fatal point of the story – that Jensen, unlike the other riders who had collapsed, was not cooled down but on the contrary was taken by first aid personnel to a tent, where he lay for about two hours in temperatures of around 50 degrees Celsius (Bøgeskov 2001: 12). This silence can possibly be explained by the fact that the tragedy has never been used for anything other than evidence that the implementation in the 1960s of an actual policy to counter doping was based on the fatal consequences of doping. The thing that distinguishes Houlihan from other people who have given an account of Jensen's death is that he retells the myth without taking the trouble to refer to even one of the earlier works that claim to know that Jensen was doped with amphetamines. If, for example, he had referred to Chapter 2 of David R. Mottram's (1996) *Drugs in Sport*, he could have laid it at the door of 'former Director of Ethics and Anti-Doping in UK Sport', Michele Verroken, who gives the impression that she has proof of the fact that Jensen's death was doping-related. With firm strokes of her pen, but with no evidence, she maintains:

> At the 1960 Rome Olympics, the cyclist Knud Jensen died on the opening day of the Games as he competed in the 100 km team time trial. Two team mates were also taken to hospital. The *post mortem* revealed traces of amphetamine and nicotinyl nitrate in Jensen's blood.
>
> (Verroken, in Mottram 1996: 19)

Verroken writes as though she has seen the *post mortem* report at first hand, but the probability is that she, too, is simply passing on hearsay. The report is, in fact, not accessible.

The vast majority of researchers studying doping have apparently had no interest in probing the circumstances surrounding Jensen's death, let alone expressed the least uncertainty as to whether there is any justification for classifying it as a case of doping on the basis of the evidence available. A reasonable explanation might be that he has become for posterity the symbol of an immoral practice. There is in any event no way of salvaging his reputation, despite the fact that there was at the time no general prohibition against doping. Just listen to Robert Voy:

> Perhaps the landmark amphetamine-related tragedy in Olympic history occurred when Danish cyclist Knud Enemark Jensen collapsed and died during the 175.38-km road race at the Summer Olympiad in Rome. It was reported at the time that, leading up to his death, Jensen was taking, supposedly on doctor's orders, a combination of nicotynal alcohol and amphetamine, sarcastically nicknamed by his competitors the 'Knud Jensen diet.' Several of the other athletes competing in Jensen's race collapsed like Jensen had at the finish; however, Jensen was the only fatality. An autopsy revealed that Jensen probably died from dehydration by the amphetamine in his system, though his skull had also been fractured.
>
> (Voy 1991: 6f)

Yet again, no evidence is provided for the claim that Jensen made use of amphetamines (and yet again we find errors of fact in the account). The story has, on the other hand, been embellished with an extra dimension, in that it is suggested that Jensen was actually notorious among his fellow competitors for using a particular 'doping diet'. Such are the webs of invention that can be weaved. But what, when it comes down to it, do we actually know about this case?

Circumstantial evidence

Under the headline 'Olympic Trainer Admits Giving Drugs to Danish Cyclist Who Died', the following article could be read in the *New York Times* of 29 August 1960:

> The trainer of Denmark's Olympic cycling team revealed tonight that the Danish bicycle rider who died after a race in the Olympics last Friday had been given a drug. The rider was Knut Enemark Jensen, 22 years old [he was in fact 23, VM]. He collapsed during the 100-kilometer (62.5-mile) team road race in Rome and died later in that day. The trainer Oluf Jorgensen told the Danish Government organ *Aktuelt* that he had given the drug Roniacol to Jensen and other members of the Danish cycling team. Preben Z. Jensen, the leader of the Danish Olympic cycling team, confirmed Jorgensen's statement in a report to the Danish Road Biking Union. Preben Jensen told the union that the trainer had given a stimulant to the team's four members prior to the race. He said Jorgensen admitted on Friday night, only a few hours after Enemark Jensen's death, that pills had been given to the cyclists. No reason was given why the report had been withheld until now. Jorgensen said the purpose of the drug was to intensify blood circulation. He said he had obtained the prescription from his doctor.
>
> (*New York Times* 1960)

It seems then to be indisputable that Jensen took a medical substance prior to the race, and in all probability in the expectation that it would improve his performance. Roniacol is, however, a vasodilative substance with no real performance-enhancing effect. It is true that it makes the blood flow more freely to the muscles, but it also has the effect that, when the body is subjected to substantial physical exertions, blood pressure falls and the blood supply to non-functioning muscles and organs is not stopped as effectively as normal. The blood supply to functioning muscles and to the skin, therefore, is not optimal. In other words, Roniacol actually reduced performance and in certain circumstances may have increased the risk of heat collapse. It contributed to a fall in blood pressure, which was probably intensified by dehydration. Falls in blood pressure bring accompanying dizziness and discomfort. In this light, the description of what happened given by the journalist, Lars Bøgeskov, sounds convincing:

> There are not many hills, but not much shade either. The pace is quick. Not long after the four Danes have cycled out for the second round,

Jørgen B. Jørgensen is suddenly gone – he just drops out suddenly. Shortly afterwards he is driven to Rome's central hospital. Cycling up the only slight slope on the way to the turning point for the last time both Knud Enemark and Vagn Bangsborg complain of stiffness in their legs. Only Niels Baunsøe still has real leg power left. 'Put yourselves behind me,' says Baunsøe, and then he pedals like fury for the turning point. And Niels Baunsøe is really travelling fast. On the sharp bend at the turning point a spectator shouts out that the three Danes are now only ten seconds from getting a bronze. Baunsøe puts himself in the lead again in the light headwind across the sun-parched plain. 'Now it's the home straight,' says Knud Enemark, prepared to grit his teeth and get through the last of his agonies, his focus on the Olympic medal. But with eight kilometres left, Knud Enemark shouts out, 'I feel dizzy!' And as the riders come within five kilometres of the finish, Enemark is only half-conscious. He loses ground and his bike lurches from side to side. Niels Baunsøe holds him up on his bike by his shirt, while Vagn Bangsborg sprays water on his head. The bike wobbles, but then Enemark regains consciousness. 'Are you OK?' asks Baunsøe. 'Yes,' says Enemark, and Baunsøe lets go of his shirt, but in the next instant Enemark faints and falls heavily onto the hot asphalt. The 100-kilometre team's car with the team manager Preben Z. Jensen immediately turned their car round and fetched an ambulance, which the riders had passed 400 metres back up the road. Meanwhile cycling teams were passing the collapsed Enemark from behind. Knud Enemark was laid on a stretcher and placed in the ambulance, which drove him to the area of the finishing line. Here an army tent had been erected, and here the unconscious Knud Enemark was laid. Niels Baunsøe and Vagn Bangsborg coasted to the finish, but Bangsborg was also feeling dizzy. He threw up and was driven to the Olympic village. Baunsøe rode his bike. In the army tent the heat was even more oppressive than on the road, and it was here that in the meantime the 23-year-old Knud Enemark died. The time was 15.30.

(Bøgeskov 1998: 14)

Great things had been expected of the Danish team prior to the race – and with good reason. Jensen had won an individual event in a Nordic championship two months before, and earlier in the year the team had been neck and neck with the Germans, who were reckoned to be among the favourites for a medal, alongside the Russians and the Italians. Conditions were the same for all teams, but if the Danes had been given Roniacol by their trainer prior to the Olympic race, then it is understandable that they became dizzy, felt ill and performed below par under such extreme conditions. The only mystery surrounds Niels Baunsøe, who was the only one not to feel unwell and who against all odds rode like a dream and after all his exertions was still fresh enough to cycle back to the Olympic village.

Two explanations present themselves. One is that he was the only one on the team to refuse to take a Roniacol tablet. The other is that in addition to Roniacol he also took amphetamine. Amphetamine has a performance-enhancing effect, and also increases the potency of the effect of adrenalin and noradrenalin – which, put simply, are the flight and fight hormones – and has a vaso-constrictive effect. Amphetamine can in other words counteract the negative effects of Roniacol. Despite this fact, no suspicion has ever fallen upon Baunsøe – and for good reason. In the first place, there was, as I have said, no prohibition against doping at the time. Second, all eyes were, of course, on Jensen.[3]

Whatever the truth of the matter, Jensen's death contributed to the European Commission adopting a resolution against doping in 1963, after which a campaign against the phenomenon began to take shape for real, and in cycling doping controls came into force two years later. Of the 102 riders tested in the course of the 1965 season, 38 (i.e. 37.5 per cent) tested positive (Woodland 2003: 116) – an indication that performance-enhancing substances were an integral part of cycling. What may give us pause for thought, however, is that when the English cyclist, Tom Simpson, died in front of the whirring cameras on Mount Ventoux in 1967, it took place *after* cycling had begun regarding doping as a problem and *after* controls had been imposed.

Death: a possible consequence of the anti-doping campaign?

The desire to impose controls did not stem from those involved in the sport. They regarded medication as an aid. That very year the five times Tour de France winner, the Frenchman Jacques Anquetil, had failed to have his improved world hour-record acknowledged because he refused to comply with the demand of the inspector to give a urine sample on the spot. Like the Pélissier brothers, he made no attempt to hide the fact that he used stimulants. He saw it as his own private choice and regarded doping control as an intrusive attack on his personal freedom. All professional riders doped themselves, he claimed (Brunel 1996: 71).

But Simpson's death intensified the attention given to the doping problem. Controls were tightened up both inside cycling and beyond. The following year the IOC introduced systematic doping tests. This marked the end of the liberal and transparent views on the doping issue that Anquetil and others had aired in previous years. A consensus appeared to spread that doping was antithetical to the image of sport.

Silence did not, however, make the problem disappear. On the contrary, systematic doping controls were, as far as can be seen, met by new and equally systematic doping methods. Naturally enough, doping tests were directed at familiar substances. This made it more advantageous to use new ones. Since, however, confidence in the use of new products is not as great as with familiar ones, this unquestionably involved an increased health risk to cyclists. This is something pointed out later by the 1966 Tour de France winner, Lucien Aimar, in a comment on the Simpson tragedy: 'They made an emblem of him. The result of pushing Simpson and the problem of amphetamines to the forefront was the tightening of dope controls and riders were pushed toward more and more dangerous medicaments' (Woodland 2003: 125).

Twenty years after the Simpson tragedy, in 1987–88, 'fourteen Dutch riders and four Belgians – all young and apparently healthy athletes – died suddenly' (Waddington 2000: 180). Their deaths were a sinister confirmation of Aimar's statement. So many deaths in such a short time among otherwise healthy riders could scarcely be the product of pure chance. As Ivan Waddington explains, 'The overwhelming probability is that some, if not all of these unexpected and unexplained deaths where associated with the use of EPO' (ibid.: 180). The new wonder drug, erythropoietin (EPO), came on the market in 1987 primarily for the use of kidney patients who produced insufficient quantities of the hormone EPO, which increases the production of oxygen-carrying red blood cells. That EPO could increase the red cell count meant that it also had the potential to enhance athletic performance. But at the same time EPO also had the side effect that the viscosity of the blood is increased, and the risk of blood clots rises (Schänzer 2005: 29f). It is therefore essential for EPO to be given in the correct dosage, haematocrit values (the percentage of red blood cells in the blood) must be monitored closely, and if necessary an anticoagulant can be given to reduce viscosity.

The 18 deaths lead us to the supposition that the awareness of the performance-enhancing effect of EPO was in advance of an understanding of its risk factors. We cannot blame people outside the world of sport for believing that the deaths brought people to their senses and reduced the use of doping. That, however, can scarcely be the explanation for the fact that similar deaths did not occur in the following years. The French anti-doping raid on the Tour de France in 1998 indicated that the use of EPO among professional cycling throughout the 1990s had been massive. And a similar raid during the Giro d'Italia in 2001 was a reminder that the use of doping remained substantial despite the international anti-doping collaboration that was subsequently set in motion. The more likely explanation was, therefore, that those involved in doping – whether they were physicians, soigneurs or the athletes themselves – had learned from the fatalities and were making allowances for the side effects. In other words, that tragic experience had made the use of the drug safer. As far as we can tell, an extremely risky competition took place between riders as to who dared force their haematocrit values highest. Nevertheless sudden fatalities had become a thing of the past. But the situation was of course highly explosive. This is something that becomes apparent when reading the book written by Willy Voet, the soigneur of the Festina team. The man who set the cat among the pigeons in 1998 by being stopped with a considerable load of banned pharmaceutical products in his car describes the situation as follows:

The years from 1994 to 1998 were crazy ones for the Festina Team: full of success, constantly growing popularity and results which took us step by step to the head of the UCI's world team points rankings. These were the years of folly. Aside from the new boys and a few other clean riders who were left on the margins, we would see the whole spectrum of drug-taking; everyone was at it, whatever team they were in. Even if some went further than others in the arms race. Remember Bjarne Riis' stunning win on the Hautacam climb in the 1996 Tour de France. The Dane, who was to win the race, literally played with his rivals before obliterating them. And the hematocrit level of his rivals, certainly at Festina, had been blithely boosted to about 54 per cent.

(Voet 2001: 98)

The fact that no rider died among whom many have later admitted to doping suggests that the medical assistance given to the riders was competent. Keeping in mind the doping deaths of 1987–88, we have to assume that, if it had been left to the riders themselves to manage things off their own bat without professional advice, the combination of lack of understanding and will to win would have driven more to their deaths. Even with competent advice on hand, it remained a problem that EPO could not be traced in a doping test. For this meant that, in reality, the sky was the limit. Each individual rider had to make a calculated risk assessment in the full knowledge that the others were all doing the same. Victory or defeat could in the last analysis depend on an advantage of a single percentage point of their haematocrit level. Regardless of the fact that all conceivable precautions were taken to reduce the risk, there was always the chance that it would go wrong at some time or other. Sooner or later one of the top stars of the sport would die of cardiac arrest in one of the major stage races. Before things got to that point, however, cycling chose a very pragmatic solution to the problem. Since there was no direct EPO test, they could at the very least introduce an indirect test by establishing a maximum haematocrit level of 50 per cent. This meant that riders would have to accept taking a blood test. That the riders did so without any resistance is a sign that, when it comes down to it, their will to win is not stronger than their will to live. Introducing the haematocrit limit of 50 per cent meant that the worst of the risk of using EPO was removed. The problem was reduced, though not eliminated. In view of the fact that most people have a haematocrit level of 42–45 per cent – a value that tends moreover to fall in endurance training – there was still a significant margin for performance enhancement. If competitors could not count themselves among those rare types who have a natural haematocrit level of around 50 per cent, they simply had no choice but to use EPO if they wanted to be sure that they entered a race with a competitive blood count. And here a new problem arose. The introduction of the haematocrit limit neutralised the chance of extracting a competitive advantage by running greater risks than your rivals. Riders who had already exceeded the doping ban in order to achieve competitive blood counts now began to look around for supplementary medication that could provide them with the edge they were looking for.

This logic is presented by the Danish cyclist Jesper Skibby, a prominent figure of the so-called 'golden generation' of Danish cycling. That generation achieved great success in the 1990s and included names such as Rolf Sørensen (winner of the classic Liège–Bastogne–Liège 1993 and the Tour of Flanders 1997), Bo Hamburger (winner of Fleche Wallonne 1998, and second place in the 1997 UCI Road World Championship after Festina rider Laurent Brochard, who was caught up in the Festina scandal the following year and admitted doping) and Bjarne Riis (winner of the Tour de France 1996). As mentioned by Voet in the quotation given above, it was Riis who, as sports director and owner of the world's leading cycling team, CSC, prior to the 2007 tour confessed to having used doping on a daily basis during his prime years 1993–98. His confession came after those of a number of his team mates who as domestiques[4] had helped him fulfil his ambition in the French race. In his unusually candid autobiography, this erstwhile rider on the strong Dutch TVM team, Skibby, recounts how, in 1991, after a couple of years with poor results he contacted a doctor who would be able to give renewed impetus to his career. He met his doctor in a hotel room during a minor stage race early in the season and was given a cortisone injection. The drug has both a restorative effect and is performance-enhancing. He took the injection without the least shadow of a guilty conscience.

> I was part of a tough profession and used all the aids I thought were necessary to succeed in it. It was as simple as that. My world was cycling, and if the sport was removed from it, then my world, everything I knew, would fall apart and leave me empty-handed. Everything would be gone. The entire basis for my existence would disappear, and everything I had achieved would mean nothing.
>
> (Skibby 2006: 121)

There was no one coercing him to indulge in doping.[5] There was, of course, an expectation that he would come up with results, but no one ever suggested to him that he could use illegal substances. It was simply and solely his own decision, and once he had made it, the rest was easy. There does not appear to be any serpent in the grass who can be given the blame. He has no bone to pick with the doctor who helped him. On the contrary, he allows him to appear in the book without naming him and when he refers to him his continued respect and admiration for the man are unmistakable.

> My contact, as I will refer to this nameless person, was a skilled doctor, who had over several years acquired a thoroughgoing knowledge of medicines capable of increasing the performance levels of a rider ... His advice and expertise ensured that over the following ten years I never

tested positive for doping. He also ensured that there was never a time when I was not optimally primed, as they say in cycling when a rider is doped.

(Skibby 2006: 122)

As soon as he set off down the doping road, he was hooked. It gave him strength to know that he had done everything he could to succeed. But he also knew that the effect of the injections did not last forever, that the treatment would have to be repeated if he was to maintain his level. And he started using drugs other than cortisone. He discovered that caffeine tablets combined with the tranquilliser Amineptine strengthened his concentration and helped calm his anxiety that things might go wrong in the heat of a sprint finish. He began to do better and to acquire a greater influence over the team. Now, after his career has ended, he can see how his decision to resort to doping caught him in a vicious circle. He brought prestigious victories home for the team. His value as a rider increased. The same went for his popularity. He had won two stages of the Vuelta a España, and entered the Tour de France with high expectations, but then had to bale out. There was something else that was missing. He knew that there was no more to give physically, since he had already trained to the maximum. He turned his gaze once again, therefore, towards improvement through medication:

At the beginning of 1992 I use growth hormone for the first time. Combined with cortisone it makes a powerful cocktail and that combination became the foundation of my use of doping for the remainder of my career. I felt I was amazingly strong, felt as though I had incredible energy … Growth hormones are muscle-building, but I noticed no change in my body. I did not turn into a superman, but I became stronger. Once again, what was most noticeable was the mental change … It was not that the products in themselves did anything to my head. It was more the awareness that I was prepared to the utmost that made me strong. And all the time I was looking for information on new methods that would be able to maintain this feeling of being insuperable, invulnerable, immortal.

(ibid.: 126)

This is the nub of the matter. At the point at which results begin to slump, riders used to doping and accustomed to winning start looking for new ways forward to secure their position. Skibby states that he came to be dependent on knowing that he was abreast of developments in performance-enhancing drugs. This he narrates in connection with his experience of an unexplained fatality that struck cycling at the end of the 1980s. He followed the rumours in the press that the cause of death had been an effective new doping substance. His fellow riders were also talking about it. Then the incident faded away, until the rumours started to circulate again,

[B]ecause some of the southern European teams suddenly started to ride like bats out of hell. Once again the press transmitted reports that EPO was in the frame. But now the correct dosage of the drug had apparently been discovered. This aroused my curiosity. It was true that the deaths that had occurred during the period 1987–90 were frightening, but a lot of water seemed to have gone under the bridge since then. After that first injection, doping had become a completely natural part of my everyday life for me, and in my eternal hunt for new opportunities I read the newspaper articles not as warnings but as signposts. A product with the characteristics that were being described and which was also impossible to trace in a doping test had to be something for me. I was so caught up in the notion that doping was the only way that it took more than a whole series of deaths to make me kick it into touch.

(ibid.: 127)

Skibby's admission helps us to understand that the values that underlie the anti-doping campaign are different from those that prevail in the sport. The will to win is far stronger than the will to stay healthy. Performance-enhancing drugs will always have an appeal for the most ambitious riders. There are without a doubt many who resist the temptation for fear of being discovered, for fear of the needle, or because they reckon that it is not worth risking their health. To say that ambitious athletes' will to win is stronger than their will to be healthy is not the same as saying that they are not concerned about their health. The truth of the matter is that some of them are willing to do more violence to it than others. This is something that neither scare campaigns nor intensive test programmes and harsh sanctions can influence. If you do not believe that a given risk to health makes any real difference to your chances, then your willingness to run that risk is evidently less than if you sense that there is a good chance that the risk will pay off. The bottom line is that, in sport, health is not regarded as something that has to be protected at all costs. On the contrary, it is seen as a resource that can be invested with a view to victory and success. Despite the fact that all professional riders had heard that EPO had in all probability killed 18 of their colleagues, many of them were still prepared to use the drug once the positive effects became known and once there appeared to be a good general idea of what dosage should be used. Its clear performance-enhancing effects, coupled with the fact that it could not be traced, made it irresistible for many riders. Seen in this light, it does not require much imagination to see that the introduction of a haematocrit limit – which takes the top end not only of the risk but also of the effect – made some riders look to other measures in order to keep their performance at a peak. Nor is it hard to see that the willingness to experiment with alternative drugs increases the instant a reliable EPO test is developed, making the hormone a real problem to use as a doping substance. The fact that the raid that took place during the Giro d'Italia in 2001 uncovered drugs still in the trial stage and not approved as substances for medical use would seem to prove this point (Schänzer and Thevis 2007: 645).

If, therefore, as WADA President, Dick Pound, claims, the anti-doping campaign's 'initial concerns were related almost entirely to the health of athletes' (Pound 2004: 55f), then we might easily conclude that the anti-doping campaign is not achieving its aims. The history of performance-related drugs in sport before 1960 throws up astonishingly few instances of doping-related fatalities. Two of the most prominent examples, the deaths of Arthur Linton in 1896 and of Knud Enemark Jensen in 1960, are, as far as we can judge, myths. The anti-doping campaign can scarcely be applauded for having achieved a reduction in the number of doping-related deaths. The question is whether it has contributed in other ways to altering the attitudes of athletes and to raising their moral standards, factors which in the longer term might bring about a reduction in the use of illegal performance-enhancing drugs.

5 The law of silence

When Jesper Skibby chose to make his confession by means of a detailed description of his use of doping over many years, the revelations naturally aroused considerable media interest in Denmark. Such was the status and profile of the golden generation within Danish society that a similar level of media attention would have been aroused if any of the riders had authored a similar confession. The fact that it was Skibby who came forward, however, had wider implications. Skibby was one of the most popular riders of his generation, always accommodating towards journalists, always cheerful and ready to respond with a funny comment. What was more, he always gave the impression of being an upright, warm person with a gentle and appealing nature. That it should have been Skibby who confessed made it difficult to maintain the illusion that sportsmen who used doping were nasty people.

The price of silence

In 1999, Denmark's Radio broadcast the award-winning documentary programme *Tavshedens Pris* (*The Price of Silence*), dealing with the systematic use of doping in cycling. If it had not been for the revelations from the doping raid in France in 1998, the programme would have been a bombshell. It came out a year after that great furore and as a result it created less of a sensation. Nevertheless it attracted well-deserved attention by underlining the systematic doping that was going on in cycling. The programme suggested that many, if not all, of the best teams in the 1990s used performance-enhancing drugs in preparing for competitions.

Before the Festina scandal, teams had an astonishingly easy-going attitude to doping substances. They were, in Ivan Waddington's words, living in a 'culture of tolerance' (Waddington 2000: 163) and did not do much to keep what was going on under wraps. Used needles and syringes were dumped in public rubbish containers or thrown in rubbish bags in the teams' hotel rooms. Sometimes the label had been torn off. In other cases not even that precaution had been taken. The journalists behind the programme, Olav Skaaning Andersen and Niels Christian Jung, therefore, could go hunting through the outdoor rubbish containers or in the teams' hotel rooms and find bags with remnants of medication, once the teams had left their hotel and before the cleaning staff arrived to remove the rubbish. They travelled round Europe finding incriminating material taken from both major and minor teams. All this was put on view. As Danes, however, it was natural that they should choose to take a Danish angle with the Tour de France winner, Bjarne Riis, as their central focus.

Before his victory in 1996, which Riis won as part of the Team Deutsche Telekom, he rode on the strong Italian team, Gewiss-Ballan. In 1995, when he took third place in the Tour, he managed to go down in history as the first Dane to step onto the podium in Paris. About a month later the modest counterpart, the Tour of Denmark, took place. Gewiss-Ballen entered the race with Riis as their captain. His phenomenal ride in the greatest arena of cycling immediately before this had, of course, made him into a superstar in his homeland, and the public poured out to see him in overwhelming numbers. The Tour of Denmark turned into a triumphal procession, and with his overall victory Riis added further to the national euphoria swelling around him.

While ordinary Danes were crowding the highways to cheer Riis and his cycling prowess, Andersen and Jung were hunting elsewhere for explanations for the strength of the Gewiss-Ballan team. Jung, who had ridden in his early youth as an elite amateur rider and later, in 1992, had started on a more modest career as a masseur, had found an opportunity to help the Gewiss-Ballan team in that capacity during the race. In one of the team's hotel rooms he found a paper bag printed with the team logo. It proved to contain bloodied needles and syringes with residues of drugs, among them EPO. Whether this was something Riis had used the journalists could not, of course, determine. However, during the autumn of 1998 they acquired access via a source to confidential documents indicating that EPO doping was widely used in the Gewiss-Ballan team during the Tour de France. On their rest day the team had been given a blood test. This was not official, for the blood test only became obligatory with the introduction of the haematocrit limit in 1997, but the team apparently had made an agreement with the Ferrari Institute in Italy to conduct a comprehensive test programme (Andersen and Jung 1999). A doctor from the institute, Ilario Casoni, supervised the test and – according to the document that came into the possession of Andersen and Jung – it revealed a haematocrit value for Bjarne Riis of 56.3. For the record, it has to be said that six of the nine riders in the Gewiss-Ballan Tour de France team were entered with a haematocrit value of over 50, and Riis was not the highest. What Andersen and Jung drew attention to, however, was the fact that another document showed that outside the cycling season Riis had registered a value of 41.1. This marked difference was a clear indication of the use of EPO that we now know for certain he engaged in after he came forward during a televised press conference in Copenhagen admitting, 'I have taken doping. I have taken EPO.'[1]

With its identification of doping as being an extremely widespread phenomenon in cycling, this documentary programme was an important supplement to the French revelations. The eye-opener as far as the Festina affair was concerned was the fact that it was not an individual rider who was caught in the doping trap but an entire team. The revelation knocked a hole in the myth that the use of doping was the preserve of villains. Instead, doping had to be understood as an integral part of the system. This placed extreme pressure on the management of the Tour de France, who could no longer restore calm in the usual way by individually excluding riders who had been caught through doping controls. And the case became all the more embarrassing for the French organisers in that their national superstar, Richard Virenque, was riding on the team that had been exposed. Virenque stubbornly denied having had anything to do with the case and implored the race director, Jean-Marie Leblanc, not to throw the team out. In the end, however, the Festina case became so damaging that Leblanc could see no way out other than to sacrifice the team in an improvised attempt to restore some form of credibility. The survival of the Tour was at stake.

This drastic decision was clearly more than anything else a way of saving the race in the long term by restoring the image of the sport. None of the riders on the team that was excluded had registered as positive in an official test. None of them had been caught in the preliminary health check; their haematocrit level lay within what was permitted. They were not thrown out on the spot on 8th July, when Voet was stopped with the medication at Neuville-en-Ferrain. Nor when the manager of the team, Bruno Roussel, and its doctor, Eric Ryckaert, were remanded in custody on 15 July, after Voet had indicated that he was acting on orders from the management of the team. It was only on 17 July, when Roussel admitted under questioning that riders on his team were using doping, that Leblanc came to the realisation that he was forced to throw the team out. The previous day, 16 July, he had still seemed prepared to fight his corner, giving assurances that the riders would not be thrown out before concrete evidence of their guilt lay before him (Jakobsen 2004: 606). Roussel's admission was not evidence of that kind. What it most resembled was the desire of a desperate man to pass the buck on to his riders after he himself had been handed the buck by Voet.

We might well wonder why Leblanc waited so long, but the reason is probably that it was clear to him that throwing Festina out would be fuelling a lie. It was true that Voet had infringed French law by driving around with prescription medicines in the boot of his car, but that was, as indicated earlier, no proof that the Festina riders had contravened the rules of cycling. The discovery in Voet's car had already provided more than a hint of what Roussel admitted nine days later. Added to that is the fact that many of the competing teams rode just about as fast. Telekom, who had won the Tour in both 1996 and 1997, rode even faster. And the quantity of EPO Voet had in his car was so large that it can only invite speculation as to whether a proportion of the vials was intended for other teams (ibid.: 609).

Whatever the truth of the matter, if we accept that EPO treatment has a performance-enhancing effect, then it hardly came as a surprise that the

Telekom team who rode (at least) as fast were using the same treatment. And the fact that Festina was not the fastest team in the peloton was undoubtedly a significant reason for Leblanc to insist that concrete proof should be presented against the riders before he was prepared to show them the door. The fact that he chose in the end to waive that principle suggests that he caved in to pressure on strategic grounds. He threw the media pack the pound of flesh they were demanding in order not to smash the cycling event completely. Once Festina had been excluded, however, the show went on, borne by the illusion of the remaining teams as less tainted, despite the fact that further raids by the police revealed that illegal substances were also found in the possession of, for example, team TVM, team Once and team Casino (Waddington 2000: 158f).

Because of the intervention of the authorities, the Tour de France of 1998 became more than anything else a revelation of the way in which the elite world of cycling was saturated with doping. This was what *The Price of Silence* underscored when the programme showed that syringes and powerful medication also accompanied the teams on minor races such as the Tour of Denmark. This was important information. However, the personal angle taken, with Riis in a starring role, pushed the systematic doping of cycling away from the centre of attention to an unfocused spot on the periphery, and the false impression of doping users as parasites threatening the life of the sport was once again brought to the fore.

The myth of the pure hero and the doped villain

At the World Congress of sports journalists, Play the Game, held in Copenhagen in 2000, Andersen and Jung were invited to talk about their research and show extracts from the programme. Their presentation was met with enthusiasm, and the question and answer session went smoothly until someone in the audience took the liberty of asking whether, during their work, they had come into possession of actual proof that Bjarne Riis was guilty. That meant proof that could hold up in a court of law. The answer was 'No'. This prompted the questioner to continue: 'What is the purpose of producing a programme that accuses a sportsman of doping without having legal proof for that claim? Is this a step on a crusade to promote a form of Puritanism that is foreign to cycling?'

This proved to be an effective form of provocation. The originators of the programme were not given a chance to answer for themselves. David Walsh from *The Sunday Times* swivelled round on his chair to deliver the reply: 'We are fighting the bad guys in the cause of the good guys.' The response was met with applause from colleagues present. A consensus apparently prevailed that the hero–villain template so effective for journalistic purposes represented a realistic picture of reality. If Riis had not ridden clean – as they had just been persuaded was the case – then it was legitimate to expose him as a villain who concealed the truth.

Unfortunately the questioner allowed himself to submit to the hostile mood of the floor and so refrained from asking Walsh to pronounce the names of a couple of those whom he thought he was fighting for. It would have been interesting to hear his response. Walsh would at the time probably have felt fairly confident in naming the British Tour de France hopeful, the time trial specialist, David Millar. For in the wake of the famous Tour of 1998, he had been making a name for himself and sending out all the right messages. It sounded impressive, for example, when in a newspaper article under the headline 'Time to stop cheating, pleads Millar', he let it be known that 'There are a lot of stupid guys in cycling. You really have to question whether they have any ethics at all.' And later in the same article he elaborated:

> Before last year's Tour you could understand why people were taking drugs, but since then we've crossed the line. We've got to a point where we can say 'OK, let's stop it'! It's become a moral issue. Before it could be called professionalism, now it is just plain cheating and that's what gets me down.
>
> (Longmore 1999)

In these statements Millar singles himself out as being exemplary. However, as events subsequently proved, he was not as clean as he claimed. In June 2004, the French drugs squad found a couple of syringes in his bookcase. The syringes had been used for EPO doping. Prior to his home being ransacked, several of his team-mates on Cofidis had been done for doping. This was a strong indication that the systematic use of doping by teams had not stopped after 1998, although the use of drugs may have become less careless. Millar later claimed only to have doped himself on three occasions. He had taken one course in 2001 and two in 2003, as part of his preparation for the World Cup in Hamilton, Canada, which he won (Fotheringham 2004d). In other words, he admitted having taken next to nothing.

The heart of the matter, however, is that the attitude expressed by Millar back in 1999 was not anchored in any firm conviction. That is the positive version of it. The negative version is that he simply told the world at large precisely what he knew it wanted to hear without feeling himself in any way tied by his own words.

The Millar example does not, of course, completely undermine Walsh's idealistic position. If he had gone so far as to name Millar as an example of one of the good guys in 2000, he could simply have admitted without compromising his idealism that he had been mistaken. That he had let himself be conned by the apparently clean-living Scotsman, who sadly proved to everyone's surprise to be one of the 'baddies'. There would have been no change in mindset. Nevertheless it is worth considering whether the idealism that Walsh represented in 2000 – and which was given the full backing of his fellow journalists – does not have a counterproductive effect, if the aim is to get a sensible anti-doping campaign running. The notion of sport as a world of pure heroes and doped villains encourages an unrealistic image of reality. This does not help to establish a sensible doping policy. Far from it.

When Millar was caught, he was given two years quarantine. Two used vials in his bookcase would scarcely be enough to win a case against him. But they were enough to have him hauled in for an interrogation:

> At first I made up a story. I thought I could still get out of it. After 47 hours they started threatening me, they were flipping out because I had not admitted to anything. It was Thursday evening, they were going to keep me, take me to Paris in a van, keep me in for three days then put me before the judge on Monday. I could have carried on. I have a good lawyer in Paris and might have got away with it. But I thought, 'Fuck this, I can't live with this.' It wasn't difficult. I was just thinking, 'I can't go through with this, I'm fucked whatever happens, it's not 100% my fault, but I'm not going to live like this.' I could have kept fighting, fighting, fighting, but fundamentally, I'm not a good liar.
>
> (ibid.)

After he had maintained his innocence for 47 hours, he could not cope with the thought of being kept in custody for a longer period. So he gave up his defence and confessed.

Outside the interrogation room he started rebuilding his reputation from scratch. In a series of articles written by the journalist and cycling expert William Fotheringham, he presents himself as a reformed character. When his French team, Cofidis, announced that the Scot would not be starting the Tour de France 2004 because he stood accused of doping, Millar's sister made a statement that she could not comment as to whether 'Millar would appeal for reinstatement if he were cleared' (Fotheringham 2004a). But after he had appeared before a judge and had admitted his guilt, she was able to make the following unequivocal pronouncement:

> He wants it known that he is deeply sorry for this … He did not want to live a lie any longer. He has told the judge the truth, but the main thing he wishes to make clear is that this was his individual decision and he has to take responsibility for his decisions.
>
> (Fotheringham 2004b)

From this statement, it seems that the use of doping was his own choice. No one else is to take any part of the blame. In the interviews he lets it be known that it was a stupid mistake, the result of the pressure he placed on himself and of his personal problems. Now he would serve his punishment, return to cycling and ride clean. In an interview, he tells Fotheringham that he had, in fact, already renounced doping in 2004. According to this article, the syringes the police found in his bookcase were kept as mementos, 'as a way of keeping myself away from it, so that I would never forget that I had become world champion at Hamilton while doped' (Fotheringham 2004c).

From an outsider's perspective, it seems an unusual explanation, not least because he claims to have felt terrible even after the first time: 'After taking EPO for the Tour of Spain in 2001 I did not feel good. For me I was a cheat; I had crossed the line and I felt bad' (ibid.). If his statements to *The Independent* in 1999 reflect his attitude, we are to understand that he was feeling bad about himself at the time after giving in to the temptation of doping. Millar's explanation was as follows: 'I doped because my job was to arrive highly placed at the finish. There were magazines, sports newspapers, television stations waiting for my results' (ibid.). The explanation is plausible but it also raises the question of how he managed to cope with all the pressure he must have felt during the run-up to him winning the 13th stage of the Tour de France 2002 which he claimed was without the aid of performance-enhancing drugs.

Also, there is the question that, if he felt terrible after he had doped himself the first time, why, in 2003, did he resort to doping, especially after he proved good enough to complete the Tour de France, and even win a stage on the way, apparently racing clean and with a clean conscience? Millar's explanation was that 2002 in general was a bad year for him despite his winning stage of the Tour. He had ended up outside the UCI top 100 rankings and that had led to a drastic reduction in salary.

> From making a lot of money I went to the basic that I had in 2002. I felt it was wrong. My salary dropped by 300 per cent. It was like, 'I'll make them pay me a shed-load of money and run this team.'
>
> (ibid.)

The second time round, then, it seems that it was the colour of money that distracted him from his high ideals. The temptation of Mammon is something we can all understand. What made him put the needle back on the shelf again after his supreme Olympic victory is harder to grasp. Maybe he felt bad about himself once again and so renounced the needle once and for all. From an outsider's perspective, however, a more obvious action would have been to make a clean sweep and throw those seductive needles away, but Millar apparently had reasons for keeping his needles. Fotheringham explained in *The Guardian* that, 'he hung on to the syringes partly because deep down inside he wanted someone to catch him, because he had lost so much respect for himself that he no longer cared if he were caught and it came to an end' (Fotheringham 2004d). Yet, this explanation is a little difficult to understand as an outsider. That a man who has finally renounced his doping past and who in his innermost soul has decided to ride clean for the remainder of his career should wish to punish himself for the sins of the past is truly enigmatic. Also, once again from an outsider's perspective, it seems strange that someone who wishes to confess to past sins is prepared to endure 47 hours of interrogation before giving in and admitting their guilt. In addition, there is the question of what he meant when he made the statement on the raid on his room – via his sister. Millar declared that, 'He did not want to live a lie any longer', which could be considered rather surprising since he also claimed that he had ridden clean for almost a year before the raid. Presumably, not wanting to 'live a lie' had also played some part in him renouncing doping a year earlier even though he hinted in the interview that he knew that he would be riding against competitors who boost their performance levels using illegal substances by maintaining: 'There will always be guys ahead of me who are one step ahead of the rules' (ibid.).

Regardless of this, Fotheringham draws the following conclusion:

> What is most bitter about the Millar saga is how unnecessary it all was. The Scot had sufficient talent at the age of 23 to beat Lance Armstrong – yes, the six times Tour winner, no less – to win the prologue time-trial of the 2000 Tour. He rose to 16th in the world in 2001 and took most of his wins 'clean'. He won a stage of the 2002 race on 'water'.
>
> (ibid.)

From Fotheringham's point of view, it appears, that Millar could have had just as brilliant a career without recourse to doping. And maybe he is right. At the same time, though, one could argue that this kind of statement contributes to the belief that doping does not make much difference and that those who use doping are weak characters or people with particularly low confidence and moral standards who bend the rules for the sake of a relatively insignificant boost to their performance. This implication is surely misleading. The reason why so many cyclists have doped over the course of time is that it can make the highly significant difference between success and fiasco.

One example is the effect that EPO can have on a cyclist's ability to continue to enhance his endurance, even under circumstances that would normally result in complete exhaustion. EPO increases maximal oxygen uptake by 5–6 per cent, but research suggests that when the riders reach around 80 per cent of the maximum, their endurance levels are increased by 30 per cent or more (Lundby *et al.* 2007). This means that riders primed with EPO can keep going at sub-maximum exertion levels for a third longer than clean riders. Such primed riders must prove tough competition for those riding clean.

The law of silence, Mark II

This was the situation which faced Millar in 2006 when he signed a contract with team Saunier Duval-Prodir. In his comeback year, he managed to complete the Tour de France a good two hours after the winner, Floyd Landis. Later that year in the Vuelta a España, he similarly fought to achieve a mid-ranking position 1 hour and 45 minutes after the winner Alexander

Vinokourov, but won the 14th stage, a time trial of 33.2 kilometres. Clearly, if athletes' will to win can be so strong that they – disadvantaged and exhausted – can force themselves to victory against all odds, then it is unsurprising that the will to win can also lure some of them into the use of potent doping means that can increase their chance of fulfilling their ambition.

Millar was not only prepared to return to cycling in the knowledge that he would have to compete on an unequal footing, he was also prepared to take all the blame for his forays into doping. Millar's insistence to take the full responsibility without any public mention of persons who helped him to get his hands on the drugs and taught him how to administer the intake suggests that the law of silence continues to be in force – only now it is the people who identify other insiders as accomplices that struggle to find a way back to cycling after their quarantine.

A recent example is the German T-Mobile rider Jörg Jaksche who did a candid interview with the German magazine *Der Spiegel* in Spring 2007. In the interview, Jaksche admitted openly that he had been one of the clients of the Spanish doctor Eufemiano Fuentes (the key figure in the doping case famously known as 'Operación Puerto'), where his identity was hidden by the code name 'Bella'. Even though he stresses that he 'did not want to incriminate other riders', the compromising things he says about his former employer were clearly unacceptable. So although he is a magnificent talent and his intention was to come back clean, he was unable to find a team that would take him on board. He had hoped that it was possible for him to get a contract with a German team because the attitude in Germany – not least reflected in the country's media coverage of cycling – has become exceedingly negative towards doping in recent years. But not even a German team would take him, so he finally gave up:

> In the last couple of months I have spent so much energy and lifeblood to find a team. I am fed up being dependent on goodwill from people who at one time say 'you can ride with us' and the next day say 'you cannot ride with us.'
>
> (*Der Spiegel* 2007)

It appears that he has become a victim of the 'law of silence' as a consequence of his outspokenness.

What is somewhat confusing is that the law of silence has taken on a new form of expression since 1998, when the Swiss Festina rider, Alex Zülle, confessed everything. The intricacies of this law were described by the former RMO rider, the Irishman Paul Kimmage, in his insider story *Rough Ride*, first published in 1990. Here Kimmage explains the law of silence as follows:

> The law of silence: it exists not only in the Mafia but also in the peloton. Those who break the law, who talk to the press about the dope problems

in the sport are despised. They are branded as having 'craché dans la soupe', they have spat in the soup.

(Kimmage 1998: 229)

But, from the discussion above, it does not appear to be like that any more. Millar has spoken reams about the dreadful doping problems of the sport without being frozen out. Apparently, everyone is free to speak for themselves, as long as they refrain from involving others.

The strategy regarding doping scandals for cycling seems to have shifted from one of denial and decrying the 'bad apples' who have to resort to drugs as losers, which would have been hard to maintain with so many revelations, to one of damage limitation. The continuous drip of exposures has led the authorities to accept that we will never put a conclusive stop to the use of doping. Another lesson has been that the sport does not, as was feared, lose its popular appeal because of doping. The large number of doping cases there have been since the Festina scandal have not destroyed people's interest, despite the fact that the media, who do after all set the tone, have been extremely energetic in fanning the perception that doping is an evil that should be combated no matter what form it takes.

When new doping revelations emerge, the prime concern for those involved seems to be that the issue should be contained in order to limit doing serious damage to the sport as a whole. Even though the gentle trickle of revelations is slowly making the general public somewhat accustomed to the thought that doping is part of the reality of sport, it is apparently not prepared to accept it.

In fear of a balanced view

Reading Skibby's book gives us an idea of how the new edition of the 'law of silence' has come into force and how it functions. It is striking then that Skibby, like Millar and Riis, takes full responsibility for his use of doping. Not only does he cover up for his helpers by letting them remain anonymous, he even speaks of them with respect and gratitude. But he is not shy about naming his fellow riders by name, not even when he has nothing but ill to speak of them. Skibby does not so much as hint, however, at any connection between his former colleagues and doping. This can scarcely be because he has never seen or heard anything. Of the media's love of the mafia notion of 'omerta', the law of silence, he has this to say:

They could just as well write about comradeship, loyalty and any instinctive human urge to protect oneself and one's family at any price. There are, of course, no agreements, no sworn declarations that everything will be kept secret. You just keep your secrets for yourself and avoid pointing a finger at others. It is no different from any other workplace. There are not many journalists, for example, prepared to stand up in front of their colleagues' TV camera and recount all the sordid details of their lives and of those of their colleagues. The difference is just that there are such a lot of secrets to keep under wraps in cycling. And behind the questions there is always prejudice and the demand that cyclists should, of course, be cleaner in body and mind than anyone else on this planet.

(Skibby 2006: 137)

The comparison with journalists is interesting because it is almost like a Freudian slip, implying that he could have provided a much more substantial testimony than he actually did. But he clearly does not place the anti-doping campaign as high on his list of priorities as considerations of loyalty towards the fellowship of which he formed a part. In accordance with the new version of the law of silence, he limits his narrative to what he has himself done. There is nothing in his presentation to show that his motive for breaking his silence was that he had become a fanatic opponent of doping after the end of his career. On the contrary, there are a number of things that suggest that – aside from the desire to divest himself of his lies – he is driven by a desire to present the use of doping as seen from the perspective of the rider. He is familiar with the sport from the inside and attempts to show in his interpretation that the situation is far too complex for any outsider to have the wherewithal to understand. Even though he (says that he) now regrets allowing himself to be tempted to intensify his quest for results by using illegal substances, because of his knowledge of the field and its working conditions he cannot formulate an overall condemnation of the use of doping. There are a billion viewers watching the Tour de France all round the world, he explains:

They want heroes, victories, highs and lows, surprises, superhuman feats, hair-raising tension and great stories. They want it all, but they bloody well want it whiter than white. That's what they demand, and as they open yet another beer and sit down in front of the box, loosening their belts after a heavy lunch, they set themselves up as the main judge of that day's stage of the race. It is often a far cry from the world of the public to the world of cycling. Hysteria reaches a climax when people get all excited at riders giving themselves sugar solution and vitamins and minerals through a drip in their arm. That sort of thing belongs in a hospital. It's got bugger all to do with sport, they say, not understanding that the riders would probably die keeping them entertained all summer if they didn't keep their reserves topped up.

(ibid.: 137)

It is probably an exaggeration to go so far as to say that riders would die, if they rode longer stages without drips or medical assistance, but seen against his own experience of levels of exhaustion, it is clear to him that the notion of the clean rider as a healthier rider is not as self-evident as it looks from the viewpoint of the armchair. It is clear that he has a burning desire to present his point of view – and that he has been longing to do so ever since the great doping scandal broke and everyone began talking about EPO. At the time, though, he found it was impossible:

> I knew ... that it was a hopeless task trying to get across an even faintly balanced message in the heated debate. It was all black or white. You were either an angel or you were Satan himself, and with that choice of options there wasn't much you could do but keep your mouth shut. So I allowed prejudice, suspicion and accusations to rain down on my head, while I tried as best I could to defend myself with one lie after the other. And in the midst of the storm I felt the enormous pain of seeing every-thing I was a part of being blackened in a hysterical witch hunt that turned fit and healthy sportsmen into drug addicts and the loveliest sport in the world into a drug-store on wheels.
>
> (ibid.: 213)

The accuracy of Skibby's judgement that there was no place for balanced viewpoints was something that Bjarne Riis' experience from 1998 exempli-fied. Pressurised by force of circumstance but presumably also driven by the same burning urge to get 'his' public to understand that the world of sport falls short of the ideal in ways that are different from the picture usually presented, he made a cautious attempt to start a dialogue. During the 1998 Tour, he gave an interview to Danish television on the rest day. The atmo-sphere was relaxed and pleasant in the garden outside his hotel, as he spoke about the tribulations currently besetting cycling and its future prospects. He replied as best he could, even when the interviewing journalist asked the unavoidable question: 'Have you yourself ever taken doping, Bjarne?' He hesitated, was evidently thinking carefully about how to word his answer, and then he said: 'I have never been tested positive ... and I believe in a sport that is clean.' This came across as an answer that was both honest and evasive. It was as though he had resolved that he would not lie, but at the same time that it would be ruinous both for himself and for cycling to tell the straight truth. He would soon discover that things were worse than he had imagined. His balanced reply provoked an outcry. His choice of words invited a positive interpretation. The chairman of Denmark's Cycling Union (DCU), the one-time world champion sprinter Peder Pedersen, stated pub-licly that: 'Bjarne Riis owes it to the Danish people and Denmark's Cycling Union to give a clear answer: In his brilliant career has he or has he not made use of doping?' (*Jyllands-Posten* 26 July 1998). There is no reason to suppose that the chairman of the DCU seriously believed that cycling would be best served if Riis went on television and told the nation:

> Of course I did not win the Tour de France on mineral water alone. As it has emerged during interrogations held in the Festina case, several of

my competitors have been using EPO since 1993 to raise their haematocrit count to a level above 50. My natural count is 41. It goes without
saying that as a part of my Tour de France preparation I have been
forced to go down the same route as my rivals. If I had not, I would not
have had competitive blood counts. This does not mean that my victory
came all by itself. I train five to six hours a day. I live an extremely
ascetic life to keep my weight down. I spend mountains of time perfect-
ing my equipment. I do not see my use of EPO as a short-cut to success,
but as a necessary part of my competition preparation, and I can easily
explain why: The drugs industry has developed artificial EPO for medical use. In combination with effective training, the hormone in question
can give athletes a significant boost in their performance levels, and,
since it is impossible to trace in a doping test, the temptation to use it is
overwhelming. This is what my rivals have fallen for. I am not saying
that everyone is using doping, just that those riders who do not in reality
don't stand an earthly chance of winning a cycle race at the highest level.
Ever since my boyhood I have dreamed of winning the Tour de France. I
have let my higher education go by the board and sacrificed my youth and
the great majority of my time since then to realise that dream. I have come
a long way with my training, but during my career I have discovered that
the final step required to join the absolute elite cannot be taken without
medical assistance. That is why I have made the decision to risk even my
health in the attempt to win, knowing full well that it was no guarantee of
success. Fortunately in 1996 I succeeded in fulfilling my great ambition.
This I am proud of. You may perhaps accuse me of winning by cheating.
That is not how I see it. As the Festina case ought to have demonstrated, I
came out as the best in a field all competing on the same terms.

(Television interview)

The fact that it was not an admission of this kind that the DCU chairman
was looking for became abundantly clear when he added in an interview:
'My request for a clear answer is not based on any suspicion' (P. Pedersen
2008). In the light of the confessions that existed from the Festina riders
about systematic EPO use since 1993, it would be strange if Pedersen was
not just a bit uncertain that Riis was not doped, when with his power performance in 1996 he made it look as though the well-prepared Festina riders
and all other competitors were struggling along on cycles made of lead. It is
more likely that in an embarrassing situation Pedersen chose to suppress his
suspicion for the sake of the sport. It seems he feels uncomfortable about
this when he continues: 'I do not personally believe that Riis has ever tried
to achieve results in an irregular manner' (ibid.). Using that form of wording
he slides round the issue. On the other hand he opens himself to the same
charge of ambiguity that he accuses Riis of. For if Riis used doping (as we now
know was the case), he did so just as systematically, that is to say just as regularly, as his competitors. So in that sense the chairman's expression is an

empty one. As soon as he turns his focus away from those areas that represent a danger to him and his own office, he becomes clearer in his choice of words:

> But the population at large, which to a large extent sees in Riis – great sportsman and magnificent asset for the DCU as he is – an idol and a role model for its young, has a right to a clear answer. What he seemed to be doing on television was, of course, evading the question, side-stepping it. Neither I nor Danish cycling can accept that.
>
> (ibid.)

The challenge is unmistakable. For the image of cycling it was important for Denmark's greatest rider and role model to deny his use of doping. But this was only to place Riis on the horns of a terrible dilemma. This was what he had just discovered when he gave the honest answer. 'I have never been tested positive.' The chairman's demand for an unambiguous answer resounded through the media like a deafening echo. In the end, the pressure was too great. The same day as he saw himself pasted across the front page of Denmark's largest tabloid branded as a coward, Riis asked the TV station to whom he had given the famous interview to give him the chance to make a direct statement to the Danish public. This he was allowed to do. Indignation and frustration were visible in equal measure when he went on screen and made his initial unambiguous statement: 'I have never taken doping'. Whereupon he launched his attack on the press.

> I refuse to accept being called a coward. I refuse to accept being constantly accused of taking doping and suchlike. I will be regarded as a serious sportsman. As I also said this morning [at the press conference]: I have raced in cycle races since I was seven. I am now 34. I feel fit and healthy. I feel as though I have never been more fit and healthy than I am right at this moment. Do I look like a junkie, may I ask? Now I would like to be left alone.
>
> (Riis 1998a)

There was no doubt that he felt himself to be unfairly treated. Whatever the press might think about him, he did not himself feel that he had done anything wrong. This is not, of course, the same as saying that he did not have anything to hide. The fact that he felt fit and well can scarcely be seen as powerful evidence for the fact that he did not use doping. The same goes for his rhetorical question about looking like a junkie. Neither Alex Zülle, Armin Meier nor any of the other Festina riders who had admitted to doping looked like junkies. Even though the examples did not prove his innocence, however, they did point directly at the difference between the public's understanding of doping and the reality known by athletes. The prejudice felt by the public at large against doping is linked at heart to a sense that doping is a risk to life and a danger to health. When a journalist asked in a follow-up question why he had not immediately given the answer the chairman of the DCU had requested, he replied:

> Now just look here: Any situation of this kind is difficult. We have reached a point in cycling right now that is very sensitive. One little wrong statement can soon be twisted and turned into ... well, into, I don't know, into a catastrophe, into anything. Everyone is on tenter-hooks, and we are in the centre of it all, us riders. It doesn't take much to make a little mistake ... to say something wrong, and then you're all down on us like a ton of bricks.
>
> (ibid.)

After he had been put through the mill like this, Riis might have been expected to choose an unambiguous denial of all accusations such as Skibby had done in his day, but Riis' passion for the sport tempted him once again to make a defence which allowed elbow room for a more balanced judgement. When the Tour was over, he was still prepared to appear in the TV2 studio to explain the cause of the whole doping mess. As can be seen from the statement given below, he had clearly learnt that doping is such a loaded word that he had to find another way to explain the need for medical assistance when it surfaced. Nevertheless he managed to express fairly clearly what it was all about by comparing the demands made on the body during a stage of a cycle race and during a football World Cup match. When riders have got through a hard stage, they only have a relatively short period of time to recuperate:

> We have to get on our bikes again the following day and ride 200 kilo-metres with perhaps two or three mountains on the way. Our problem, however, is that we do not have six days for it. We have to ... I'm not saying we have to resort to doping. We are forced to have, shall we say, a form of security. That is why we have doctors with us. That's why I have, for example, an acupuncturist along. That's why one year I had a specialist masseur with me. That's why our doctors make sure first and foremost that we get the right food, the right vitamins, minerals, salts and sugar, extras. Because I burn around four times as many calories as you do. You swallow a Multi-tab every day. I can't swallow a handful of Multi-tabs like that every day. My kidneys and my liver simply cannot cope with it – I would come to a complete standstill. I am forced to have some aids that can enable me to keep my standard up and keep me fit and well. That's why we have doctors with us to give us, if needed, a ... let's say simply a drip, such as you might see sick people get in a hos-pital, with salts and minerals in. [Doctors give] us extra things that we need to keep us in good health. Of course there are some things we have to deal with. We all agree about that. But we must not forget that it is also important for us to get to Paris fit and healthy.
>
> (Riis 1998b)

By constructing a health angle on the matter, he places a mine under the anti-doping campaign. If we accept that cycling teams make use of doctors to ensure that riders recuperate properly, maintain their levels and so protect their health in order to get them through the race fit and well, then we can scarcely avoid the conclusion that restrictive doping regulation impedes doctors in their work at the expense of the cyclists' health.[2] By using the wording: 'Of course there are some things we have to deal with', he signals his opposition to the deregulation of doping but at the same time lets it be understood that the current doping rules stand in the way of riders protecting their health. Between the lines of Riis' statement is an openness to discuss whether medical assistance can be integrated into the sport in such a way that the health risks to athletes are reduced as far as possible. Maybe he thought that with his authority as winner of the world's toughest cycle race he could reverse the inflamed popular mood by entering the debate. He had spent his life in the sport and was surely living proof that medical assistance was not the health-destroying business it was made out to be. In the wake of doping revelations that had left behind the impression of a sport that was rotten to the core, Riis' argument for the need for medical assistance fell on stony ground. The time was not ripe for reflection but, on the contrary, for the intensification of the anti-doping campaign, which manifested itself in the creation of WADA.

Irrespective of how Riis prepared for his triumphs, what underpins everything he says after the Festina scandal is that he does not feel that he has done anything wrong. In this he appears to be at one with Skibby. But in contrast to his older colleague, he chose to speak openly. He even lets himself be interviewed by Andersen and Jung for *Tavshedens Pris* (*The Price of Silence*), even though he has been told in advance that he will be asked to comment on the famous test print-outs that show that his haematocrit levels had risen from 41.1 to 56.3 between January and June. When they present the blood counts for him in front of the live cameras, he starts off by denying that they are his counts. Once again he was caught in a situation in which the alternative to denial was an abyss. It was an abyss towards which the experienced interviewer enticed him closer and closer. As though Andersen had not heard the denial, he repeated his question in a slightly different wording.

Andersen: A count of 56.3 – what does that tell you?

Riis: Off the bat, I'd say that I would never have been that high.

Andersen: What does that tell you? That the count could be so high on a rest day?

Riis: But I have told you, those are not my counts – I mean, you won't get me to say much more than that.

Andersen: If we talk about 1995 now, during the Tour de France – what do you think your count was then?

Riis: I don't know … I don't know … And if I did know, it is not certain
I would tell you.

Andersen: What count would you usually have, when you are on top
form?

Riis: Well, that's not something I am going to tell you, because you will
just use it.

This last reply is made by Riis right out on the edge of the abyss, and he
delivers it with a cheeky smile playing on his lips. The reply implies that if
the journalist had had a different agenda, then he might have talked more
openly about these things. But he has discovered that every time he tries to
pave the way for a measure of insight into the conditions experienced by
cyclists, it is used to throw dirt at his moral standards. He is forced to take care
what he says. If he does not, he risks being paraded before the public as a
common cheat. That was where he ended anyway. Not as a cheat but as a liar.

Lie upon lie

In the summer of 2006, Riis once again hit the front pages of the same
tabloid that had accused him of cowardice in 1998. This time the headline read:
'The Master of Lies'. Behind the headline was the great Spanish doping case,
the so-called Operación Puerto, which exploded with accusations that leading
riders had had consultations at the clinic run by Dr Eufemiano Fuentes.

After Riis retired from his active career, he bought a controlling share in
the professional Danish cycling team, Jack & Jones, in 2000 with the express
aim of creating the world's best cycling team. Even this crazy ambition was
one he managed to fulfil. At any rate, five years later under the new name of
Team CSC they won the international cycling union UCI's team competition, the Pro Tour 2005. This was a victory repeated in 2006, which looked
like being a golden year when the team's biggest star, Ivan Basso, won a
crushing victory in the Giro d'Italia. A Tour de France victory was set to be
the crowning glory. That dream, however, bit the dust in dramatic fashion
when Riis found himself forced to send Basso home the day before the start
of the race. The reason was that the Spanish authorities had linked Basso to
the Spanish doping affair. He was alleged to have used Fuentes as his doctor.
A raid on Fuentes' clinic revealed clear evidence that he was running a
comprehensive doping practice, which resulted in a charge of conducting a
business that was harmful to health, since Spain had no law prohibiting the
doping of athletes.[3] During the raid code names were found on sachets of
blood and documents that apparently implicated a number of leading riders.
In itself this was no reason for Basso to be excluded from the race. Nevertheless, despite the fact that Basso denied having anything to do with
Fuentes, Riis sent his star home. It was no consolation that Telekom also

had to say goodbye both to their best cyclist, Jan Ullrich, and to their strong domestic, Oscar Sevilla. Nor was there comfort in the fact that Astana's top favourite, Alexander Vinokourov, was also heading for home – without even being involved in the case himself – alongside the rest of his team mates, since too many of them were involved in the case for them to fulfil the requirement to start the race with six men.

In his time as sports director, Riis had not had a single doping case on his team. Operación Puerto appeared to throw suspicion on more than 250 athletes from a variety of branches of sport. Basso was the only member of the Team CSC to be drawn into the affair, and the evidence presented against him was so weak that the Italian Olympic Committee later withdrew the case against him. From the moment he took over the management of the Danish cycling team, Riis had proclaimed and practised a zero-tolerance policy towards doping. His treatment of the Basso case was in line with that policy. Nevertheless it gave rise to fresh attacks against him personally. His Tour de France victory in 1996 was compared to Basso's formidable strength in the Giro in 2006 and used as a basis for renewed doping accusations. He could, for example, read the following about himself, 'At the time Bjarne Riis was, according to a number of Italian studies, involved in cheating with EPO. His haematocrit counts showed massive variations, and the large irregularities indicate doping. But Riis never confessed. Instead he acquired the image as "the master of lies"' (Werge 2006).

Despite the article being on the verge of slander, he did not respond to it. After the Tour, it is true that he agreed to appear on the TV programme *Ugens Profil* (Profile of the Week), which is modelled on BBC's *Hard Talk*, a programme in which a public person is critically interviewed about a current problem they are involved in. There was no mention here of him being fed up with the new accusations. He argued that it was vital to the survival of cycling that it established an even harder line on anti-doping, and he would himself take the lead by appointing the highly respected Danish anti-doping doctor Rasmus Damsgaard to the team with a view to making a watertight control system, and he would be happy to do so in collaboration with Anti Doping Denmark. In this interview, too, he was asked if he had ever used doping himself, to which he answered with a firm negative and without the suggestive asides along the lines of 'Do I look like a junkie?' such as he had used previously. Nor were there any balanced viewpoints presenting the need for riders to get through to Paris fit and well. Riis still finds it necessary to have doctors attached to the team, but to judge by his statement this is no longer to provide the riders with a drip containing the required salts, vitamins and minerals, since this is now accounted as doping.

Riis has apparently chosen to focus on creating results with his team on the basis of conditions as they are. The requirement for this is, it goes without saying, a solid economic base, and in so far as that depends on the goodwill of sponsors, both his credibility and that of the team are important. The political correctness he now displays to the world serves that purpose.

Because of his past as the doping-denying winner of the Tour de France during the scandalous 1990s, he continues, even after his recent confession, to be seen as a villain in the eyes of the press. This, of course, presents a problem for him, since the biggest asset of the sponsorship business is positive media coverage. He cannot, therefore, simply cut off his links to the press. On the other hand, he refrains from discussing anything but his team, its results and the tasks ahead, and otherwise is unswerving in taking resolute action when doping cases are in the offing to ensure that they cause the least possible damage. In other words he abides by the new edition of the law of silence, a law that was expressed in exemplary fashion when he was asked for his comment when Skibby's biography hit the bookstores. 'This is his book, and I have no comment to make about it. He is old enough and sufficiently grown-up to stand by what he writes. Keep me out of it', demanded Riis, but then could not help adding: 'We shouldn't sound as though this is a bomb that has exploded here. That there was doping in cycling in the 1990s – that's only what you journalists have been writing all the time.' The journalist was not content to let that one pass but once again asked the question that had been thrown at him a thousand times before in different guises: 'What about you? Surely you were one of the riders who rode faster than Skibby?' The answer he gave first in 1998 and most recently in 2006 was: 'No, I have not taken doping.' Since this is apparently not acceptable, he chooses instead to kick it into touch: 'To think that you haven't moved on! That is not something I'm going to make any comment on. My life has moved on' (Riis 2006). Not a harsh word about Skibby, no word of rebuttal on the use of doping in the 1990s. Just a refusal to speak about himself in relation to the book when he still thought he would get away with it.

In contrast to Riis, the rider from the golden generation with the most wins to his name, Rolf Sørensen, chose to defend himself and cycling in line with the old version of the law of silence. Without naming the book directly, Skibby was dismissed with the following: 'I haven't got much time for people who spill the beans afterwards and say that they have done something or other. And that there's nothing but corruption in cycling. That's because they couldn't keep up anyway. I don't give a monkey's for that sort of thing. They are hypocrites' (Sørensen 2006).

In other words, those who open their mouths are to be despised, exactly as described above by Kimmage. That form of treatment is, however, a thing of the past. Over the past ten years so much has come to the surface that it seems directly counter-productive to throw mud at colleagues who break the silence. That was a lesson taught to Sørensen by Brian Holm, a rider of the same generation, who wrote his biography before Skibby (see Chapter 1), in which he also – though to a more limited extent – admits to using illegal substances. Holm, who now acts as sports manager for Telekom, defended Skibby in the following forthright manner, when he was asked about his view of Sørensen's denunciation:

I have read it and I think Rolf Sørensen seriously needs to put a cork in it. Jesper Skibby was one of the most serious riders I have seen in my career. He had a body fat percentage of five at the start of the season. Even his base level was high. Rolf on the other hand turned up with a little beer paunch. I would love to see the training programmes Rolf went through in Italy. I'd like to see what they did in their training that we didn't do in ours. It was common knowledge that Italian riders couldn't win a veteran race one month but that they won classics the month after. I'd like to see how Rolf trained, and I'd also like to say to Rolf that if he really wants a discussion about doping, then I'm happy to meet him. He can just name the day. Those high-tech Italian doctors, Rolf – we can easily take a chat about them. You just say when.

(Fjeldgaard 2006)

Following that challenge, Sørensen immediately made it known that he had been misquoted, and that he harboured great respect for both Skibby and Holm. He had been thinking about other riders. The law of silence Mark II prevailed. The question is, however, whether it contributes to making the sport more honest. There are plenty of signs that the doping inquisition gets athletes used to seeing the truth as something dangerous and teaches them to approach it with caution. This can scarcely raise ethical standards, let alone contribute to the development of a sensible doping policy. For a sport to give its complete backing to the exorcist strategies of the anti-doping brigade solely for financial reasons is likely to result in its moral standards being even further debased.

6   When good intentions turn bad

The intensification of the campaign against doping over the past ten years has left its marks on the attitudes of athletes. It is evident, not least in cycling, that the silence of times past no longer helps to keep the doping issue out of the media spotlight. With the huge amount of attention devoted to the phenomenon, attempts to play down cases of doping no longer work. There is a big difference between the reception of Paul Kimmage's book *Rough Ride* (1998) when it first came out in 1990 and the way such confessions and revelations would be received today. Kimmage describes the doping situation in cycling as an insider. He confesses his own initiation as a doper and he even mentions the name of a rider, whom he saw charge himself in a race. Today such a revelation would undoubtedly hit the headlines, whereas in 1990 it went almost unnoticed.

High-profile revelations together with the media's cultivation of doping into a self-contained area of news have given the public the impression that doping is the rule rather than the exception among top-class athletes in certain sports. In other words they have become *usual suspects*. As suggested in the previous chapter, it is doubtful whether this role has improved the athletes' moral standards. It is true that a number of them have begun to speak out and to openly declare their support for the anti-doping campaign. It has become common to keep a healthy distance from competitors who use doping. At the same time, however, it is a fact that several of those who have publicly condemned the use of doping have themselves been caught with banned substances in their bodies. This arouses the suspicion that the new line being taken may represent a new strategy – a new posture – but not an alteration in fundamental attitudes. And in so far as it can be said to be an expression of a change in attitude, it is far from certain that that change is in the favour of the anti-doping campaign. In any event, it is not unknown for people who are treated with mistrust to tend to begin to live up to it (Becker 1973).

A blow to the image of sport

Increasing awareness of doping and critical attention focused on doping cases are, however, not only problems for athletes. It is the entire sporting system as a lucrative business that is being put under pressure. For that business depends on the impression that sport is a positive activity that promotes health and develops character. That, at any rate, is the consensus among those in charge of the system, notwithstanding the fact that, despite the string of glittering scandals over the past 20 years, the sports industry has grown explosively during the same period.

In the beginning it made sense to present cases of doping as manifestations of the individual athlete's immoral behaviour. Positive action was taken against these unworthy sportspersons by using an ever more refined form of doping control. Both decreases and increases in the number of positive doping cases recorded could be interpreted as signs that the latitude permitted to cheats was being reduced. Both served to support the illusion that the fight against doping would soon be won. In that way doping could be said to be a problem *for* sport not a problem *in* sport. But this has changed.

There are two pressing problems. Incidents of doping can no longer meaningfully be reduced exclusively to a discussion of the individual athlete's low moral standards; nor can they any longer be seen as symptoms of the healing process in view of the fact that faith in doping control has been undermined by a whole series of unfortunate episodes. If faith in the effectiveness of controls was reinforced, for example, immediately after Ben Johnson's fall from grace, it was weakened again when in 2003 it emerged that Carl Lewis, to whom Johnson's gold medal passed, tested positive in the USA for three banned drugs two months before he ran in Seoul (Magney 2003). According to former WADA President, Dick Pound, the American Olympic Committee (USOC) had turned a blind eye to the positive test result on the grounds that Lewis had not taken the drugs with the intention of doping himself, but just been negligent (Pound 2004: 53). It could, of course, be said that in Lewis's case it was not the control that failed but the USOC that proved unworthy of its responsibility. If we consider that none of the other tests that Lewis had taken in the course of his career had shown positive, we must accept that Lewis's one test was an innocent mistake or that doping controls do not work effectively.

It could, however, just be a further indication of the powerlessness of doping controls when faced with resource-rich athletes. A view that is given extra credence if one considers the number of debatable cases that have followed in the wake of Lewis. In fact, Linford Christie, the silver medallist after Johnson's exit, also gave a positive test some years later. In 1999, he tested positive for Nandrolone. Clearly, the discovery does not prove that he used doping during – or during the preparations for – Seoul. However, it does raise further questions about the effectiveness of doping controls. It is a common cliché in anti-doping circles that it is only a matter of time before doping offenders are exposed. If they are lucky enough to cheat the controls today, they will be snared tomorrow, and if not tomorrow, then the following day. Although, Christie's positive test could be construed to confirm this cliché, at the same time it could also indicate the opposite, which highlights another way in which doping controls may be failing. What is particularly interesting about Christie's positive test is that it actually took place at a time when as a 39-year-old he had, in fact, given up his career. If he had not allowed himself to be persuaded by his training group to enter an insignificant indoor race in Dortmund, his career would have remained without a blemish. And it is hard to believe that a retired athlete would dope himself only with the aim of running a minor race.

The British Athletic Federation did, in fact, clear Christie but was overruled by the International Association of Athletics Federations (IAAF), who penalised him with two years exclusion. The affair was, however, far from convincing proof that doping controls were working. For if he really had taken Nandrolone as part of his preparation for that minor race in Dortmund, then it is possible to imagine that he had taken similar steps with a view to performing well in competitions earlier in his career when significantly more money and prestige and honour were at stake. It is possible, therefore, that when he was caught, it was because a banned drug had ended up in his bloodstream through negligence. Christie defended himself by saying that the drug must have been present in a food supplement without it being declared. This sounds credible when we take the situation into consideration. And that supports the idea that positive tests not only occur as a result of systematic doping but also through thoughtlessness, carelessness or incompetent help or advice. In this context the IAAF's overruling of BAF that led to the 'retired' Christie being suspended for two years was an attempt to demonstrate efficiency and zero tolerance in anti-doping. That is not to say, however, that all cases of one-off positive tests result from mistakes. But when athletes manage a whole series of amazing clean performances while some around them occasionally are being caught doping, doping controls may in fact be legitimising 'superhuman' feats that could later be called into question.

One such performance that has caught the attention of those observers with a more cynical stance is that of Florence Griffith-Joyner who improved dramatically during the same period as Lewis and Johnson tested positive. The world records she set at the time in the 100 and 200 metres still stand. Another example is Lance Armstrong's seven successive wins in the Tour de France between 1999–2005, in which he beat a whole host of riders who have since been caught or who have admitted using banned substances. Although there is no clear-cut evidence to link these athletes to the doping scandals occurring in their respective sports, and there is nothing to say that these athletes were not simply at the top of their sport, the number of clean super-performances must raise some doubt regarding the effectiveness of the controls. In addition, mistrust is given a further boost when athletes make their confessions in biographies or are exposed through police actions when for years they have been handing in an endless stream of blood and urine samples without ever testing positive. The recent revelation that the WADA-accredited laboratories do not have a reliable test for EPO, the most efficient performance-enhancing drug for athletes competing in endurance sports (Lundby *et al*. 2008), only goes to strengthen suspicions about the effectiveness of doping controls.

A crusade that must not fail

WADA was set up as a consequence of the threat posed by doping revelations to the image of sport. The initiative was not only about making the anti-doping campaign effective. That process had been going on since 1965 without any apparent reduction in the doping problem. What motivated this huge initiative was rather the desire to resurrect the moral standards of sport by restoring the ideals of fair play, health and purity of soul. In that sense, the establishment of WADA heralded a crusade against a world of elite sport that – in step with increasing commercialism – had become ever more corrupt (Simpson and Jennings 1992; Lenskyj 2000). What was special – and risky – about the initiative was that it was elevated from being exclusively the preserve of sporting organisations to being a political issue as well. The fact that those governments that backed WADA also took on 50 per cent of the responsibility and liability boosted the credibility of the enterprise. This constellation made it difficult to maintain accusations against the IOC and international sporting associations that 'drug testing was little more than a cosmetic procedure designed to reassure the sporting public that something was being done about drugs' (Hoberman 2005: 243). The anti-doping campaign turned into a high-prestige project. While earlier attempts had revolved around keeping opportunities for doping in check through constant advances on the testing side, the object now was to eliminate the evil altogether. The measures that were adopted were twofold, on the one hand, more frequent and tighter controls both during and outside competitions and, on the other, tougher sanctions.

At the level of politics and rhetoric, things went swimmingly. With WADA President, Dick Pound, leading the fray, the organisation soon showed itself to be energetic and single-minded. The broad backing given to the WADA codex that was adopted in Copenhagen in 2003 paved the way for a uniform global anti-doping campaign. The only associations that bridled and refused to sign were UCI and FIFA. These organisations continued, however, in negotiations with WADA and within about 18 months both had signed up for the codex. The successes on the political level were, however, less than half the battle. In reality, it does not matter how much unity there is about testing programmes and sanctions, if testing methods are not really effective. No amount of good will or signed paperwork is going to improve testing techniques on their own. In other words, the core element of the anti-doping campaign continued to be the Achilles' heel of this latest attempt to purify sport.

The uncomfortable fact for both sporting organisations and for politicians is that if an organisation based on a collaboration between the governments and sports organisations of the world cannot manage to make progress in its attempt to end the doping culture of sport, then the battle appears to be lost for good. If WADA turns into a fiasco, then sport – to use the dominant discourse of the area – will be at the mercy of the needle. The WADA project can, therefore, not fail. As Lincoln Allison remarked in a commentary written in the UK newspaper *The Guardian*: 'The orthodox view is that doping is cheating, that it is a minority activity and that the system of testing that operates under the auspices of the World Anti-Doping Agency (WADA) can, and must, succeed in eradicating drugs from sport' (Allison 2004). An unfortunate consequence of the official anti-doping policy having to be a success come what may is, Allison claims, that the agency tolerates no challenge to the official view: 'If you are to get any official research co-operation from WADA and the International Olympic Committee (IOC), blanket opposition to drugs is the only view you are allowed to take.' And that is not all. 'Three of my colleagues in the academic study of sport', he continues, 'were threatened with legal action by two different international sporting organisations last year, simply for stating aloud some truths about the extent of drug use in top-class sport' (ibid.).

Allison had himself experienced this kind of opposition at a conference in Sweden in 2003, when the chairman of the IOC's medical committee and member of WADA, Arne Ljungqvist, had called Ben Johnson a traitor to the ideals of athletics. When Allison challenged him with the question of whether or not 'it was reasonable to believe that most of Johnson's peers had used steroids in some form and at some stage in the development of their bodies', Ljungqvist denied the suggestion, remarking that no proof for it lay to hand. The implication was that the question was the expression of unacceptable doubt as to the general purity of sport. Ljungqvist's evident discomfort at the question is, according to Allison, related to the fact that it directs a poisonous barb at sports idealism. What is at stake is 'the core of our concept of sport and its values' (ibid.). If the presumption became generally accepted that Johnson's competitors had prepared themselves medically exactly as he had done, but just without being discovered, if in other words the idea took root that the use of doping was the rule rather than the exception among the stars of world sport, then there would be a risk that popular backing for the anti-doping campaign would crumble. At that point the sports idealists would stand to lose the ideological battle for sport that must not be lost. In this light, Ljungqvist's swipe at Johnson and the subsequent distance he takes from the question about Johnson's rivals can be interpreted as a necessary defence of the illusion that the rot lies in individual athletes not in sport as such. The insistence in (sporting) politics that doping is a consequence of the low moral standards of individual athletes and not of the logic of sport, means that athletes caught in the trap are turned into scapegoats. This is the price to be paid if sports idealism is to be kept alive. Sadly, sport in the real world appears to deny idealism. There has been no shortage of scapegoats since Johnson, not even after the global anti-doping campaign was launched. There is, therefore, ever increasing insistence on questions as to whether the failure of the anti-doping campaign – the one thing that absolutely must not happen – is not precisely what is happening; and whether, in fact, the leading lights of the anti-doping campaign saw the writing on the wall quite early on in the latest attempt to curb doping in elite sport. At any rate their reaction to critique appears to be symptomatic. Discussion is not welcome – and that not only applies to sceptics on the outside like Lincoln Allison. Even when sportspersons dare to question the sense of the doping ban as it is now enforced, they refrain from discussing its substance. Instead they round on the individual.

This was something the experienced alpine skier Bode Miller discovered when he told an American sports magazine in 2005 that EPO should be allowed in alpine ski sports. Condemnation fell like a hammer: 'He has not thought this through. He is enjoying his 15 minutes of fame and he can say what he likes. But it is irresponsible and wrong' (DR.dk 2006) thundered the WADA President without taking the least account of Miller's reasoning.

Miller won the World Cup that same year and found himself at the top of the international ski sports hierarchy, so Pound's insinuation that Miller's statement was motivated by the wish for a brief moment of fame seems not to be very well-founded. Pound, however, was clearly furious, and we can see why. Because, in his statement, Miller is criticising the moral stance WADA has taken to the doping question. It is bad news for the agency. Whether it is bad news more generally is, however, doubtful. There are several things that indicate that the discussion is badly needed. Not all aspects of the anti-doping campaign are equally sensible, and it is difficult to maintain a belief that it is being conducted primarily for the sake of the athletes. Listening to the reasons behind Miller's viewpoint, it becomes clear that Pound's rebuttal does not in this case spring from any concern for the health of the athletes. If that was the objective, Miller's argument should have made an impression. Miller said:

> I'm surprised it's illegal. Because in our sport, it would be pretty minimal health risks, and it would actually make it safer for the athletes, because you'd have less chance of making a mistake at the bottom and killing yourself. That burn you feel in your legs at the bottom of a course indicates anaerobic oxygen depletion of your blood. Your brain is similarly affected. Endurance boosting drugs such as erythropoietin, which is very much banned in Olympic sports, would help keep oxygen flowing to the brain, allowing skiers to make safer decisions. You have to make four or five decisions every second in skiing, every turn. [These are] conscious decisions, plus there's another hundred that are instinct. And when your brain starts to slow down, as if you're holding your breath for two minutes, it makes it damn hard to make those decisions.
>
> (Vinton 2005)

Miller, then, is arguing for legalising EPO on the basis that it would make downhill racing, for example, safer for participants. It would reduce the risk of athletes losing concentration and making fatal mistakes. If there is no evidence for what he is saying, then he should at the least have been refuted in a proper manner. Whereas the agency which promotes its battle against doping by citing the health and safety of sportspersons, apparently dismissed the suggestion with the wave of a hand. Instead of responding to Miller with evidence for the damaging effects of even limited amounts of EPO on competition and on health, the organisation seemed to prefer a knee-jerk response. Nor did the IOC show any inclination to discuss the matter with Miller. They chose to follow WADA and, from an outsider's perspective at least, it seems that they sent trusted athletes out on a mission to convert the heathen. With the world record holder in pole-vaulting, Sergej Bubka, as its spokesperson, the organisation announced: 'His statements are downright madness. We are shocked.' Bubka is a member of the IOC's Executive Board and, according to him, 'Miller's colleague, Pernilla Wiberg, will contact the American. She can explain our view to him and find out why he thinks the way he does' (B.T. 2005).

The reaction and the rhetoric are in some ways reminiscent of the practice of religious sects reaching out to the strayed sheep to convert them and lead them back to the path of righteousness. Wiberg does not contact Miller to have an open and unprejudiced dialogue about problems in the current approach to the doping problem. She comes to lead him back onto the WADA path. But, as has been discussed already, it becomes an ever more urgent question whether that path is indeed the only right one.

Marching on the spot

Ten years after the setting up of WADA and six years after the implementation of the codex, doping is still a hot potato. New cases turn up constantly without anyone getting the impression that it is the result of a systematic elimination of the last pockets of incorrigible cheats. The net may have been tightened. With the demand that they notify their place of residence, athletes have been submitted to a regime of constant surveillance.[1] They are tested during and outside competitions as never before. Nevertheless only few test, and when that does happen it (still) seems rather to indicate negligence on the part of the athletes and doctors than proof of the net becoming finer. It is certainly true that a number of big names have been brought down in recent years, but when large-scale doping cases have come to public notice it is because government authorities have started to be interested in the case and carry out judicial enquiries and police raids.

When details of big cases come to light, the anti-doping organisations can rub their hands with joy, of course. But their joy can only have a bittersweet taste as long as the raids go to show that sport's own doping controls are not up to the job and apparently only catch a small proportion of those who break the rules. It was precisely in response to the fact that doping was taking place systematically and to a far greater extent than had been imagined that the IOC took the initiative to create a world-wide anti-doping collaboration. And since the anti-doping work that really brings in results takes place outside the framework of WADA, it is natural that considerations arise as to whether it makes any sense to throw further resources in the direction of traditional anti-doping measures.

Governments could perhaps make a bigger difference by devoting these resources to anti-doping work using the customs and the police instead. It goes without saying that this presents a frightening scenario for sporting organisations, since it would fundamentally alter the perception of sport as something positive and instead paint a picture of it as a nest in which criminal elements are hatched. For the same reason this is hardly a road that politicians would be tempted to take.

When in the run-up to the Winter Olympics in Turin, the IOC urged the host nation to suspend its doping laws because they might involve athletes who were caught risking a prison sentence, their motives were just as much to do with the damaging effect that pictures of sports personalities in handcuffs would have on the image of sport as they were with the risk of the Games being hit by competitors cancelling. In an interview with *Associated Press*, Dick Pound gave his backing to the IOC's viewpoint using the following wording:

> It's always been our view that sports should settle its own problems ... Doping in sport is a serious problem and it will be dealt with seriously but it is not criminal ... Maybe it will have the deterrent effect that they hoped. But it's a wrong message to send to people that sport is going to be run by criminal authorities. That's not what Italy promised.
>
> (*Associated Press* 2005)

On the face of it, it seems somewhat surprising that the man who stands at the head of the anti-doping campaign for world sport should be against the criminalisation of doping. It was, after all, only because the authorities stepped in and treated riders suspected of using doping as criminals that confessions started to roll during the Tour de France in 1998, which led, as we have seen, to sport rearming its anti-doping campaign through the establishment of WADA. Pound's pronouncement starts, then, to look like an indirect critique of the 1998 action in France and from the police action that caught Scottish cyclist David Millar. This was scarcely the intention. The situation meanwhile provides evidence for the suggestion that the campaign against doping is about other – and more important – matters than consideration for fair play and health. There are other things – not least commercial interests – at stake, things which not infrequently involve ideals being kicked into touch, which makes the idea of fairness in the enterprise end up looking secondary. In any event, it is easy to come away with the impression that the anti-doping campaign conducted by the sport itself is working primarily to reassure the world outside that the doping problem is being dealt with in a single-minded way on the basis of a zero-tolerance policy. In other words, that the main concern is the image of the enterprise. When the powers-that-be of the sporting world feel it necessary to show that they can act, then they do so without bothering their heads much about the rights of athletes or about considerations for the 'level playing field', whose praises are otherwise so proudly sung. Taken as a whole, such numerous examples leave behind the impression that the anti-doping campaign is conducted according to the precept that the end justifies the means, and that in so doing it has stepped out into the moral morass.

Morality, gone by the board

For example, in the wake of its success in creating a consensus about the code WADA was still short of proof that the institution was able to achieve concrete results in the battle against doping. But by a stroke of extraordinary fortune they suddenly found themselves with a case to pursue.

The case arose about six months after the signing of the code, when the head of the American anti-doping agency (USADA), Terry Madden, stepped forward and pronounced that a series of American athletes had tested positive for a hitherto unknown synthetically produced anabolic steroid, tetrahydrogestrinone (THG) (Rasmussen 2005). The manner in which WADA dealt with the matter of the new drug gives the impression that the chance of a break-through in the anti-doping campaign weighed more heavily in their deliberations than consideration for the athletes. At any rate the agency would not wait to put sanctions into effect against the athletes who tested positive for THG until scientific proof had been produced that the drug really did have a performance-enhancing effect. Not even when leading medical experts working with anti-doping had raised serious doubts as to whether the drug really ought to be regarded as a doping substance did WADA hold its hand, and this aroused concern. One of the absolute heavy-weights in anti-doping work, the Swedish Professor Bengt Saltin, pointed out, for example, that: 'As long as it is not established that THG is doping, it is wrong to announce that a series of athletes are doping addicts on that basis' (Brandt 2003). And he provided the following analysis of the situation:

> There exist many steroid hormones that have no effect. The precondition for breaking the rules is a documented performance-enhancing effect, but it looks as though the international doping agency (WADA) together with the Olympic committee (IOC) have taken up the case to prove to the world at large that they are on the ball. WADA and IOC are hell bent on cleaning up athletics in USA. My only hope is that WADA have a basis for their case.
>
> (Saltin 2003)

Instead of following the advice of medical experts and treading softly, WADA chose to soften the definition of doping in their code and in that way ensure that athletes testing positive for THG – regardless of the effect of the designer steroid – would not have support for their case in any future legal action. For that reason the wording is no longer that new drugs, analogous to those that already are on the doping list, have to have a corresponding pharmaceutical effect *and* chemical structure but that they have to have a corresponding pharmacological effect *or* chemical structure. In a press release, WADA explains:

> The discovery of the 'designer steroid' Tetrahydrogestrinone (THG), has made clear that the definition of 'analogue' as defined under sections S4 and S5 of the former List is inappropriately restrictive. In fact, in its former version, the List required an analogue to have both a similar chemical structure and similar pharmacological effects. However, contrary to good medical and pharmaceutical practice, these 'designer steroids' are administered to athletes despite the lack of any studies on their pharmacological effects. Therefore, in order to be able to cover new 'designer steroids' in future and to prosecute such cases quickly, it is important that substances that have a similar chemical structure or similar pharmacological effects be prohibited. In consequence, the references to 'analogues' and 'mimetics' in sections S4 and S5 have been deleted and replaced by the same wording that is used in sections S1 and S8 namely: ' ... and other substances with similar chemical structure or similar pharmacological effect(s)'.
>
> (WADA 2004)

This means that WADA no longer needs to concern itself about the precise effect of THG. In its chemical structure it resembles other drugs on the doping list with anabolic effects and therefore its use – after the change in wording – has to be considered as doping under any circumstances. If, on the other hand, WADA had not changed the wording, THG could not have been added to the doping list, and the case would in all probability have been lost. By making the alteration, WADA fended off the problem of having perhaps been a little too quick off the blocks. In the future, the agency will be able to act quickly and effectively when any new and suspicious drug sees the light of day. On the other hand, the problem has arisen for athletes that the number of drugs that can potentially be viewed as doping has become considerably larger. In principle, cholesterol now falls inside the definition of doping, which is patently absurd.[2] Four years on, it is clearer than ever that Saltin had a point. We still wait for evidence that THG has a performance-enhancing effect. And, if we leave out this affair, sports' doping control work continues to have no more than a modicum of success, despite the increases in resources and effort. The fact that more than 200 athletes were in treatment with Dr Fuentes when his clinic was raided in the aforementioned Operación Puerto seems at least to suggest that it is only a small fraction of doped athletes who are caught by the official control system.

The suspicion that positive doping tests are more the result of laxness and mistakes than of the effectiveness of the test programme – even after the establishment of WADA – was given support during the Tour de France 2006. The winner of the race, the American Floyd Landis, had been tested positive after the 17th stage, which he won with an awesome display of power cycling. He had been tested five times earlier in the race without problems (Landis 2007), but in its third week he was suddenly discovered to have an unusually high level of testosterone in his body. It seems utterly improbable that Landis should have taken the decision between the 16th and 17th stages that he would begin to dope himself. It is true that the previous day he had fallen so far behind and lost so much time that it would need an almost superhuman performance to bring him back on course to win. It was also true that he had huge ambitions of winning the race. True, too, he appeared for the 17th stage as a changed man. Nevertheless, it is difficult to believe that, if any rider had previously raced clean, that they would go to their doctor at this stage in the race and ask for an illegal drug that could make them ride like a rocket knowing full well that if they won the stage they would inevitably be asked for a doping test. Furthermore, it would be curious for a doctor to regard treatment with testosterone as being the most appropriate means with which to achieve a dramatic improvement in performance. A far more obvious measure would be to increase the number of oxygen-transporting blood cells if the doctor had a quantity of compatible blood to hand. In accordance with this, the chief physician at the National Hospital of Denmark, Professor Bente Klarlund Pedersen, suggested an alternative explanation for Landis's positive case. In a feature in the Danish daily *Berlingske Tidende*, she wrote:

> When Landis tested positive for testosterone at the Tour de France in 2006, it made no sense. Testosterone has no immediate effect on performance. In the milieu it is rumoured that Landis may have had his own blood collected earlier in the year when he was in the process of building muscle. What a mistake! Since it was impossible to detect blood doping because he had his own blood transfused, the testosterone was picked up in the test [as if it had been administered recently].
>
> (Pedersen 2008)

Even though this may sound far-fetched in the ears of biking enthusiasts, the theory harmonises well with the finds made by the Spanish authorities during Operación Puerto.

So if Landis's test result is not a false positive as both Landis and his physician maintain,[3] there is the possibility that Landis could have had a blood transfusion using his own blood, taken earlier in the year. According to Pedersen, this is at least one possible explanation as to how Landis could have put the rest of the favourites behind him and kept them at bay across three mountains. Clearly, this is just a theory. The point in mentioning it is that *if* that was what happened, it further supports the hypothesis that positive tests among top athletes come about as a result of lack of attention to detail. Moreover, the only real alternative to the false positive that makes sense implies that if the doctor had not blundered by taking blood while it still contained doping materials, Landis would not have been exposed. His victory could have been celebrated as a success for the concerted anti-doping effort. The government authorities – in this case, the Spanish police who, when they carried out their major raid, had found bags filled with blood and other material at the clinic run by the Spanish doctor Fuentes – could be praised for having put a spoke in the wheel of a set of the most hard-boiled cheats, while sport's own doping control could be praised for having had a suitably deterrent effect on the remainder of the participants, which had resulted in a race with such drama as had not been seen since the beginning of the EPO era, with ups and downs that caused havoc with the rankings. But Landis's exposure did more than destroy this optimistic story. It also exposed the worryingly random nature of the entire anti-doping campaign. And worse than that, it also demonstrated that moral issues in anti-doping work are ignored for the sake of the cause, as though every anti-doping initiative were by its very nature morally justified.

If the Spanish authorities had not carried out a raid against Fuentes, if the three big pre-race favourites, Ullrich, Basso and Vinokourov, who due to suspicion were denied participation, had all taken part, then the race would without the shadow of a doubt have taken a different course and would have had a different winner. If this is worth mentioning here, it is as a reminder that whatever may be the truth in Landis's case, it is highly unlikely that Fuentes is the only doctor in the world who is doping. If the raid had targeted a doctor – in Switzerland, Italy, the USA or wherever – it might have been other riders who would have been excluded in advance. That would depend, of course, on whether the authorities in the country in question had been just as unspeakably lax in their dealings with the press as the Spanish authorities were, while the investigation was going on. If, for instance, it had been Landis who had been excluded in advance, the Tour would in all likelihood have proceeded without any scandal.

If Fuentes deserves praise for anything, it is that he apparently is carrying out his work with circumspection. At any rate, the top cyclists excluded for being Fuentes's star clients have never tested positive in a competition.[4] It was only in the May before the Tour that Basso had won the Giro d'Italia in such sovereign fashion that his Italian rival Gilberto Simoni could not resist commenting that his power was inhuman: 'I've never seen anyone dominate like him, never seen anyone that strong. He seems like an extraterrestrial.'[5] A thinly veiled insinuation that Basso was doped. And if Simoni was right, we have once again to conclude that doping control is not good enough to produce fairness. On the other hand if he was *not* doped when he rode his competitors into the ground during the Giro, it is incomprehensible why he found it necessary to prepare to blood dope for the next great race, as he admitted was his intention during the Operación Puerto trial which had brought to light the fact that his blood was found in Fuentes' clinic (*International Herald Tribune*, 7 May 2007). The whole affair seems to bear witness to the arbitrariness of the current anti-doping measures.

The injustice becomes even more glaring in Vinokourov's case. He was also prevented from entering, but he was not even mentioned in the Spanish investigation launched at the end of May 2006. His controversial sports director, on the other hand, Manolo Saiz, was mentioned, along with 15 of his team mates on Liberty Seguros/Würth, and this had two serious consequences (http://www.cyclingnews.com/news.php?id = news/2006/jun06/ jun29news, accessed 7 March 2007).

The first was that the team's main source of finance, the American insurance company Liberty Seguros, cancelled all sponsorship agreements on the spot, which presented a direct threat to the team's existence. That threat was, however, fended off when a number of companies in Vinokourov's home country of Kazakhstan stepped in as replacement sponsors. Under its new name of Astana/Würth (Astana is the capital of Kazakhstan), Vinkourov's dream of winning the Tour was given financial security. The second and more serious consequence, however, was that ASO, the organisation behind the Tour de France, announced that the team would not be welcome at the race because of the case that was pending. According to UCI rules, Astana/ Würth could not be excluded just like that. The team's Pro-Tour licence ensured it an automatic right to take part. Astana/Würth brought the case, therefore, before the international Court of Arbitration for Sport (CAS), which ruled that the team ought to be allowed to take part. The grounds given by the CAS were that 'there is currently more uncertainty than facts established concretely'. But the ASO were not in a mood to roll over and accept the legal decision and in doing so run the risk that the Tour would get a bad press. They therefore used another way to get around it. The fact of the matter is that Pro-Tour teams – presumably for the sake of upholding the reputation of cycling – have produced an ethical code of conduct that ostensibly involves riders being able to be excluded solely on suspicion of doping. A rider whose name has come up in connection with a doping investigation can, according to the code, be summarily suspended until the person in question has been given a penalty or has been cleared. This was the code of conduct that was to be put to the test in connection with the Spanish case. That was how it was presented. Since, as far as the ASO was concerned, it was unacceptable to have Astana/Würth start the race, they put pressure on the Pro-Tour teams to make them live up to the code of conduct. In so doing they paved the way for a legitimate exclusion of the team, whose credibility lay in tatters after their sports director was arrested as one of the principal figures in the case at the same time as a substantial group of his riders were implicated as suspects. By insisting that suspended riders whom the team had entered in advance could not be substituted, the organisers managed to exclude Astana/Würth by referring to the rule that teams must have a minimum of six riders entered at the start.

Despite the fact that Vinokourov had fought tooth and nail to be included, there was nothing he could do about it once the remainder of the Pro-Tour clan chose to stick together and keep to their ethical line. By the time it emerged that several of his team mates had been named in the case by mistake, the party was, literally, over. The exclusions, which were announced to a loud fanfare, had been imposed without legal basis. They were, therefore, in direct contravention of one of the pillars of WADA's work, namely the ideal of the level playing field and the athletes' right to have 'a fair shot at it' (http://216.46.1.34/WADA/WADA_ang.mpg, accessed 6 January 2007). That this was actually unfair has only emerged since. The fact that Vinokourov was caught blood doping during the following Tour de France is ironic but does not make it just that he was expelled from the Tour 2006.

The Pro-Tour teams' ethical code of conduct

The ethical code of conduct was an internal document. It was not for public consumption. The public was told of its contents but was not allowed to see it. The chairman of Anti Doping Denmark, Jens Evald, told the participants in a seminar entitled 'The Press and Doping', held at Åarhus University on 16 November 2006, that he had tried to obtain a copy but without success. The code was apparently confidential. This aroused some amazement, and one of the journalists present set himself the task of investigating the matter. Presumably because of concerns that it would mean yet another tiresome affair for cycling if a meddlesome journalist began to write column after column about closet secrets and arcane ethics, it was by dint of an anonymous source that he came into possession of the code, whereupon he had it printed in his newspaper.[6] When we read it, we can well understand why the Pro-Tour teams would wish to keep it confidential. For it contains no requirement that riders should be excluded on the basis of circumstantial evidence.

Although the document can scarcely be said to be written in accessible language, it can be seen that the sections that might be cited as giving grounds for exclusion are paragraphs VIII and IX, which state:

> UCI Pro Teams make the following undertaking:
> VIII Subject to the right to terminate employment because of a serious offence, not to employ for races a licensed rider who is the subject of disciplinary action for infringement of UCI's regulations regarding anti-doping, carried out by any competent instance in accordance with the international code of anti-doping.
>
> IX Subject to the right to terminate employment because of a serious offence, not to employ a licensed rider for races who is the subject of an

investigation or of criminal proceedings on the grounds of circumstances relating to the sporting activity, i.e. either an action that constitutes an infringement of UCI's regulations regarding anti-doping or some (other) intentionally criminal offence.

(*Jyllands-Posten*, 25 March 2007)

Yet on close reading it appears that no such grounds actually exist. Since none of the riders who were suspended in the Fuentes case were 'subject to a disciplinary action', the condition relating to paragraph VIII is not fulfilled. Nor was this the case with paragraph IX. None of them were 'subject to an investigation or of criminal proceedings'. The investigation was directed at Fuentes with a view to taking criminal proceedings against him. The fact that famous cycling names appear in this connection naturally gives grounds for assumptions that those involved were following a doping programme with the Spanish doctor, but the ethical code of conduct does not go so far as to claim that riders should be excluded on the basis of nothing more than assumptions about their doping.

When Evald, who in addition to being chairman of Anti Doping Denmark is a Professor of Law, was presented with the code of conduct, he also came to the conclusion that the paper contained no legal basis on which to exclude the riders. He was, then, in agreement with CAS. He has no objection to the first seven requirements. He regards them as fine ethical norms. The remaining points, however, he sees as unfortunate, because here 'elements are mixed in that have nothing to do with ethics', which have had the unreasonable consequence 'that a series of riders have been excluded on a questionable legal basis'. And he adds:

[T]he excluded riders should have been allowed to take part, and then one could see later whether evidence became available. If anyone thinks that the lesson to be learnt from this story is that this is the way things should be done, then they signal at the same time that practitioners of cycling have to have less favourable treatment than other athletes, and that, if they want to exclude someone, anything is permitted ... Our successors in anti-doping work will ask what we were up to back in 2006, and with good reason will bring up this question: Where was the legal basis? ...

The idea behind working with anti-doping, of course, is on the one hand that there should be effective doping control and on the other that all athletes should be treated equally as far as that is possible, and that everyone understands the consequences of using doping. It should not be left to the powers-that-be in sport to exclude a man from doing his job in the heat of the moment and under pressure from the media, when that man proves such a short time after not to have been involved at all. That sort of thing sends shivers down my spine.

(Evald 2007)

For the chairman of Anti Doping Denmark to express concern about the legal position of athletes is significant. His concern is, unfortunately, not reflected in the views of those who set the agenda in the global campaign against doping, which became apparent the following year when the Dane Michael Rasmussen was withdrawn from the Tour after he had won the last mountain stage and put himself in a position where only bad luck could prevent him from winning the race overall. There was nothing in the rules that could justify his involuntary withdrawal, but because sensation-seeking media found out that he had lied about his whereabouts, the media pressure piled up around him. So to prevent bad publicity the Tour organisers put pressure on his team Rabobank to take him out (*NRC Handelsblad*, 2007). It may be that Rasmussen had exploited the whereabouts rules, which allow two missed tests in an 18-month period, but UCI had not initially identified him as breaking these rules otherwise he would not have been allowed to enter the race in the first place. So basically the whole affair appears to support Evald's statement quoted above, that: 'if they want to exclude someone, anything is permitted'. Most disconcertingly, WADA did not challenge the decision to force Rasmussen to leave the race.

The aim justifies the means

WADA's past President is also a man of law, which raises questions since one may have expected him to have expressed concern about the fact that there was no justification in the sporting rules for the tough decision to force Rasmussen out of the Tour in a winning position. Perhaps he regards the fight against doping as a war in which a form of emergency situation prevails and in which *in practice* the rules governing appropriate legal conduct can be followed with a certain latitude. We have already seen how, in order not to risk losing the THG case because of the detail that the drug might not have been performance-enhancing, WADA chose to alter the conditions governing whether a drug should be regarded as doping with the consequence that cholesterol is in principle now included. On the other side there has been incredulity at the fact that Pound was involved in putting pressure on the Italian authorities with a view to getting them to put their harsh anti-doping legislation temporarily on ice during the Winter Olympics in Turin (*The New York Times*, 2005). These very different episodes give the impression that inside WADA there thrives a belief that the agency is equipped with the moral right to act as it pleases – even to discount the rights of athletes – as long as it does so in the service of the cause.

When *L'Equipe* printed an article on 23 August 2005 with the claim that Lance Armstrong had used the banned drug EPO during the Tour de France in 1999, it was a severe blow to a sport that was already under scrutiny. The credibility of cycling was so low it was almost non-existent. If there now existed evidence for Armstrong having cheated, all attempts to restore faith in cycling would be in vain, and the bombshell would blast UCI back to where it started in 1998. It was almost impossible to get the message across that the tests were evidence of nothing whatsoever, since there was not one but six different Armstrong B-tests taken in 1999 that had apparently been found to be positive. It is, therefore, understandable that UCI felt itself under threat from these revelations and reacted angrily. Confidential information had been leaked from a WADA-accredited laboratory. A number of things were unclear. Why had Armstrong's six-year-old urine become the object of new tests in the first place? It was usual, so the explanation ran, for old urine samples to be used for research in new testing methods. Several unnamed riders' urine had been tested at the same time, and besides Armstrong six others had also tested positive for EPO. There was, however, still no explanation given for why urine that was to be used for the purpose of research was passed on with the old code numbers allowing the riders to be identified. According to the UCI rules, the test records that 'caught' Armstrong should have been destroyed after two years. For the information to be leaked to the press was not exactly by the book either and reinforces the suspicion that there was an agenda here that had nothing to do with research. Seen in that light it was understandable for UCI to harbour thoughts of a conspiracy and to be furious at Pound's reaction. It was not just that he took the newspaper article on trust without bothering to verify it and used it to question the credibility of the recently 'retired' Armstrong. There was also the fact that the tests that had been investigated had been taken before the establishment of WADA and when it came to it had nothing to do with the agency. Nevertheless Pound felt it incumbent upon himself to put pressure on the UCI with words to the effect that he expected the organisation to take the opportunity offered by the revelations to get to the bottom of the matter (Mackay 2005).

It was a challenge that UCI could not, of course, ignore. The organisation reacted, but not in the way that Pound had hoped. UCI sent out a press statement that looked more like a declaration of war than anything else, in that it emphasised all the irregularities in the affair. The UCI statement went as follows:

> We have substantial concerns about the impact of this matter on the integrity of the overall drug testing regime of the Olympic movement, and in particular the questions it raises over the trustworthiness of some of the sports and political authorities active in the anti-doping fight.
> (http:/www.cyclingnews.com/news.php?id = news/2005/sep05/sep16news,
> accessed 8 January 2007)

The organisation had, therefore, decided to launch an investigation with a view to finding out:

> Who commissioned and directed this research and who agreed to the public dissemination of the results?
> How could this be done without the riders' consent?
> Why was the UCI not informed?

How is it that the journalist apparently received WADA's official reaction on the possibility of continuing the research with the remaining urine samples, and on possible sanctions, on 22 August (see *L'Equipe*'s article of 23rd August), when WADA apparently received the information on these results only on 24 August?

The dissemination of the results being a breach of WADA's anti-doping code, did WADA itself authorise this step?

Has this apparent research on the 1999 Tour de France been widened to other sports events in France in the same year (Roland Garros, football World Cup) – why was the Tour de France chosen?

(http://www.cyclingnews.com/news.php?id = news/2005/sep05/sep09-news3, accessed 12 June 2008)

The move seems to be a clear attempt to undermine the credibility of WADA that, if it succeeded, would be a serious blow to the anti-doping campaign. That notwithstanding, it cannot be denied that these are relevant questions. The moral problem, namely that Armstrong was sentenced by a people's court with no opportunity to defend himself with anything but his oft-repeated assurances that he had never doped himself, was left untouched by Pound. Nor apparently did he find the motives that might lie behind the revelations worth qualifying or investigating. It was as though the UCI, in its insistence on sticking to the established rules, was, in Pound's view, demonstrating its opposition to the anti-doping campaign and must therefore be regarded as an enemy. Pound then reacted to the proposed investigation by publicly insinuating that in reality it was the UCI Chairman, Hein Verbruggen, who had leaked the confidential information to *L'Equipe*.[7]

It is hard to see what motive Verbruggen could have for doing so. If the information had been leaked from the world of cycling, then it would be more natural to suspect individuals who might have envied Armstrong his seven-year hegemony over the Tour and who had taken objection to his abdication without defeat. But whoever was behind it, it would appear to be inappropriate for the WADA President to allow himself to be carried along by the media scrum instead of referring himself to the doping laws that he himself had helped to formulate. The remarks coming from him put not only his own credibility at risk but also that of the whole of WADA, which could only be to the detriment of the anti-doping campaign.

UCI did not allow itself to be intimidated and, undaunted, initiated an independent investigation of the course of events headed by the Dutch lawyer Emile J. Vrijman. The report's conclusion was deeply damaging both for WADA and for the WADA-accredited laboratory, the *Laboratoire Nationale de Dépistage du Dopage* (LNDD). Without getting lost in the detail of the 130-page report, the following are noteworthy:

1   That the French ministry that owned the laboratory, LNDD itself and WADA would apparently not cooperate in shedding light on the case by

acceding to the request of the investigative commission to hand over relevant documents (Vrijman 2006).

2   That it is 'difficult to understand how WADA and/or the LNDD could believe their discussions with the media regarding the LNDD's research report could be consistent with their agreement to treat those reports confidentially' (ibid.: 18).

3   That it was WADA who had put pressure on the laboratory to get it to include the infamous information, and that 'LNDD representatives made it clear that they were afraid to resist WADA's demands for including the "additional information" in their research reports' (ibid.: 21).

4   That criticism of the handling of the matter had been raised internally in WADA, on the one hand through the Vice-President, the Danish Minister of Culture, Brian Mikkelsen, denouncing it, and on the other through the director of the WADA-accredited laboratory in Montreal, Dr. Christiane Ayotte, making it clear that the affair was an infringement of the WADA codex (ibid.: 25).

5   That 'IOC president Jacques Rogge acknowledged the unfairness and made public statements in the fall of 2005 criticizing the manner in which this situation had been conducted, and stated univocally that Lance Armstrong should not be placed in a position where he would have to prove these allegations to be false' (ibid.: 19).

6   That organisations representing the interests of sports professionals, the General Association of Summer Olympic Federations and IOC Athletes Commission 'expressed their joint concerns regarding the violation of athletes' confidentiality' (ibid.: 21)

These uncomfortable statements come on the heels of the report pointing out the ethical responsibility that lies with those in charge of the monitoring work, which the CAS has expressed with clear emphasis:

> The fight against doping is arduous and it may require strict rules. But the rule-makers and rule-appliers must begin by being strict themselves. Regulations that may affect the careers of dedicated athletes must be predictable. They must emanate from duly authorised bodies. They must be adopted in constitutionally proper ways. They should not be the product of an obscure process of accretion. Athletes and officials should not be confronted with a thicket of mutually qualifying or even contradictory rules that can be understood only on the basis of the *de facto* practice over the course of many years by a small group of insiders.
>
> (ibid.: 12)

Apparently Pound's management of the affair ran directly counter to the exhortations of the CAS. The quotation, which was worded four years prior to the establishment of WADA, is for that reason an effective sounding board for the report's specification of irregularities and rule infringement. It shows how, before the establishment of WADA, it had been understood that the campaign against doping, however important it might seem, had to be carried out on fair terms. After the great doping scandals and the establishment of WADA, however, it is as though the hunt has come to take on a higher priority than ethics. This is at heart what the Vrijman report says, and its proposal is as bold as it is logical:

> That WADA changes – if necessary – its governance structure and policies to ensure that concerns like those expressed by Mikkelsen, Ayotte, the ASOIF, and the IOC Athletes Commission are timely identified, considered, resolved, and remedied and that a mechanism will be devised as soon as possible to deal with any grievances any WADA stakeholder might have who is adversely affected by alleged misconduct either by WADA, a WADA-accredited laboratory, a WADA official or any other individual or organization involved in international doping control testing and results management system. Whether this should be achieved by instituting a 'Code of Ethical Behavior' applying to all WADA staff and personnel or having an 'Ethics Committee' not unlike the IOC Ethics Committee, is for others to decide. However, just as athletes are accountable for their behavior, so should WADA.
>
> (ibid.: 22)

The report, it goes without saying, is something that WADA would prefer did not exist, and the organisation rejects it as being full of mistakes, describing it as both an insult to their reputation and a farce. In addition, it announces that 'WADA has taken legal advice regarding its recourses against the investigator and any organization, including UCI, that may publicly adopt its conclusions' (http://www.cyclingnews.com/news.php?id = news/2006/jun06/jun03news, accessed 12 January 2007). The report has, however, never had any legal repercussions. And Pound, whose reputation had been seriously damaged by the affair, had further reason for finding himself in the court of law in order to clear himself of an accusation of misusing his office, when Lance Armstrong used the conclusions of the report as a basis for a personal attack on him. In an open letter addressed to Pound, he wrote, among other things, that:

> The report established that WADA had forced the laboratory to prepare an improper report, and had promised the laboratory that the report would be kept confidential and would not be used against any athlete. However, as soon as the report was leaked to the French tabloid, WADA President Dick Pound went to the media and claimed, contrary to what he knew to be true, that the research was reliable and showed that I had cheated. The investigator concluded that Dick Pound's conduct against me was motivated by a desire to discredit me because I had publicly challenged his improper conduct in the past and that WADA

made false statements to the investigator in an effort to conceal its wrongdoing.

> (http://www.cyclingnews.com/news.php?id = news/2006/jun06/arm-strongstatement, accessed 12 January 2007)

If Pound really believes that he has acted according to the book in this matter, it is difficult to understand why he did not take Armstrong's comments to court for defamation of character. Nor is it clear why WADA as an organisation did not do the same. For, on the one hand, he makes serious accusations against the agency as such for having used threats to make LNDD break the rules, and, on the other, it is not just Pound's reputation but also the Agency's that were compromised by Armstrong's final salvo against Pound:

> Dick Pound has already told the media that he does not acknowledge the authority of the IOC in this matter. That is the fundamental problem here. Until the IOC steps up and makes it clear that they are responsible for misconduct by IOC officials and all misconduct by sports officials, no athlete will be able to take seriously the rules and protections of athlete rights in the rules of sport. It is in that spirit that I ask you to read my letter.
>
> (http://www.cyclingnews.com/news.php?id = news/2006/jun06/arm-strongstatement, accessed 12 January 2007)

According to Armstrong's presentation, the case has brought about a breach of trust between athletes and the organisation that ideally should serve to protect their health and their sport. It is a serious problem for those seeking to have a sport free of doping that the people who are fighting doping seem to have lost sight of the notion that sport first and foremost exists for and depends upon the athletes themselves. Currently there is colossal pressure on them. As has been mentioned, they have to provide accurate, current whereabouts information and be prepared to provide urine and blood samples on demand. It is, therefore, essential that athletes retain faith in the fact that rules are adhered to on both sides. Once immorality creeps in – and it is no excuse that it takes place in the service of a greater cause – the wind is taken out of the sails of the most powerful argument for the retention of an active anti-doping campaign, namely the wish to see fair play. And since it becomes ever more evident that the health argument in itself is not particularly strong, lack of moral standards in the anti-doping camp paves the way for those who argue for the deregulation of doping. By way of preparation for that discussion, it is worth considering what lies behind the fact that doping, which until 1960 was not particularly seen as a problem, has today become, according to the governing consensus, an evil to be combated with such vehemence.

7   The fear of modernity

At first glance, the anti-doping campaign would seem to be a rational defence mechanism. However, as previous chapters have shown, the rationale behind the scheme is questionable. History teaches us that doping is not something new that has suddenly invaded sport. Approaching the subject from the viewpoint of the history of ideas, and taking as our starting point the role of money, may help to throw light on the change in mentality that generated the anxiety about the doping phenomenon. It took hold in the 1960s and is today more extreme than ever. In what follows focus is on cycling – modernity's sport *par excellence*. An attempt will be made to provide a sense of the complexity of the issue as well as the overall structure.

Not for the money

The most common explanation for sportspersons doping themselves is that they do it for the money. The explanation for that stares us in the face. The difference between success and failure can be measured in millions in several branches of sport. The emphasis on economic motive does nothing, however, to solve the riddle of why people doped themselves before the sums involved became so huge. Nor does it account for the fact that athletes dope themselves in sports such as weight-lifting where the prize-winning sums are small and can scarcely be used as an argument for reaching for the needle. This explanation leaves the driving forces of sport out of the frame. However, the attraction of doping throughout history cannot be understood unless we appreciate the significance of the central characteristic of sport: the will to win, which in the final analysis is about positioning yourself at the top of the hierarchical ladder (see Chapter 2). Even though there is no doubt that fewer athletes would resort to illegal performance-enhancing drugs if the contracts and prize money did not provide financial inducement, it is a misunderstanding of sport to believe that a return to amateurism would make doping disappear. And such a misunderstanding could further lead to the mistaken belief that the anti-doping campaign was an obvious way for sport to defend itself against a monster created by the power of money.

In his dramatic introduction to *Mortal Engines*, John Hoberman describes the death of the West German heptathlete, Birgit Dressel, in 1987 (Hoberman 1992). The official cause of death was given as infection of the spinal cord, but the real cause was, as far as can be ascertained, an abuse of doping stretching back over a year, which had destroyed her immune system. At her home the police found a wide range of medicines and performance-enhancing substances. Furthermore, she had collaborated with the sports physician, Armin Klümper, who is apparently said to have given her more than 400 injections with a range of substances, among them 'proteins known to be immunologically hazardous' (ibid.: 2). Dressel's father believed that she was a victim of the drugs industry, but that explanation, according to Hoberman, is too black-and-white. The explanation 'absolves too many people who share responsibility for her drug abuse, not least the athlete herself' (ibid.: 2), he says, and he provides his version of the complex causes of the sad affair.

> The Birgit Dressel affair offers a comprehensive portrait of modern high-performance sport in miniature. The cast of characters is complete: the ambitious athlete and her trainer-companion, both hoping to escape from their cramped attic apartment into the brightly illuminated world of stardom; the sports officials who take the necessity of illicit drug use for granted and therefore tolerate or even encourage the use of performance-enhancing drugs, and the physician whose need to associate with famous athletes rendered him unfit to distinguish between maintaining the body's health and boosting its performance with medically reckless procedures.
>
> (ibid.: 2)

Hoberman is undoubtedly right when he says that individuals in Dressel's network must bear a share of the responsibility, some of them by assisting in the procurement and dosing of the drugs, others by looking the other way or even going so far as encouraging it. But Hoberman keeps his focus metaphorically speaking firmly on the shell surrounding the core of the problem. He does not get to its nub: the nature of sport. This is incidentally a recurrent feature of anti-doping literature, which can be linked to the widespread – but erroneous – perception that doping is a threat to sport.

It may be that the business of sport *is* under threat, but the threat does not come from the use of doping as such. The threat derives from the prevailing view of doping as a destructive abomination, a view that, as I have said, is relatively recent. When Hoberman points to the ambitious athlete as the first in the line of 'guilty parties', he comes close to voicing the significant perception that when talented athletes are hooked on a sport, it tempts them to optimise their performance levels by using all means at their disposal. He immediately buries what is for sporting idealists an uncomfortable insight, however, when he adds his comment about the trainer-lover and their shared desire to achieve a higher standard of living. In so doing, he manages to convey the impression that ambition is directed towards the external world. In other words the ambition that drove Dressel to her fatal abuse was not sporting but economic. What is seductive in this explanation is that it makes it possible to define abuse as unsporting. If, on the other hand, we allow ourselves to entertain the notion that the will to win was the driving force behind the abuse, then the notion of sport as a healthy and noble force for good is cast into doubt, since it could suddenly be argued that the abuse was sporting in its nature.

As mentioned, there is no doubt that financial motives play their part in relation to doping. The assistants who wait in the wings with medical support are not doing so for nothing, nor because they harbour a burning ambition to win a sporting competition by proxy. Maybe they offer their services simply because they are driven by scientific curiosity as to how far they can push the athlete's performance levels, but there is no doubt that the good money to be made out of doping is a contributing factor. And the more the campaign against doping intensifies, the more the athletes' need for expert assistance will increase, and it stands to reason that according to the law of supply and demand the rewards will continue to increase with it. The fundamental problem remains that the athletes' ambition to take the lead in the sporting hierarchy can be so powerful that they fall for the temptation to invest in the 'resources' that those behind the scenes have ready to hand. If the decisive motivation for athletes to use drugs was the desire to earn a fortune during the brief period they are at the top, then it is hard to understand why they continue once that fortune is in the bank and they could retire and live in luxury for the remainder of their days. A Danish interview study provides support for the conclusion that doping is not motivated primarily by financial ambition. One rider, who under cover of anonymity admitted using EPO, explained his motivation:

> I would like to stress that [doping] is not something people do for the money. That just isn't possible. It is simply too hard for that. No one is injecting themselves with this or that drug for the sake of the money. What are the driving forces are ambition and passion.
>
> (Christiansen 2005: 121)

Enlightenment and Romanticism

Sports idealists who advance the cash motive as the cause of doping present an argument that is in line with the Marxist sports criticism of the 1970s. The emphasis was, it is true, quite different then. That critique was directed at the tyranny of time and achievement that athletes were subjected to, as a consequence of which sport resembled a form of training for and legitimisation of the working conditions of the factory (see Chapter 2). The weakness of this critique of sport is that it could not account for the attraction of sport, which was evidently different from that of the factory, and this same weakness is to be found in the critique of doping coming from sports idealists. Both have to give up on the attempt to explain the athletes' desire of their own free will to risk life and limb for their sport.

It is no accident that both critics and idealists of sport are quick to criticise the power of money, even though it provides an incomplete explanation for the attraction of either sport or doping. For the logic of capitalism gives further impetus to the intrinsic forces of sport and makes them stand out with greater clarity. This is why it seems so obvious to regard it as a corrupting influence. If we appreciate that economics plays only a secondary role, then our faith in the golden opinions which sport attracts gives way to a sober recognition that they are based on a set of ideological precepts invested in sport that are motivated by a wish to civilise and that are in the last analysis untenable.

While sporting competitions in pre-modern times were often conducted in a raw and brutal fashion (see Chapter 4), in their original modern incarnation they were stage-managed as noble contests, as one gentleman throwing down the gauntlet to another. As long as sport was cultivated as a pleasant pastime by the educated, well-heeled middle class, this ideal could be maintained. Even so there was a clear sense that restrictions had to be placed on its development if it was not to degenerate. The idealisation of the amateur was part of that attempt.

But there was yet another reason for amateurism to be promoted by the middle class, who in other respects were the standard-bearers of capitalism. It excluded the lower classes from taking part (Krawzyk 1977). With the spread of capitalism and the development of industry, fanned by the rationalist thinking of the Enlightenment, the middle classes began in an economic sense to make inroads into the domain of the nobility. The sport of gentlemen displayed similar tendencies towards social climbing. Bourgeois wisdom has it that time is money. By 'spending' time on the sports field, the middle class could in some sense imitate the show of excess and extravagance which was so characteristic of the aristocracy and which in every other respect was anathema to it. In addition, sport became overlaid with significance as a character-building activity. Being a 'good sportsman' became the sign of nobility. The way sport was stage-managed reflected the manner in which the bourgeois classes wished to see themselves. The deeper nature of the bourgeoisie revealed itself, however, in the fact that what it cultivated was a culture of the body in which competition was deeply ingrained, a culture quite different from the hunting, shooting and fishing cultivated by the nobility. It is no accident that modern sport has its origins in England, from where it gradually spread to the Continent as industrialisation gained momentum there. Whereas the gentlemanly ideals of the amateur and of fair play looked backwards at a pre-capitalist universe of values, the logic of sport pointed forwards towards the competitive capitalist societies of modernity. Professionalism was, then, no perversion of sport but rather a liberation that fitted hand in glove with the dynamism of modern society. The family resemblances between sport and modernity lie in their shared urge towards expansion, which was given telling expression in the motto of the modern Olympic Games: Faster, Higher, Stronger. And it was further demonstrated in the linking of the Olympic Games to the World Exhibition in Paris in 1900, in St Louis in 1904 and in London in 1908.

Seen in that light, we might expect professionalism to have come about more quickly and across a wider range of sports than it did, for as a rule retrograde tendencies find it difficult to withstand the pressure of the time. The development of modernity took place, however, at such a pace and with such transformational power that it rapidly provoked a significant counter-reaction in the form of the Romantic movement, whose underlying idea was that modernity had an unnatural and dehumanising effect (Cranston 1994). Rousseau's rallying cry 'Back to Nature' became emblematic for the movement. An ideological split arose between the Romantics critical of the development of modern society and the progressives who regarded progress positively. This split became visible in their respective cultures of the body. The Romantics preferred a culture of the body that emphasised naturalness and the development of 'the whole person'. The progressives, on the other hand, welcomed technological progress and were happy to integrate it into the culture of the body as an indication of the potential of modernity to develop 'the superman'. This split can still be felt in our time. If the use of doping is far more widespread in cycling than in other endurance disciplines such as the marathon and the triathlon – and this seems to be the case – then this can be related to the fact that this is a genuinely modern sport.

The origins of cycling

The perception of sport as a whole being a product of the industrial revolution is not new. All sporting disciplines are, however, not equally modern. Phenomena such as boxing, running and tennis, unlike cycling, have their roots back in pre-modern times. And considering the differences in forms of behaviour and social conventions that can be observed between different disciplines, it seems to be a reasonable assumption that their origins are reflected in their present cultures.

For, while it is true that sport is dynamic in its striving to optimise performance, it is at the same time conservative. Sporting disciplines change only slowly. When we attend Wimbledon, for example, we do not need to know that tennis was once a pastime for the nobility enjoyed in the castle grounds of England to sense the heavy hand of tradition at work. The conduct of the players, the umpire's manner and the behaviour of the public are markedly different from those we experience watching football. The introduction of the 'tie break', which made competitions more TV friendly, like John McEnroe's recurrent breaches of the accepted norms of propriety, are examples of the pressure for change exerted by changes in society and by the altered norms associated with them.

A corresponding development – albeit in the opposite direction – can be seen as regards the sport of boxing. The use of a helmet became *permitted* as late as in 1985. The rule making the use of the helmet obligatory in amateur boxing followed later as a response to pressure to have the sport banned in the interests of health. But even though they may undergo social adaptation, it remains the case that tennis and boxing are different in their appeal and in their recruitment base. And those who are recruited will be socialised into that particular environment and be stamped by the values and traditions that predominate there.

Many of the popular sports disciplines of our day carry in one way or another the stamp of pre-modern traditions, but this is not true of cycling. Cycling was born with the invention of a machine. It is, therefore, history's first thoroughgoing modern sport and, as if symptomatic of that fact, it was run professionally right from the start. The bicycle was a confirmation of the optimism for the future felt by early modernity in that it represented a substantial increase in the potential geographical perimeters of a person's life. Even though the first bicycles – the so-called penny-farthings with pedals mounted on the front wheel – were monsters that cost a fortune and weighed in at 30–35 kilos, they made it possible to make lengthier and more arduous journeys than ever before using human power. In 1870, the Englishman Michael Kemp, for example, cycled across northern India with the curious result that when the Hindus saw him astride his wondrous machine, they took him to be God and locked him up in a temple, from which he was only freed after considerable exertions on the part of British diplomats (Rabenstein 1991: 14).

Cycling adventurers, for example, demonstrated through their feats that technical developments could effectively shift the bounds of possibility. Travellers were often sponsored by manufacturers and financed by newspapers who received in exchange sole rights on the travellers' stories, and readers enthusiastically kept up with the serialised accounts as real-life supplements to the popular futuristic tales of Jules Verne (Woodforde 1970). By around the turn of the century round-the-world cycling tours had, however, become so common that the readers' interest waned and with it the incentive for newspapers to pay their expenses. The age of round the world cycling was slipping away.

But interest in the bicycle remained undiminished. Manufacturers worked to improve its construction, and with the development of the cycle with a chain-drive to its back wheel (the low, rear-wheel-driven safety model), the road lay open to its breakthrough among the ordinary public. The safety bicycle was easy to ride. It was also relatively cheap. It could be purchased for less than half the price of a penny-farthing, and tough competition between manufacturers drove the price even lower. During the period 1890–1904 the price fell from being what roughly corresponded to a high school teacher's monthly salary to a worker's weekly wage (Rabenstein 1991). The profit margins on bicycle production were marginal, so producers focused heavily on increasing sales. Marketing by means of cycle races was an effective sales strategy.

The cycle race was not, however, invented for that purpose. The first velocipede was created in the late 1860s and the first longer distance race was between Rouen and Paris in 1869, a distance of 123 kilometres (Gronen and Lemke 1987). The bicycle was, then, from the very first used for sporting purposes. The rapid increase in the number of organised cycle races, on the other hand, came about clearly as a consequence of commercial interests. The races were arranged by manufacturers, who paid professional riders to compete on the track or the highway to demonstrate the superiority of their products (Woodforde 1970). There was no doubting the interests of the manufacturers, but they were not the only ones to see a chance for making a buck out of bicycle races. Entrepreneurs invested in bicycle tracks, and the public poured in to see the races in large numbers. The press also played a significant role, for the interest of the general public ensured that it was lucrative for newspapers to write about the races. The long distance road races, in particular, that were organised during the 1890s provided the press with the opportunity to make idols out of the riders, which further stimulated public interest, creating the basis for magazines that wrote predominantly about cycling. The need for modern legends in a secularised world was evident.

The ordeals to which the organisers submitted the riders were colossal. Bordeaux–Paris, which was raced for the first time in 1891, offered the riders a distance of 577 kilometres. Pacers were allowed. Nevertheless the average speed of the winner, George Pilkington Mills, who clocked in at 21.5 kph, indicates an impressive power performance given the equipment and the state of the roads of the time. Another of the legendary classics of cycling, the Paris–Brest–Paris race, was founded in the same year. The race was more than twice as long as Bordeaux–Paris, 1196 kilometres and was open to both amateurs and professionals. A field of 575 riders applied to take part, several of them no doubt attracted by a first prize of 25,000 francs, which would have represented a fortune at the time. The rules did not allow pacers, and cycles were sealed at the start to prevent the riders swapping them along the way. In the event of a fault the cyclists had to wait for their bicycle to be repaired, if that were possible. The winner of the race, the Frenchman Charles Terront, completed the race in 71 hours and 16 minutes, or in other words with an average speed of about 17 kph (approximately 10 mph) including the periods when he held (in)voluntary breaks. His longest break was 45 minutes, while he waited to have his bicycle repaired (Gronen and Lemke 1987).

Paris–Brest–Paris is regarded as being the start of the era of the highway hero and Terront is seen as France's first great sporting star. His phenomenal riding skill and his impressive list of victories (in 1885 he entered 65 races and won 55 of them) inspired thousands of younger riders. Competition was, however, tough. Only a minority succeeded in creating a rewarding career. One of them was Constant Huret. In 1900, the very year in which the UCI was founded, he won the first official World Championship for professionals. It was no surprise. He had already made a name for himself when he won the Bordeaux–Paris race and at the same time cut four hours off the previous record. His performance bears witness to the unbelievable spirit of sacrifice that cycle riders possessed even in those days. He arrived in Paris drenched in blood due to crashes and almost unconscious from exhaustion.

Record mania and the drive to experiment

Huret also set a world record in 1898 when he rode 909.072 kilometres in 24 hours. In other words he was able, using pacers, to maintain an average speed of just under 38 kph (Gronen and Lemke 1987: 153). Six years earlier another Frenchman, Stéphane, managed to cover 651 kilometres in 24 hours. The following year he attempted to improve on his record, but without success. On that occasion the doctor and sporting enthusiast Philippe Tissié was present. He took the opportunity offered by the attempt to experiment with the effect of a variety of stimulants on human performance. Stéphane had decided to make his attempt without consuming any solid food on the way, which seemed to have a negative effect on his attempt at the record. He took nourishment only in the form of milk and the various liquid concoctions that Tissié gave him, along with milky tea, peppermint drink, lemonade, rum with milk, and champagne (Hoberman 1992).

This collaboration between the doctor and the cyclist gives the impression of bringing together two issues of the day. Tissié was driven by an interest in investigating possible ways of pushing human performance levels to their limits. Stéphane for his part had hopes of pushing the limits of his own capacity.

Cycling as a whole bore all the marks of record mania, as though an enthusiasm for speed had become an obsession. Records were sent soaring using all available means. The reason that Huret could ride so much further than Stéphane was because he used pacers, the use of which, it was discovered, was the ideal way to improve speed and so break records. So pacemakers were developed. Bicycles were constructed for several riders, windshields were mounted and later auxiliary motors were added. And speeds rose faster and faster. Between 1890 and 1909, the hour record increased from about 38 to over 100 kilometres.

This record mania was an expression of a form of curiosity in exploring human potential. Where were the limits? The rapid growth of records fed the idea that human potential was almost limitless. The realisation that humans could transport themselves three to four times faster than they could run represented a real and fundamental shift of consciousness. This meant that they could transport themselves faster under their own steam than they could on horseback, and this superiority was put on show at curious competitions. For example, in 1893, one of the fastest road racers of the day, the German Josef Fischer, won a 4000 metres track race against a trotting horse by five seconds with a time of 6.47 minutes. Earlier the same year Fischer had won the Vienna–Berlin race, which actually had its origins in a horse race held the previous year over the same route. The winning rider, the Austrian Graf Wilhelm Starhemberg, covered the 580 kilometres in 71 hours and 35 minutes, after which the horse died. In spite of the fact that the cycle race was held on poor roads, that the weather was oppressively hot and that the route had 250 climbs, 28 cyclists completed the race and Fischer only took 31 hours to cover the distance. In other words, he took less than half the time Starhemberg had taken only the year before (Gronen and Lemke 1987). Events such as this demonstrated the 'extra-biological' superiority of humankind.

The bicycle was seen as a victory over restrictive nature, and ever since the first machine saw the light of day there have been continuing efforts to improve it. Reduction in weight, gear systems, various initiatives aimed at reducing wind resistance – all these have contributed to making the bicycle more efficient. Changes in the bicycle reflect an offensive technological development that can be found in countless other areas. What is special, however, about the bicycle is that it is never more effective than its rider manages to make it. Forward progress is dependent on the transference of power from 'man' to machine. The rider is the bicycle's motor. It is an easy step, therefore, not only to look at material improvements to the bicycle, but also to be interested in potential ways to optimise the performance of its 'motor' – at any rate if you are interested in improvements in sporting results (as cyclists are) or in optimising the functional levels of the human organism (as doctors and physiologists are). It is, therefore, understandable that from the very beginnings of cycling, riders have looked to achieve improvements in performance with the assistance of a variety of medical substances. Nor is there anything strange about doctors, as human mechanics, having an interest both in studying and in contributing to the development of athletes as the Formula One specimens of the race. Tissié's presence during Stéphane's attempt at the world record (mentioned above) was neither an accident nor was it exceptional. In his day there was nothing shady about the idea of using medicine to contribute to the performance of sportspeople. On the contrary the doctor–athlete relationship was of mutual benefit and could even prove to be of benefit for the wider population in so far as the athletes' focus on performance and their willingness to consume drugs – even when they had potentially fatal effects as in the case of cocaine and strychnine – provided doctors with good opportunities for experimentation. Over the past centuries athletes in their thousands have benefited from medical support in something that resembles a gigantic experiment with the human organism (Hoberman 1992). Athletes who have donated their physiques to that experiment have nurtured a faith in the robust strength of the body, while physiologists and doctors have had faith in the invigorating power of medicine. Fundamental for both parties has been a mechanistic view of the body. From that perspective, doping is to be seen as medication directed towards optimising the physical capacity of the body, a form of bodily tuning to the highest pitch.

The reason for the doping problem in cycling

Cycling seems to be an invitation to doctors and physiologists to research the mechanics of fatigue. The Monarch bicycle, which is still used at a number of sports science institutes, can be seen as a symbol of the successful but currently discredited alliance between science and sport. If it were not for the curiosity of science, for its marvellous freedom from narrow-mindedness, its absence of blinkers, we would scarcely have such a widespread doping problem as now confronts us. As has been shown, the close relationship between science and cycling is nothing new. What is new is the fact that that relationship has become the subject of suspicion. The heavy-handed way in which authorities across Europe have begun to take action with regards to the use of doping gives pause for thought, signalling as it does the current scepticism towards medicine. But the scepticism is qualified, even ambivalent, since it is not directed towards the production of new medicines or towards the sharp increase in use of medication by the rest of the population. What is seen as unacceptable is the specific link between sport and medical enhancement. The doping scandal in 1998 brought the reality home to the authorities. Even though the revelations came as a shock, the discoveries were, strictly speaking, no surprise. What was found was only what could have been expected, namely a set of the most powerful performance-enhancing drugs available on the market. Any raid of the kind undertaken at any time in the history of cycling would probably have given the same result. In Terront's days no amphetamine would have been discovered – and for good reason – just as in Jacques Anquetil's days no EPO would have been found. But it is likely that at any time what would have been found were the most effective drugs on the market. In his book *Supermen, Heroes and Gods*, first published in German in 1962, Walter Umminger underlines the point:

> Championship cycle-racing places exaggerated demands on the physical and psychological staying power of the competitors. During a recent Swiss track championship meeting at Zürich, the police made a surprise raid on the contestants' changing rooms. In one of these they seized no less than 77 Weckamin tablets, a stimulant available on prescription only. In addition the same source yielded 100 caffeine granules, two ampoules containing a vitamin preparation for injection, ten doses of a powerful sedative, three tablets of a local anaesthetic for injection, and ten hypodermic needles of various sizes. The total haul of drugs in all the rooms by the police would have been sufficient to poison the population of a small town.
>
> (Umminger 1963: 241f)

The evidence before us cannot be explained away. It seems indisputable that performance-enhancing drugs have been a natural part of the cyclists' equipment. The difference between the drugs found around 1960 and those being discovered in raids 40–50 years later does not give the impression of there having been any fundamental change in the milieu of cycling. If the substances found today appear more dangerous than those found earlier, this is not due to any corruption of the moral standards of riders. Cyclists have not become hard-nosed criminals from one decade to the next. Or if they have, then it is because the law has been tightened in such a way that they can now be defined as such. As policies in the area have been tightened, they have been caught in a dilemma between their sporting ambitions and the desire to live in peace as law-abiding citizens.

The dichotomy of modernity

When we find that the drugs being unearthed by the authorities today are different from those that might previously have been found, what is being really disclosed is the core problem of modernity. Riders use what modernity makes available for them. This has been the general practice from the very start. As has been said, the bicycle has been improved in many ways. Cycling has, in the spirit of modernity, adapted the great majority of these innovations. In addition to improvements in the construction of the bicycle, the sport has also been open to other forms of technological progress, which have revolutionised cycling for better or for worse. When in recent years people have spoken about the crisis of cycling, they have then in reality been pointing towards a crisis of modernity. As far as economics, the media and public interest are concerned, cycling is as vital as ever it was.

Uncertainty revolves, however, around the degree to which the innovations of modernity can really be regarded as progress. For those people who place an emphasis on authenticity and the inviolability of physical health, the use of medication in sport may be progress but in the wrong direction and constitutes nothing less than an assault on sporting ideals and something that has to be combated at all costs. But to fight against the use of doping is tantamount to wanting to fight against the idea of modernity. It is the great paradox of our time.

For at the core of the foundation stone of modernity, of the Enlightenment, lies the ideal of making it possible for humankind to make its own choices and its own decisions on the basis of rationality. Faith in the individual's own power of reasoning and judgement – and by extension in the Enlightenment project – is visibly crumbling, a development that has to do with modernity in many cases having proved itself to be ambivalent. Those forms of progress that it has given rise to have in many cases proved to constitute both promise and threat. New discoveries that are accounted positive in one context are often judged negative in another. And at times they will be judged to be positive and negative in the same situation by parties with discordant viewpoints. What determines the matter are basic attitudes, values, matrices of belief. An exception can be found in enforced medication, which is seen as something good, or at least as a necessary evil. The explanation for this might be that such treatment relates to patients who are assumed to be a danger to themselves or to others unless they are treated. At the point at which the institution responsible for treatment assesses a psychosis to have robbed the patient of his or her reason, the therapist, following the dictates of good sense, adopts the role of guardian and initiates medical treatment.

In sport, the situation is the opposite. Here there is no question of force. Here medication is available as a possible option that the athlete sees as an advantage and therefore wishes to be treated with. If this view cannot be accepted unquestioningly, it might be because it is argued that the athlete is not sufficiently aware of the consequences and of the risk that he or she is taking in the long run.

Intervention and the necessity of surveillance

In the 1960s, a number of new perspectives opened up that led away from the main highway of modernity. One that is central to our concerns here is a questioning of the mechanistic perception of the body. During the Enlightenment, when that perception began to take hold, it was linked to a view of a God who, so to speak, tightened the springs in the clockwork of the human body and got it to work. But the Enlightenment and the progress of science eroded that perception. As early as in the eighteenth century there were many doctors who believed that the reason individual parts of the body functioned was to be found in the parts themselves. In other words, to uncover the workings of the liver or any other part of the body it was sufficient to investigate that part in isolation (Cassell 1992). That paradigm has since led to celebrated successes in the form of surgical reconstructions and other forms of replacement surgery (such as the sewing back on of detached limbs), including the transplantation of vital organs like the liver, kidneys, lungs and heart. At the same time, however, it has become clear, especially as regards these major transplantations, that such solutions are not ideal but can be associated with serious side-effects and involve a dramatic reduction in quality of life. Treating the body as a machine is, then, something that is no longer seen as unequivocally acceptable (Porter 1997: 622).

This results in a frustrating uncertainty, which found expression the moment it was clear what the situation was in cycling. The impression given by the manifest assault on sporting practice launched by the authorities is above all of a form of compensation for their sense of powerlessness in the face of that momentum in society as a whole. As far as can be judged, there is nothing that can be done about the overall development of society, where the endless upping of competition has made 'happy pills', beta-blockers and the like into essential measures to combat stress, fear and high blood pressure. Measures against doping, however, signal that, while the mechanistic view of the body may be applied with undiminished strength on the macro-level, sport ought to constitute a kind of set-aside, a safe haven. In this area it is no longer acceptable for individuals to exert control over their own body as though it was a machine, which is otherwise so much the norm in the world of cycling that it even leaves its mark on the sport's own discourse, as seen, for example, when Edmund R. Burke of the American Cycling Association writes: 'All racers are concerned with nutrition. Food is fuel and, to extend the analogy, quality food is needed to supply high-octane fuel' (Burke 1986: 200). If the analogy is no longer a fortunate one, the reason is, of course, that as time has gone on 'fuel' has been produced with a higher 'octane' than even the most nutrient-rich food could match. To live and move in modernity is like crossing a minefield. People cannot be allowed to access it at will. The way modernity has developed has meant that it becomes increasingly indefensible to rely upon the individual's own judgement. Increasing levels of interference are necessary in the form of the 'nanny state' and state surveillance. The notion of progress and the Enlightenment's ideals of human knowledge, which were closely associated with the ideal of individual freedom (including freedom from interference on the part of the state) have ended up completely counter to their original intentions, requiring a restriction of personal freedoms. And this tendency appears to be on the increase. Since the 1960s anti-doping surveillance has been tightened to a remarkable extent. Jean-Marie Brohm from his neo-Marxist perspective was quick to see this tendency and in the 1970s described a development that is now as clear as day:

> Thus in the fight against the scourge of doping, which as cycling has shown, can easily give rise to serious and even fatal accidents, the sports authorities are introducing more and more preventive measures, threats, surveillance of athletes, blood tests, urine tests, new techniques for detecting banned substances and of course disciplinary measures. In other words, within the institution of sport, generally described as educative, liberating and fulfilling, we see the outbreak of the same contradictions to be found in the police-style regimentation of hearts and minds in capitalist society in general – a society haunted by the totalitarian dream of absolute control over people's private lives. The sports and medical authorities, reigning hand in hand over a system governed by the logic of competition and productivity, inevitably give birth to a strengthened judicial and police apparatus. Do we have to face more and more supervision, all year round both of the competitions themselves and of training? That would mean turning the world of athletics (and of all other sporting events) into a huge police operations area, and would seriously infringe on the athletes' private life.
>
> (Brohm 1978: 22–3)

What we are seeing at the moment – albeit in miniature – is at one and the same time the culmination and the bankruptcy of modernity. Once a new technique, a new medicine or a new treatment has proved to be usable, there is no turning back. As a rule, new discoveries add new conditions that it is fruitless to try to oppose. In direct opposition to its nature, however, sport has apparently been ascribed a significance as the potential sanctuary of mental hygiene, as a place in which the dream of paradise and pre-modern authenticity can develop inspired by the health and strength manifested in it. At heart the anti-doping campaign serves as a defence of sport's function of preserving mental hygiene. Once that has been acknowledged, it is not hard to understand that anti-doping basically derives from a religious impulse, even though, paradoxically enough, it mobilises all the aids and methods of modernity.

The Protestant Ethic and the Spirit of Capitalism

The analysis in *The Protestant Ethic and the Spirit of Capitalism* provided by the German sociologist Max Weber and published for the first time in 1904–05 helps to illustrate the point. According to Weber, the success of western capitalism was founded on the Protestant notion of a 'calling' that developed in and through the Reformation in the sixteenth century. Luther told the world that if people worked hard and their work yielded good results, this was a sign of God's grace. A flourishing business was, then, tantamount to an assurance that one was acceptable to God. The importance of secular life in society was thereby dramatically re-valued. The next most important reformer after Luther, Jean Calvin, made even more of the same doctrine in his teaching. For the central pillar of Calvinism was predestination, or the idea that man's destiny was preordained. From the moment of birth, man's fate was sealed, and one was either among the saved or the lost. For each individual the most burning question of their lives was whether they had drawn a long or a short straw. According to Calvin, this could not be seen in this world. Man was simply to live trusting in God's judgement. In practice this was, of course, utterly unsatisfactory – a feature that would prove to have a productive consequence. For instead of committing suicide or passively awaiting their fate, which is what, strictly speaking, the doctrine of predestination invited, Calvinists endeavoured to achieve wisdom. If faith in good deeds as a way to salvation was invalidated by Luther's arrival, it was once again given a central psychological significance by the practical observance of Calvinism as a way to ensuring that one belonged to the chosen. Calvinists worked assiduously and single-mindedly in their secular lives. What mattered in one's calling was to show oneself to be acceptable to God, which was measured using three criteria: moral value, implications for the general good and, most important, profitability (Weber 1985).

Protestant esteem for hard work along with its injunctions towards puritan frugality are perfect accompaniments to the development of capitalism. The prescription unavoidably results in an accumulation of capital, which the calling requires be reinvested:

> Wealth is thus bad ethically only in so far as it is a temptation to idleness and sinful enjoyment of life and its acquisition is bad only when it is with the purpose of later living merrily and without care. But as a performance of duty in a calling it is not only morally permissible, but actually enjoined. The parable of the servant who was rejected because he did not increase the talent which was entrusted to him seemed to say so directly.
>
> (ibid.: 163)

With his Fall, man was condemned to earning his bread by the sweat of his brow. Work is the tried and tested ascetic means to that end. As such it has always been valued by the occidental church. It is not surprising, therefore, that the origin of the capitalist ethos should be found in the Church. Ascetic leaders are, however, clearly aware of the dangers of the consequences of this ethos, namely that it creates a wealth that tempts the owner to give up his striving for a pious life. In other words that the vertical ambition towards God's salvation might be weakened and turn into a horizontal ambition towards worldly luxury and delight. The Methodist, John Wesley (1703–91) gives a precise description of this:

> I fear, wherever riches have increased, the essence of religion has decreased in the same proportion. Therefore I do not see how it is possible, in the nature of things, for any revival of true religion to continue for long. For religion must necessarily produce both industry and frugality, and these cannot but produce riches. But as riches increase, so will pride, anger and love of the world in all its branches.
>
> (Weber 1985: 175)

What is interesting in the present context is that the conflict of interests that Weber's analysis uncovers is to be found once again in the dominant valorisation and evaluation of the practice of sport. Sport's injunction to hard work, a regular life, discipline and a strong sense of purpose, in other words, its ascetic imperative, harmonises well with the Protestant ethos. The same is true of its outcome, that is to say the financial rewards and professional contracts that show that athletes manage their divine talents profitably. Only at the moment when financial rewards and princely contracts acquire their own attraction as a road to a life of luxury – in other words only when the spirit of capitalism is corrupted into the worship of Mammon – does immorality show itself. It was precisely this constellation of ideas that we saw on display at the beginning of this chapter with Hoberman's presentation of the fate of Birgit Dressel. In the explanation that the doping problem is caused by the large quantities of money that have flowed into sport we find the same ambivalence towards the logic of capitalism that Wesley so tellingly expressed in the eighteenth century.

It is surprising that those people who regard money as the root of the whole doping problem are not calling for a return to amateurism. That they refrain from doing so is not necessarily due to a lack of faith in the possibility of reversing the current of developments but can easily be coupled with the idea that professional sport in itself is not what creates the evil that it gives impetus to.

This explains why the notion of doping as an evil that has prevailed since the beginning of the 1960s can also be explained as a manifestation of the Protestant ethos. In the earlier phases of modernity secular attitudes had the upper hand. The attitude to the medical and technological developments of science (which money also provided impetus for) were positive and, since these developments were used offensively, they helped to keep religious attitudes in check. However, religious energies continued to play a role. Faith in reason and progress is also itself a faith. What was new was that energies were directed more towards the underlying aims of modernity rather than towards the heavenly domain. In a natural extension of the Protestant ideological tradition, once sport took root, athletes were cultivated for their striving for success. Seen through secular eyes, however, success was not regarded first and foremost as a sign of God's favour. Sporting success led instead to a deification of the athletes themselves. Superhuman significance is attributed to successful athletes, and this is reflected in the fascination with records. The pursuit of records promoted in the Olympic motto contributes to the belief that humankind is making progress, and it functions – albeit in the form of an illusion – to provide assurance that man can transcend himself. And in so far as records are achieved by means of technological aids and improved equipment, they only go to show that progress is both physical and mental. The offensive attitude dominant in the earlier phases of modernity meant, therefore, that there were no significant scruples to the effect that new aids ease work and so undermine its character-building qualities. It is true that the originator of the Tour de France, Henri Desgranges, was deeply unhappy at the invention of the freewheeling hub, which meant that riders could rest their legs on downhill runs (Jakobsen 2004). Nevertheless it was introduced as the first step towards the advanced Derailleur gears that made racing even 'easier', which in practice simply meant that races became even faster. The pressure on the body's physique remained in the nature of things at a maximum.

During the 1960s, however, the realisation began to spread that modern breakthroughs could not unequivocally be viewed as progress. The thalidomide catastrophe, for example, made people understand that medicine could have side-effects. This gave the religious instinct a further opportunity to develop in a vertical direction. Once it was discovered that medicine could both help and harm, the road was open to a consideration of 'unnecessary' use of medicine as being the work of the devil. It is a natural reaction for the Protestant thought process to condemn doping as an expression of a lack of 'moral fibre', a weakness of the will to strive for success. As an undesirable short-cut, doping becomes morally reprehensible.

Using Weber as a form of lens we have been able to see, therefore, that the current opposition to doping is not simply a self-evident and rational response to an unavoidable problem, but can be understood as a reaction deriving from a religious feeling that is imbued with a Protestant way of thinking.

The irrational aspect of the anti-doping campaign has generated opposition in the form of those who support the deregulation of doping. To judge from their form of discourse, this opposition see themselves as supporters of rational modernity as formed by Enlightenment humanism. According to the philosopher John Gray, liberal humanism has today the same power over people's minds as religion once had.

> Humanists like to think they have a rational view of the world; but their core belief in progress is a superstition, further from the truth about the human animal than any of the world's religions. Outside of science, progress is simply a myth.
>
> (Gray 2002: xi)

With this in mind, the view that doping should be liberalised will be explored in the next chapter.

8 Legalisation of doping

The official fight against doping is in trouble. There are a number of reasons for this. The first thing we can point to is the fact that there exists no obvious, clear-cut definition of what doping is. Those attempts that have been made to come up with a meaningful definition have come unstuck. As we saw in Chapter 1, WADA has chosen to take as a basis for its work an *ad hoc* definition that gives the anti-doping campaign the hallmarks of arbitrariness. A second reason is that the agency does not manage to provide a consistent justification for the necessity of the anti-doping campaign. We have seen the fight against doping presented as a defence of the spirit of sport. However, when the agency describes its characteristics, the ones it mentions are almost all compatible with doping. And those that are not appear to be contradicted by the practice of elite sport (see Chapter 2).

Of all the characteristics that are highlighted, health is probably the one with the widest appeal. But the health argument only holds as long as it is taken for granted that doping is unhealthy. When the doping methods prohibited include the use of intravenous drips containing sugar, salts, vitamins and minerals – all of which can have a positive contribution to health – the argument loses its power. The health argument is also powerless when faced with, for example, small, compensatory doses of testosterone in endurance events like the Tour de France.

To support the campaign against forms of medication conducive to health, the second argument with broad appeal is arguably arbitrary, namely that competition has to take place on an equal footing. As was pointed out earlier, however, it is less than convincing as a justification for the ban on doping, since legalisation of doping would bring more equality into the competitive situation than there is now, because the risk of being tested positive is considerably greater for athletes who do not have the means to go to the most skilful doping doctors for advice and treatment. In this context we come upon a third reason for the troubles that beset the anti-doping campaign. This is that the modern world has managed to produce performance-enhancing methods other than medicine that create that uneven playing field for athletes. These include, for example, the disputed hypobaric chambers that are banned in some countries, but permitted in others. The lack of consensus about them illustrates the confusion rampant in the world of anti-doping.[1] The modern world has, however, also created things that are accepted without a murmur, such as specially manufactured sportswear and equipment that not all athletes have access to.

The naturalness of artifice and the artificiality of the natural

The use of hypobaric chambers for the purpose of improving performances illustrates the difficulty in finding a logical and consistent demarcation line between acceptable and unacceptable means and methods. In the absence of clear rules athletes have taken advantage of the possibility to gain a competitive advantage by using these artificially low oxygen pressure environments. In April 2006, WADA's Ethical Issues Review Panel provided its response to WADA's assessment request arguing that,

> The use of artificially induced hypoxic conditions to modify performance as an invasion of technology that does not require athlete's insight, effort or significant active participation of any kind. As such, artificially induced hypoxic conditions to modify performance are a violation of the spirit of Olympic sport, which celebrates natural talents and their virtuous perfection.
>
> (http://www.gbshaun.com/altitudeforall//wada_statement.html)

The panel's assessment rests on the understanding of sport as a contest between natural talents who by training and other efforts actively pursue to perfect their performance ability. Accordingly if athletes take advantage of means by which they can passively increase their performance capacity it is contrary to the spirit of sport. In light of WADA's doping definition, hypoxic devices could be banned without any implication of inconsistency. But despite the panel apparently advocating a ban, to date, WADA has continued to accept this performance-enhancing method. Maybe the agency's decision was influenced by a journal editorial endorsed by 76 scientists from 24 countries that challenged the panel's view suggesting among other things that the passivity argument is flawed (Levine 2006). However, it might as well be the panel's report itself that opened the decision-makers' eyes to the unfortunate implications of a ban based on the passivity argument. Because there is a vast sports industry that produces sports equipment designed to – and advertised as tools that – passively enhance athletes' performances. Hence improved running shoes and so on might be labelled doping on the same grounds. The report's attempt to bypass that problem – by claiming a distinction between technologies and expert systems that operate on the athlete as merely a passive recipient, versus technologies with which the athlete actively interacts as part of the process in training and competition to enhance performance – is far from convincing as should be apparent in what follows. The general problem that we are faced with has in fact been rumbling on for a long time, and discussions regarding the (un)acceptability of artificial performance-enhancing environments began before WADA was formed.

In 1997, a debate blew up in Norway about the use of hypobaric chambers. By living in a chamber of this kind, the athlete can increase the number of oxygen-bearing cells in his blood. The debate hotted up when the winner of the gold medal in the 800 metres running event at the Olympic Games in 1996, Vebjørn Rodal, criticised his countryman, the skier Bjørn Dæhlie, for using the method: 'As far as my sense of morals goes, he is cheating … For me there are no grey areas in sport, only ruthless training. Sport has to be a natural activity, without artificial methods' (Arneberg 2001).

When Rodal mentions 'grey areas in sport', he is referring to disputed performance-enhancing means and methods such as creatine, vitamin injections, and hypobaric chambers, usually called 'grey area products'. In an article in the Norwegian newspaper *Dagbladet*, the sports historian Matti Goksøyr pointed out that the demand for naturalness is an expression of a lack of understanding of the history of the development of sport. There will always be uncertainty, he claims, as to where the line should be drawn between what is banned and what is not (Goksøyr 1997). His argument goes that if people wish to lay down hard and fast rules for top sport, it will soon become an archaic museum piece, and more than likely die out in the same way as happened in the case of games played of old on the village green, which really have become outdated. The fact that sport is modern means that to a large extent it follows social and technological progress. Top sport by its very nature transcends limitations and for that reason it is hard to set limitations on it. In addition, it is by nature, says Goksøyr, unnatural, which is why it comes across as a contradiction in terms to speak of 'natural' training methods. Historically it can be shown that for as long as sport has been practised, athletes have sought ways to improve their performance. That is how things were in ancient Greece, and that is how they returned to being in the nineteenth century when sport once again assumed a dominant role. It is 'competitive sport's own rationale' (ibid.), he says, whereupon he provides two challenging examples that demonstrate that the core of the problem is not artificiality. In a number of sports it is an advantage to weigh as little as possible. Athletes who compete in these sports strive, therefore, to maintain an abnormally low weight. It is clear that the authorities could prohibit slimming pills and start testing for them. But athletes can also lose weight simply by stopping eating. The result is the same, namely, an unhealthy weight loss. Even though athletes can lose weight naturally by refusing to eat, it is a performance-enhancing practice that we can scarcely applaud, but which is nevertheless accepted (see Chapter 1). On the other hand, when we look back over the development of sport, there are a number of artificial performance-enhancing innovations that it would be impossible to imagine being without today. 'When certain clever individuals introduced something as novel as rubbing wax under Norwegian cross-country skis just before the First World War, the practice was met with all sorts of raised eyebrows' (ibid.). It was, of course, an unnatural practice. But if traditionalists had managed to prohibit its use, it is unlikely the sport could have survived for long, since the public, who were not bound by the same restrictions, would have been able to ski faster than their sporting heroes. Today there can surely be no one who thinks of waxing skis as cheating. It has become a natural part of the sport of skiing. Seen in this light, Goksøyr concludes, what is natural is determined by history and culture, which makes it impossible to establish clear limits: 'What is acceptable and what is "natural" will be constantly changing' (ibid.).

The article opened up an abyss. It let it be known that the fight against doping was a product of the spirit of the age. This viewpoint presented a challenge that caused the philosopher of sport Sigmund Loland to try to present a reasoned argument for the limits of sport. He goes a long way towards accepting the historian's reasoning, but believes that it is necessary to maintain a discussion about grey areas, and supports his argument as follows: 'The debate is important because it continuously places question marks around the limitless notion of growth, the "inner rationale" of top sport according to Goksøyr, which threatens the most important qualities of top sport' (Loland 1997).

We can already glimpse the difficulty of the project Loland has taken upon himself in his justification for grey areas. By announcing that the most important qualities of sport are threatened by its inner rationale, he would have us believe that the qualities of sport are in conflict with the logic of sport. That sport should be the enemy of its own most important qualities is a paradox that makes us suspect that Loland is not looking at sport in its own right. If he did so, he would find such qualities as excitement, commitment, mastery, courage, efficiency and dedication that are in no way threatened by sport's 'limitless notion of growth'. Loland does not, however, set out down the trivial road of normativity by hitching sport to the wagon of health or character formation. Instead he directs his attention towards the question: What is sporting performance? And he answers: 'The starting point for any performance is the practitioner's talent and effort. Talent relates to our genetic make-up, to the straw we drew in the lottery of nature' (ibid.). Even though he recognises the historian's viewpoint that what is artificial or natural is to a large extent determined by history, he argues for a demand for naturalness. In order for sporting performance to have value, it must derive from innate or natural talent. There is an echo here of Rousseau's call 'Back to Nature' (see Chapter 7). Talent alone is not, of course, sufficient, but the athlete must be prepared to make a substantial effort. There has to be 'the will to train, to give everything in competition, to develop his potential to the utmost', he says, and adds: 'A practitioner who cultivates his talent through his efforts has the primary responsibility for his own achievements. In this way elite sport can be the bearer of an optimistic message about human greatness and potential' (ibid.). Loland is not, however, a thoroughgoing Romantic. This quotation expresses a line of thinking that bears features of the tradition of Enlightenment philosophy. In Kant's programmatic essay of 1784 'What is Enlightenment?', the Enlightenment ideal is formulated as follows:

> Enlightenment is man's release from his self-incurred tutelage. Tutelage is man's inability to make use of his understanding without direction from another. Self-incurred is this tutelage when its cause lies not in lack of reason but in lack of resolution and courage to use it without direction from another. *Sapere aude!* 'Have courage to use your own reason!' – that is the motto of enlightenment.
>
> (Kant 1995: 83)

This ideal has played a central role in the development of modernity. It provided fertile soil for the secular powers' 'optimistic message about human greatness and potential'. And cycling – the first entirely modern sport (see Chapter 7) – cultivated that message with a ruthless intensity. This it did until the critique of modernity gave its response in the field of sport and forced a more moderate attitude to prevail, on the discursive level at least. When pressure began to be exerted on riders to accept doping tests, Jacques Anquetil demonstrated the modern approach in the stance he took, by rejecting doping controls as unacceptable intervention. In his view, 'compulsory dope tests were an infringement of individual liberty ... racing cyclists and other athletes should be free to use whatever was legally available' (Woodland 1980). His message was in other words – in line with Kant – that athletes should have the right to self-determination without intervention from above. In view of the fact that the use of doping does not harm anyone else, there is no self-evident objection to Anquetil's position. If we wish to defend intervention as liberal humanists, we have to do so as a defence of particular values, because, as long as individual responsibility and the right to self-determination do not affect a third party, this point of view provides no other foundation for limiting individual freedom.

Loland bases his defence of the restriction of athletes' rights to make use of the creations of modernity on values such as self-responsibility and personal effort. His defence seems to be at odds with itself, since by making use of modern values he places himself on the side of modernity while at the same time objecting to the human autonomy that it espouses. Strictly speaking, he is arguing with modernity against modernity. This indicates a significant degree of ambivalence with regard to what it is to be modern. On the one hand, he applauds the Enlightenment ideal of freedom, while on the other he does not trust the ideal of the limitless freedom of the responsible individual to decide for himself, and this lack of trust is reflected in the view that, if sport is allowed to develop in accordance with its own inner logic, it will be self-destructive.

This ambivalence makes itself felt when he recognises that the day of the solitary natural talent is gone, and that there is not necessarily anything wrong with that. There is, in fact, he points out, a support system of trainers and other experts in Norwegian elite sport, which can create a good network around the athlete. 'Performance arises in a social interplay with the practitioner at the centre' (Loland 1997). So it is fine to have trainers, psychologists, physiotherapists, biomechanists and others capable of advising and treating athletes so that they can take part in competitions optimally prepared on the tactical, technical, physical and psychological levels. But he then adds:

> Support systems can take on too great a significance. Elite sport can go from being a contest between practitioners to being a contest between total systems with substantial resources when it comes to finance, skills and practical and scientific know-how.
>
> (ibid.)

The view presented here is, then, that athletes are welcome to have support systems at their disposal, but they must not be allowed to grow beyond the point at which the philosopher thinks that they have gone too far. Loland gives no precise estimate as to when these support systems take on too great a significance. Presumably because this cannot be done.

If we take English football as an example, we can see that top clubs have become business enterprises with turnovers measured in many millions of pounds and with a vast array of experts in all relevant areas capable of seeing to the players. In addition, they have at their command a world-wide network of talent scouts, who ensure a constant influx of natural talent into the pool of players. In the total picture each individual player is without particular significance. It is a rarity today for a player to remain in the same club for an entire career. Even the biggest stars are regularly bought and sold in the managers' endless striving to optimise their team. In other words, clubs have become total systems. As Loland so rightly says: 'The survival of the system does not depend on individual players but on improvement in performance in an absolute sense' (ibid.). But does this mean anything for the sporting quality of the contest itself? Is it not the case that, once the ball has been kicked off, it is still natural talents like Cristiano Ronaldo, Fernando Torres and Lionel Messi who perform the work and who through their efforts contribute to the result? They have been given help and advice from a group of professionals before going onto the pitch, but once the game has got under way, everything depends on them, just as it has always been in football. They 'have primary responsibility for their own achievements'. That is something systems do not alter. If they think that conditions in the world of top professional football are too tough and impersonal, then they are free to hang up their boots or join an amateur association where things are done as they were in the old days. So what is the problem? 'In its most extreme form the system will make use of any measure. Performances can be given an edge by using biochemical products and different forms of technology' (ibid.). The desire to set interventionist limits for sport is the product of a fear that modern technology dehumanises.

This view is not born of pure and simple nostalgia. The invention of what we used to call 'spectacles' is so old that it seems natural to leave it out of our account. They are not, however, the best things to wear when playing sport. Sweat mists the lenses and blurs the vision. The invention of contact lenses came, therefore, as a major help to many sportspersons without putting them in the firing line, despite the fact that they provide an increase in performance that does not demand any personal effort. A number of people now use laser treatment for near-sightedness. No criticism is raised here either. When Loland recommends a ban on hypobaric chambers with the argument: 'Here performance levels are increased without personal effort in technologically manufactured environments. It is artificial because it removes responsibility for the performance from the practitioner' (ibid.), he could use the same justification to recommend a ban on contact lenses and laser surgery to correct near-sightedness. As with hypobaric chambers, what we have here are technological advances that improve performance without personal effort. The argument cannot be refuted by saying that lenses and laser surgery do not give the athlete a competitive advantage, but simply assist to overcome a handicap. For, if performance has to derive from 'our genetic make-up' in order to have value – 'the straw we drew in the lottery of nature' – then there are unfortunately those who have chosen the straw that involves being near-sighted. Without technological help they would have no chance of making their mark. If it is argued that it is acceptable to assist in overcoming a handicap as long as this does not give a competitive advantage, it would be difficult to justify a *blanket* ban on the use of hypobaric chambers and EPO. Athletes whose genetic make-up means that they have a sub-normal haematocrit level ought surely to be allowed to use hypobaric chambers or EPO to bring their levels up to the norm. It cannot be otherwise if the line of argument is to remain consistent. The example shows that the ban lacks an adequate foundation. The reference to the fact that it is artificial will not do. Nor is it any use to speak of these measures removing responsibility for performance from practitioners themselves. For it is a misunderstanding to think that doping measures work all by themselves. In reality, it takes a lot more to become a winner in a high performance sport than to live in a hypobaric chamber or use EPO. If athletes do not put effort into training, any amount of medication or sleeping in a low oxygen tent will be in vain. Correspondingly no one will become a superman by taking testosterone without pumping iron in the gym. Hypobaric chambers and hormone preparations, like waxing skis, only help in optimising the effect of training.

With that statement we arrive at Loland's differentiation between acceptable and non-acceptable performance-enhancing innovations. The differentiation is introduced to distance the writer from the notion of 'sport as museum piece' and it plays a central role in the argument. Not everything that is new is to be banned. What is decisive is whether new things increase the value of sport:

Scepticism about hypobaric chambers does not mean that we want to see cross-country skiers returning to wooden skis and bamboo sticks. On the contrary. Advances in ski construction such as specialist skis for ski skating can provide new possibilities and more enjoyment in skiing.

(ibid.)

There is no doubt that the innovations that have come about in ski sports, in everything from bindings and waxing to the way in which skis and sticks are shaped and what they are made of, have made a positive contribution to the development of ski sport. They have made the sport more fun by making skiing easier and faster. In fact, it is quite difficult to find examples of innovations that have not contributed to the enjoyment of the sport. The attractive elements that, according to Loland, have provided more enjoyment in skiing are elements that have made the sport faster and at the same time less technically demanding. The first quality, speed, is clearly a sporting one. The second on the other hand – that it has become less technically demanding – is not. If we take the innovation of the hypobaric chamber, it makes no difference to technique. On the other hand it enables – all other things being equal – a higher speed, and for that reason it adds quality to sport. The athlete who discovers that he is able to maintain a higher speed over a longer time-span as a result of an increase in levels of oxygen-bearing blood cells will undoubtedly also experience an increased enjoyment of skiing.

Loland is clearly aware that his own argument in this specific case cannot withstand rigid analysis. This shines through when he says, '[Rodal's] gut feeling has something to be said for it' (ibid.), where he makes it clear that resistance to technological progress need not be rational to be valid.

The difficulties of conducting a consistent critique of the use of performance-enhancing technology in elite sport forces him in the end to seek refuge in values which, while they may be recognisable in the broad spectrum of recreational sport, are not characteristic of elite sport, which is where such technology first – and often exclusively – makes itself felt. He indicates, then, that an important reason to go along with the suggested normative criteria is that:

A sport in which the practitioner has the greatest possible responsibility for the development of his own performance becomes more fun, more exciting and more engrossing. In a word it becomes more human. A sport that prioritises powerful and good experiences ahead of the ideal of limitless growth is a playful sport.

(ibid.)

With this justification the conclusion to his defence of interventionist limitation ends up as a retrogressive project, despite the fact that in his introduction he points out that his aim is the opposite, namely to protect the future of sport.

For, if the ideal truly is to ensure the greatest possible personal responsibility for the development of performance, this would mean that the sport would have more value if skiers themselves bore the responsibility for making their own skis. According to Loland, sponsors, trainers, physiotherapists, sports psychologists and product developers all make sport less fun, less exciting, less engrossing – regardless of his acceptance of certain technologies and his emphasis on the possibility of athletes being surrounded by a positive team of experts. Whether this is correct can be debated. On the other hand it is hard to argue against the statement that 'a sport that prioritises powerful and good experiences above the ideal of limitless growth is a playful sport' (ibid.). What this, in turn, effectively means is that the activity in question is not, in fact, elite sport.

A telescope to the blind eye

If it is, as it appears, impossible to make a cogent argument for limiting performance-enhancing technologies in sport, the question raises its head as to whether we could not just as well suspend restrictions and surrender sport to its own inner logic. A number of people in recent years have taken up the controversial standpoint that proposes a complete deregulation of doping (e.g. Savulescu *et al.* (2004) in the *BJSM*; Kayser (2007) in the *Lancet*; Tamburrini (2000), and Beamish and Ritchie (2006)). Not surprisingly, perhaps, this provokes many people, which makes it an easy way to gain attention. To make a consistent argument in favour of the deregulation of doping is considerably easier than to argue against it. All it requires is that we take liberalistic principles as our starting point and argue for the responsible individual's inviolable right to self-determination. Individuals bear the responsibility for their own happiness and should be restricted as little as possible in their efforts to achieve it. The limit should be established at the point at which people abuse their freedom and violate the freedom of others, depriving others in the process of the chance to pursue their happiness. This is not something that doping users can be said to do. From a libertarian point of view the argument that dopers damage the interest of clean competitors does not count because in the last analysis doping is a free choice that neither hurts nor restricts the freedom of athletes who do not use doping. In the name of unrestricted competition, therefore, doping should be permitted.

Strangely enough, this is not the argument that is put forward. Proponents of the deregulation of doping do not apparently care to construct their argument on the political ideology that lies closest to their position. This is presumably because they find it distasteful. Instead they either opt for a sceptical position methodically presenting the inconsistencies in the current anti-doping policy as an argument to abandon it or they, more enthusiastically, throw themselves into sophisticated forms of argument that are curiously no more consistent than the position they fight. A glance at the line of reasoning pursued by the Argentinian philosopher, Claudio Tamburrini, illustrates the difficulty in arguing pro-doping consistently.

Tamburrini introduces his (2000) article 'What's wrong with doping?' by pointing out that some of the forbidden substances are injurious to health but that this does not apply to all. The health argument cannot, then, be decisive. He goes on to point out that blood-doping, which gives an increased oxygen uptake, is banned, while training at heights (and we could add hypobaric chambers to take account of the discussion above) is permitted. Ergo, the effect is not decisive either. What is at issue here, according to Tamburrini, is a set of arbitrary restrictions that reduce the athletes' performance opportunities, and he allows this to stand as the first argument in favour of the deregulation of doping.

It is true that there are things on the doping list that give the impression that the doping ban is arbitrary. The ban on drips with water, sugar, salts, vitamins and minerals belongs clearly to this category. But it is not tenable to argue for a lifting of the ban on doping on the grounds of the arbitrariness of the anti-doping programme. Pointing out such discrepancies only serves as an argument for removing them. The fact that the doping rules are arbitrary does not necessarily mean that they are mistaken.

The second justification that Tamburrini presents is that due to the ban we lack knowledge about the potential health effects of the use of doping. Tamburrini himself believes that this is extremely pertinent because doping is practised even though it is banned. If the ban was lifted, it would be possible to conduct research with a view to reducing the detrimental effects of the hidden doping currently going on.

In other words, doping is assumed to be associated with detrimental effects. This would seem to speak for a retention of the ban, since significantly fewer would let themselves be tempted to use it than if it were deregulated. Experience from other policy areas such as alcohol, weapons control and traffic suggests that restrictive legislation does at least reduce the extent of undesirable behaviour. But no. Because a relatively small number of elite athletes make use of doping substances that contain a health risk, everyone is to be allowed to experiment with doping that is detrimental to health so that science gets some material to work with in order that they – it is hoped – can find ways to remedy these harmful effects. Tamburrini has, however, overlooked a few things.

In the first place, doping has been widespread in leisure sport for years. In the USA it is estimated that there are 3 million users of anabolic steroids (Parkinson and Evans 2006). By and large, there has been no regulation and the use of the substance has brought with it a significant number of victims. This means that in the fitness arena science has had the experimental station that Tamburrini is suggesting should be introduced in the area of elite sport. The world of body-building has produced unfortunates who have contributed to the knowledge of science by exhibiting the destructive effects of anabolic steroids on the body's organs, without this resulting in the use of steroids becoming less dangerous. Furthermore, experience from such environments suggests that if people are given the free run of the shop then, metaphorically speaking, they will take a sample from every shelf. In a study of the habits of steroid users more than 95 per cent indicated that their dosage consisted of a cocktail of different drugs. The study also showed a tendency for users to become careless. Over half of the respondents indicated that they used at least 1000 mg. of testosterone per week; and over 10 per cent reported that they shared needles (ibid.). There is no reason to believe that things would have a different outcome in the area of elite sport – not least because the number of potential doping drugs is huge, and the drugs industry is constantly coming up with new drugs and variants of drugs that, if this proposal were to be accepted, athletes would be free to experiment with.

In the second place, effects and side-effects of medical doping substances are studied before they are let loose on the market. What we 'lack' knowledge about is the effect of various doping regimes in different branches of sport. But a precondition for being able to procure this knowledge is that science has to have information about precisely which substances and in which doses and intervals they are administered. Furthermore, a number of athletes have to follow the same programme in order for results to be accorded any validity. That athletes might be willing to take part in this kind of trial is a hypothetical possibility that ignores the fact that the athlete's motivation to dope himself is that it provides a sporting advantage. And if it were possible, it still remains highly uncertain whether any scientific committee would give permission for that kind of trial.

Third, if we leave aside the long-term effects of relatively new substances such as EPO, there already seems to be reasonable familiarity with the effects and side-effects of the drugs being used. As Waddington (2000) pointed out, when EPO made its entry into sport at the end of the 1980s, it apparently led to a number of deaths among young cyclists. Despite the fact that massive use has been made of the substance, nothing similar has been seen since, which indicates that the doping world has learnt to manage it appropriately. Familiarity with the drug has, as far as can be judged, reached such a level that despite the development of the EPO urine test, the drug can now be given in doses that cannot be traced (Lundby *et al.* 2008).[2] And, it must be stressed, this can be done without compromising its effect. Thus Lundby and his colleagues have managed to increase their research subjects' haematocrit level to 50 per cent by giving micro dosages of EPO (ibid.).

The final justification that Tamburrini gives for proposing a deregulation of doping is that it reduces sport's transparency. It is damaging to the sporting experience, he believes, that we do not know whether the winner was doped, and he poses the rhetorical question: 'Who hasn't sometimes felt that his admiration for a sport hero was darkened by the doubt whether the victor really was clean?' (Tamburrini 2000: 201). It is certainly true that sporting enthusiasts cannot deny having a suspicion from time to time that a contest has been won on something other than talent and hard training. But it would seem a pretty drastic solution and a curious justification to say that because as a spectator one can sit with a sense that one of the victorious athletes has been lucky enough to cheat the doping controls, the controls should be removed so that we can put an end to all doubts. A corresponding argument could be made for removing the prohibition on the black economy because there is a widespread suspicion among the population that the at times extravagant life led by builders and the like is financed by means earned without the knowledge of the taxman.

Having given his reasons for proposing the removal of the ban on doping, he expresses his amazement: 'In spite of all these reasons, the ban on doping apparently has wide support among athletes, sports officials and the public. It thus seems reasonable to ask: What's wrong with doping?' (ibid.: 201). This is a surprising statement in that it is difficult to imagine that the motives behind the support for anti-doping measures of the groups he mentions, are in any way similar. Concern about what modernity brings with it is certainly a central factor in the reluctance of the general public to support loosening the controls on doping. Meanwhile, the attitude of sports managers reflects the opinions of the public, which in fact is setting the agenda. For if the public lose interest in sport, then sport will lose money. The support of athletes for anti-doping measures has other roots, however. This is where the key to the muddle lies, as we shall see in the following chapter, but instead of considering why it is that athletes generally support the ban on doping at the same time as many of them break its rules, Tamburrini starts showing that the prevalent anti-doping arguments are untenable and forgets all about the athletes' underlying motives.

Paternalism

The primary objection to the doping ban is that it is paternalistic. In his words, 'the ban on doping is justified in order to secure the wellbeing of sport practitioners. Thus, sportsmen are impeded from practising their activity, in the way they find more appropriate' (Tamburrini 2000: 202).

But he has just been expressing his surprise at the fact that athletes support the doping ban! If his viewpoint is that sport exists first and foremost for athletes, it must be reasonable for those leaders elected to administer the rules to do so in accordance with the general wishes of those athletes. And if his view is that, by signing a contract and delivering themselves into the hands of professional sport, athletes renounce their ownership of sport – athletes have instead signed themselves away to the owners of sport – then it must be admissible for those owners to administer sport according to what-ever is best for business. In either case the ban on doping is well-founded.

Tamburrini would like to demonstrate that the paternalism to be found in sport is unique. He claims, therefore, that in all other professions prohibition serves directly or indirectly to protect others. In doing so, he avoids taking on board the full consequences of the liberalism he is advocating in the area of sport. That he is aware that he is skating on thin ice can be seen from his subsequent line of argument:

> To this it might be objected that this is not true of safety working reg-ulations, which are compulsory and intended to prevent workers from getting injured. Are they not paternalistic also, then? In a sense they are, for workers are compelled to wear helmets in their own best interest. But this is not why safety regulations are relevant here. If there were none, employers could coerce workers not to wear helmets; in fact they might even make it a condition for employment, in order to reduce costs. Safety working regulations aim to prevent this unfair coercion. So their ultimate rationale is not protecting workers from their own decisions, but rather protecting them from being compelled by others (employers) to take risks they don't want to take. This justification is totally in line with the anti-paternalistic principle.
>
> (ibid.: 203)

Not just 'in line' but 'totally in line'. With this final emphatic flourish Tamburrini does everything in his power to hammer his argument home. Under-standably enough; for without nailing it into place his argument will not hold. The potential objection he presents in his opening statement is undoubtedly relevant. And he is correct when he answers affirmatively that the rule that safety helmets must be worn on building sites is interventionist. His subsequent magicking away of the paternalistic element on the other hand looks more than anything else like a failed attempt to avoid identification with the ultra-liberalism that his crusade against doping control so closely resembles. His justification for the requirement to wear safety helmets could be reworded (without being watered down) to become a defence of the doping ban. For if doping was permitted, sports directors and football managers could, for example, force riders and players to take drugs that would increase the chances of success – and with it profits. They could even make it a contractual condition. Bearing that scenario in mind, the ultimate justification for banning doping would not appear to be the desire to save athletes from the consequences of their own decisions but to prevent others legitimately being able to pressurise them into running unwanted health risks.

A number of people have fallen for the temptation to knock paternalism in their arguments for lifting the ban on doping. The concept is well suited as a weapon in this ideological battle because of its association with negative values. One problem with it, as just demonstrated, is that it does not work unless there is a willingness to take ultra-liberalism on board hook, line and sinker, which only few are prepared to do. In addition, its weakness lies in the fact that it presupposes not just that one or two, but that the majority of athletes in reality practise their sport with an unspoken desire that the ban should be lifted. We can safely say that is beyond the range of probability.

Nevertheless Rob Beamish and Ian Ritchie (2006) make a brave-hearted attempt – and what is more they do so taking as their starting point the greatest imaginable challenge, namely the former East German sports system. With the fall of the Berlin Wall, documents became available that revealed that the republic's formidable ability to hold its own in the international sporting war was founded on a scientifically designed programme. Talented children were boarded at sports schools and unwittingly brought up on doping substances. By way of introduction they wisely assure the reader that their intention is not to defend the East German regime of horror and that they, of course, oppose the exploitation of children:

> Court evidence shows that GDR politicians and sports leaders initiated or permitted practices that were, and remain, completely unacceptable by any standards. Most disturbing of all, much of the criminal activity in the system concerned young athletes who, as minors, were placed in positions of trust with their coaches and other sport leaders.
>
> (ibid.: 127)

Having thus condemned the system's exploitation of innocent children, they set about demonstrating that not even East European athletes were forced to dope themselves. There were, they say, some who refused: 'some chose not to take part in the "anabolic program"' (ibid.: 126). That some individuals refuse and thereby demonstrate that there is a choice is, however, a far cry from proving that those who submitted to the system actively wished to dope themselves. It is probably more a matter of them wanting the privileges that went with life as an elite athlete within the system and that they paid the price by following the regime. Seen in that light, it seems doubtful whether the authors are right when they believe that their examples have shown that, 'the claims that athletes of majority age in the GDR were forced to take steroids or they were unaware they took them do not stand up to closer scrutiny' (ibid.: 126). And if they are right, then they have still to make a plausible case for saying that athletes who followed the regime would prefer doping, if an elite sporting career free of doping had been a possible alternative. The examples they give seem better designed to support an argument favouring the expediency of a paternalistic system that attempts to prevent the possibility for doping, in as much as ambitious athletes do not need to be forced but can apparently, lured by the prospect of success, be tempted to take medication whose long-term consequences they are unaware of.

Beamish and Ritchie continue their argument by pointing out that even if we do assume that East German athletes were, in fact, being forced to take doping, it is a historical fact that the paternalistic anti-doping initiatives that the IOC was responsible for before 1989 were powerless in the face of the GDR system. And if it still existed, the situation would in all likelihood be that WADA would also have been found wanting: 'Even with a ban on performance-enhancing substances in place, it would be difficult to provide paternalistic protection for athletes developing within high-performance sport systems inside totalitarian regimes' (ibid.: 126). The argument here is that because the doping ban does not work effectively anyway against totalitarian regimes that can force their athletes to submit to a health-threatening doping regime, the paternalistic attempt to protect athletes should be given up.

Instead they propose, in line with Tamburrini, that the ban on doping should be lifted while at the same time research work is set in motion in the area that can provide knowledge as to how health deficits can be reduced. As it is now, they complain, it is not possible to conduct systematic peer-review research into the various doping substances.

Beamish and Ritchie explain that resistance to the use of doping and to research into such use stems from the fear that the knowledge generated would be abused by evil powers. But, as they disarmingly write, the fear of the abuse of technology will always be with us. And this is something that research into such areas as stem cells, reproduction technology and gene therapy have suffered from.

> The single greatest danger to progress in any of those issues is the uninformed arbitrary banning of practices, procedures and research in any of those areas. Research on, and the use of, performance-enhancing substances in sport are not even in the same ballpark as those three examples although, to individual athletes, the impediments to sound research could have long-term consequences. The steroid hobgoblin distracts attention from the real unknowns that can and should be investigated.
>
> (ibid.: 142)

These authors clearly subscribe to the view of science as progress. And they are right in saying that the scepticism that applies to research into stem cells, reproduction technology and gene therapy puts the brake on scientific progress. On the other hand it is debatable whether these forms of scientific progress should be regarded as progress in the sense that they strengthen the human animal in the long term. It is for that very reason that they are regarded as controversial. But these authors have apparently fallen prey to the myth that scientific progress is synonymous with progress for the betterment of the world, and they express a faith in reason that has no foundation in reality.

From the beginning of the 1980s until well into the 1990s, Professor Francesco Conconi headed an anti-doping laboratory under the Italian Olympic Committee. However, as it has been documented, he used his position to develop performance-enhancement programmes (Donati 2004: 51ff). The Conconi trial provides just one example of many that illustrate the unpredictability of science, its amoral pursuit of its own interests. It is hard to believe that consideration for the well-being of athletes would take a higher priority because doping was deregulated. It is far more probable that a scientific race to create superhuman sporting performances would ensue, with the result that it would become a condition for even being considered for competitive sport that athletes had to accept submitting to a system similar to that practised in former East Germany. There would be no compunction. But the moment talented sportspersons decided to attempt to develop their talent at the highest levels they would have to choose to put themselves in the skilled hands of the doping doctors.

The most curious aspect of their line of argument is that they conduct it with an eye to the interests of athletes. Athletes cannot look after themselves. That is a job that has to be done by doctors, drug researchers and other external agents. In other words, the state-society has to make its contribution to avoid the use of doping having negative consequences for the athletes in the longer term. In this the authors prove themselves to possess a paternalistic attitude comparable to the paternalism they argue against.

Both supporters and opponents of doping legalisation appear to be in agreement that the interests of athletes should carry considerable weight. In light of this it does seem an obvious step to take the athletes' own views into consideration and we do this in the next chapter.

9   The athletes' viewpoint

The former Italian athletics trainer, Alessandro Donati, who has since become one of the world leading doping experts, has provided significant insights into the complex psychology of doping use and in the following I am drawing heavily on his work. In 1981, Donati was contacted by Professor Dr Francesco Conconi, who had a proposal to make. Conconi had become familiar with a performance-enhancing technique in Finland, which he had then developed further. By using a 'transfusion of selected red blood cells, in which these cells were stored at −90°C, enriched with particular substances and then transfused into the athlete two or three days before a major event' (Donati 2004: 46), it was possible to achieve performance improvements of 3–5 seconds over 1500 metres, 15–20 seconds over 5000 metres and 30–40 seconds over 10,000 metres. This improvement was hugely significant, and the technique was not yet on the doping list.

Donati just did not find the idea very appealing. He chose to present the proposal to the seven athletes he was responsible for without concealing the fact that he was against the idea. It would, however, be up to them to decide whether they wished to collaborate with Conconi. There was no doubt that their chances of winning would improve. And if they chose to opt for Conconi's programme, then Donati would withdraw as trainer without making a fuss and return to his position on CONI, the Italian Olympic Committee. The athletes were training with an eye on the Olympic Games in Los Angeles three years later. Nevertheless all of them expressed the view that they would never dream of going along with the transfusion technique. After a few weeks had passed, Conconi wrote to Primo Nebiolo, who was President of both the Italian Athletics Association and the International Association of Athletics Federations, to say that Donati was refusing to cooperate. Shortly afterwards Donati was contacted by the chief trainer of the national athletics team, who attempted without success to put pressure on him to change his position. Donati replied that he would have to find a new trainer, if he insisted on using the programme. And there the matter rested. For a time. Once the Olympic Games started to loom closer, the association became more aggressive. The athletes were now called to a meeting and asked directly whether they would be prepared to increase their performance levels in the run-up to the Games with the assistance of the blood transfusion technique. Donati was also present but was obliged to keep his opinions to himself. Once again the athletes declined.

Incitements to doping

Donati's account gives the impression that the attitude of the trainer has a decisive influence on the choice of the athletes. If the key people around the athletes clearly distance themselves from illegal or dubious medication and methods for enhancing performance, athletes will follow their lead and stay away from them. There is no doubt that trainers and managers often share the responsibility for their athletes' use of doping. Nevertheless we should beware of drawing the conclusion that, if only trainers and other key individuals would one and all keep the moral flag aloft (which is at least a theoretical possibility), then the use of doping in sport would disappear. The pressure of expectations, tacit acceptance and naïve enthusiasm at sudden and unexpected progress can be enough encouragement to make an athlete turn to the needle. The inner driving forces of sport are so strong that some athletes will under any circumstances regard doping substances as an irresistible temptation to go that extra mile. Athletes way down the sporting league tables can get to experiment with caffeine tablets, ginseng and such substances that are taken orally out of sheer curiosity.

When athletes include medical performance boosting as part of their preparations for a competition, however, they do not do so lightly. Weighty considerations precede the decision. This can be seen from an interview study of cycling undertaken by my colleague, Ask Vest Christiansen. One cycle rider, for example, talks about the first time he was to do something so taboo as to give himself a completely legal vitamin injection:

> I was shit scared. I sat in my hotel room and stared at the needle for half an hour before I stuck it into my arm ... The sweat was pouring off me. All of a sudden I was going to stick a needle into my own arm. Hell, it feels almost like running into a wall or hitting yourself. It's like doing an injury to yourself. That's how I felt anyway.
>
> (Christiansen 2005: 81ff)

Later, once he had got used to it, he taught a friend how to give himself an injection:

> He did fine really ... He pulled the needle out and put a piece of cotton-wool on. Then he got up and said, 'I feel rather dizzy now'. And then he walked over towards the bedroom, and halfway there his knees suddenly gave way and fell forwards, his head hitting the stone floor ... That was an unpleasant experience, I can tell you.
>
> (ibid.: 82)

It subsequently became a matter of course for his friend, too. It is only at the start that sticking a needle through your skin seems to be breaking a taboo. Even though the injection only contained vitamins, it gave the impression of being on the verge of doping. He had had vitamin injections before, but they were given by a doctor and that was not the same thing. No doubt because the ministrations of doctors are associated with healing and health promotion, the injection the doctor gave seemed to be a help and support, something not essentially different from a vaccination. Doctors who agree to give athletes vitamin injections do so because they have a more powerful effect than vitamin pills. In doing so, such doctors are in effect recognising performance-enhancing medication. Since doctors are not always on hand, it is naturally an advantage for athletes to be able to treat themselves. And even though it evidently requires them to overcome serious reservations on the first occasion they do it, the doctors' recognition of the method makes self-administration easier to manage. It is clearly still far from easy. But once they have got used to injecting themselves, however, and felt that it benefits their performance, the transition to doping boils down to a question of what substance is contained in the syringe. The rider explains further:

> It was a huge relief to be able to do it yourself. And then it just becomes a routine. I wouldn't say that it becomes so much a routine that you become indifferent to what runs through the syringe, but it was still the business of sticking a needle in yourself that was the big barrier to overcome.
>
> (ibid.: 86)

As an athlete at the highest level, you live with a huge pressure on you to perform. The competition is colossal. Among the very best the distance between average and excellent performances is only marginal. Tiny things can decide the outcome. A career does not begin with doping. If an athlete needs that extra boost from the very start in order to get on, it stands to reason that, as competition becomes sharper, you will fall by the wayside. Most people begin to practise a sport in all innocence because they enjoy it, and they continue because they find it fun. Sooner or later they may discover that they have exceptional talent, which can arouse an ambition that makes sport much more than mere fun. It also becomes ruthless training directed at more or less clear goals. Those of them who as seniors even get anywhere near the absolute elite are super-talents who have succeeded in cultivating their skills with intensity and focus. These are people who physically and mentally are totally geared to achieving their sporting ambitions and are tuned to do so. They do not live like the majority. Their perception of their body is different. This is what we have to appreciate if we are to understand the temptation to use doping.

When an athlete is optimally prepared in the traditional way and still finds it insufficient to allow him to fulfil the goal of his dreams, then he is only human if he looks to less traditional means that promise renewed progress. As one of the riders in the study says:

> I have wanted to be a professional cycle rider since I was a boy, and now I have got the chance. If the consequences are that I have to take medication, that does not make me stop pursuing the dream. I have not ridden for so many years just to stop now that I have reached a point when the dream can be lived out in reality.

> (ibid.: 105)

Here, too, ambition is the driving force behind the use of doping. As long as a rider can get by among the top flight of their peers without using medicine, it is no temptation. But once he becomes aware that this is what is required if he is to stay up with the field at the highest level, he perceives it simply as the next necessary step in his career development. The motive is, then, somewhat different from the official explanations given by riders like David Millar, for example, who after they have been caught claim that, for no reason at all really, they chose to take doping in a weak moment to secure themselves a chance of winning.

Doping is not something athletes suddenly clutch at in a moment of uncertainty and return to the shelf once their self-confidence has improved, only to fish it out again when self-confidence nose-dives again. Christiansen's study shows up quite a different scenario, in which doping takes place in a far more calculated manner. Treatments are scheduled just as systematically as training. In some races, riders compete at 'low heat' or, if possible, with no medical assistance. In other events, however, where they are particularly reckoning on making a mark, the 'heat' is turned up. One rider, for example, relates: 'When it really mattered, I might have had slightly higher levels. You could say that I wanted to ensure that my blood count was competitive in comparison to those I was going to compete against' (ibid.: 114).

The ambition to get out ahead is the principal motive behind the use of performance-enhancing substances. Many people have a tendency to condemn doping users as morally corrupt. This is an easy mistake to make, but nonetheless a mistake. The belief that doping can be put down to weak or immoral character involves an underestimation of the attraction of sport. Some people have pangs of conscience, others do not. But it is not even the case that those who are without scruples are evil individuals without a conscience. If, as is the case with the rider just mentioned, you see nothing wrong in using illegal medicine, the reason lies in the fact that you perceive doping in a different light from those who condemn it. This rider saw it as a step in the process of becoming professional. If what he wanted was to excel, then this was one of the pre-conditions. His own moral code told him that he should do it in a proper fashion. He had no time for those riders who got caught. They were unforgivable losers who deserved their punishment, because they got the sport into disrepute and ruined it for everyone else. In his view a sense of responsibility to the sport went hand in hand with doping. You must not be caught. Seen from the outside, this can easily come to sound like the viewpoint of a 'bad' character, but it is understandable enough given the fact that the increasingly negative way in which doping is seen by the world at large is developing, as far as riders are concerned, into a greater and greater threat. And there is nothing odd about people trying to defend the milieu in which they live and work. It can, of course, be objected that, since riders know that doping is prohibited, defending doping without the least trace of a guilty conscience is still an expression of low moral standards. But in that case we choose to ignore the fact that athletes are encouraged by their sporting environment to perceive doping as acceptable medication in spite of the fact that it is, in reality, illegal.

Kelli White

Kelli White, the American sprinter who tested positive for modafinil and was subsequently banned from competition by USADA, articulated this clearly at the conference Play the Game in 2005, when in the midst of her enforced quarantine she made an appearance to talk about how she had ended up going down the doping road. She started by stating: 'Those who do use drugs are not bad people, we just have made a bad mistake' (White 2005). Her aim was not to absolve herself or other 'doping cheats'. If we want to understand why people begin to dope themselves, however, we have to throw the facile image of rotten apples in sport out of the window.

Her involvement in athletes had started when she was 10. As a 12–13-year-old she started training with the famous Ukrainian-born trainer, Remi Korchemny. He came to play a significant role in her life over the subsequent ten years or so. Having competed in athletics at the University of Tennessee for a period of four years, she decided to go professional and in 2000 returned to California, where she once again started training under Korchemny. Shortly after this, he introduced her to Dr Victor Conte. At that point she did not know what he stood for. Ostensibly the reason for going to him was to seek his advice about legal nutritional supplements that might help her improve her performance. She had no idea that she might get involved in anything illegal. He gave her, she said, flaxseed oil among other things. She used it for some weeks. Then she was invited once again to his office, where he told her that what he had given her was, in fact, not flaxseed oil but a substance that could give rise to a positive doping test if it was not used correctly. She stopped taking it immediately, and did not touch the other things he had given her again either. After a dreadful season in 2002 plagued by injury followed by a subsequent failure to qualify for the world championships in indoor athletics in 2003, she decided to seek out Conte again. He proposed a treatment that would be able to bring her back, which she accepted well knowing that it contained THG and banned substances such as EPO and other stimulants. With Conte's help, she managed within a relatively short space of time to become the world's fastest woman while at the same time undergoing 17 doping tests both during and outside competitions without testing positive. On the one hand, she was pleased with her progress. On the other, she was plagued by feelings of guilt. She explains the psychology behind it:

> It not only took Mr. Conte's help, it took my coach making me believe it was okay, and I think that a lot of the time what happens to athletes is that people make you believe that what you are doing is OK because everyone else is doing it.

> (ibid.)

Despite the fact that the feeling of guilt apparently is negligible among cyclists doping, this explanation fits in neatly with the points made above. When doctors sanction the use first of vitamin injections and then later of actual doping substances, athletes can be led to believe that there is nothing wrong with it, that cheating the doping controls is simply part of the professional game. This is, however, far from saying that athletes wish to see the controls done away with in order that they can throw themselves into unlimited experimentation with drugs.

Attitudes of elite athletes to performance-enhancing methods

Elite athletes are not in agreement as to where the boundary between legal and illegal methods should be set. They also disagree as to how the fight against doping should be addressed. Nevertheless there seems to be a general agreement that limits and a system of control are needed if sport is to function in an acceptable fashion.

In an interview study that I conducted with Christiansen into elite athletes' attitudes towards the use of methods for enhancing performance, no athlete advocated the deregulation of doping. The study was constructed around 19 in-depth interviews with anonymised athletes competing at the highest levels in a variety of sports. A similar kind of study carried out by Christiansen into cycling (mentioned above) which comprised both young talents and senior riders in the national and international elite, also found no athletes who were sympathetic to the idea of lifting the doping ban although some expressed the opinion that the doping controls and their implied suspicion were a nuisance they ideally would rather be without. Combined, the two studies involved more than 50 athletes and not a single one, whether they had doped or not, believed that the anti-doping campaign should or could be abandoned in the real world. We cannot, of course, conclude on that basis that there are no athletes in favour of deregulating doping, but these studies allow us to presume that they are clearly in the minority.

Another striking aspect of these interviews was that, regardless of the sport that was represented, the athletes interviewed had almost identical perceptions of what constituted the essence and the ideals of sport – although, it has to be said, without being able to unite these values into a consistent idea of what was sporting. We heard athletes say, for example, that of course sportsmen had to be fair, and then without a pause for breath explaining the next moment how from time to time, as an integral part of the game, they used intimidating tactics against their opponents to gain a psychological advantage. They attempted throughout to unite ideas about what was sporting with their own experiences of sport, which often resulted in glaring inconsistencies and self-contradictions, as ideas and experiences conflicted with each other. The way in which they related to methods for enhancing their performance, too, often resulted in their line of reasoning leading them into dead ends. This was particularly evident with athletes who had a clear sense of right and wrong. The following example from our interviews (italicised to distinguish our own material from other quotes) illustrates the point:

> *Of course, the basic principles of sport are quite clear. You have to stick to them. Competition has to be on an equal footing. The athlete who has prepared himself best, physically and mentally without the use of artificial stimulants, he is the winner. He is the best.*

When the athlete in question is then challenged about his views and asked to specify what he means by 'artificial stimulants', the answer comes:

> *For me these are substances produced chemically or in other artificial ways that have a passive effect on physical development. To take an injection to get into better shape while you are asleep, that's wrong. And then there is the debate about hypobaric chambers … In my view, altitrainers [hypobaric chambers] are cheating, because they are a form of passive chemical manipulation that mean you get into better shape. Whether you take EPO in an injection or a tablet or whether you change your blood levels using an altitrainer, it's all one to me.*

Since he himself has not at any point felt the need to increase his haematocrit values in order to be competitive, he can easily reject all of the methods mentioned above. However, when asked whether high altitude training was an acceptable method for increasing haematocrit values, he replied:

> *Then it's not artificially influenced. You can say that it gives the same effect, but it's not artificially produced, and that does not give a competitive advantage to those with the money and the technology. If you have clear limits for what is artificially produced manipulation, then you can get rid of all the grey areas. The athletes will know what they can and cannot do.*

There are two things here that are worth looking at more closely. The first is the desire for clear demarcation, so that the discussion about grey zones can be put to rest once and for all and athletes can know what they have to comply with. The second is the desire that everyone should be on an equal footing. Both fall under the heading of the idea of fair play. Unfortunately, reality is not so simple, and attempts to create simplicity, clarity and clear demarcations, as a rule, tend to end up running into paradoxes – which is precisely why WADA has chosen to refrain from making a verbal definition of doping. It goes almost without saying, therefore, that the athlete's brave attempt to create clarity ends in self-contradiction.

There are two things about hypobaric chambers that he objects to. They seem to be an artificial method for preparing an athlete for a competition, and they cost money. The use of them is, therefore, unfair on those athletes who wish to compete on natural premises, or those who do not have the money. Taken in isolation, the viewpoint seems reasonable. The problem arises when we try to explain why it is acceptable to live in a hut at high altitude, where the oxygen content is just as low as that set in a hypobaric chamber and where the body's reaction is the same. Athletes who live at sea-level do not get up there free of charge, and they transport themselves by means of technological inventions such as the aeroplane or the car. If the energy consumption were to be compared for these two performance-enhancing methods, the hypobaric chamber would, undoubtedly, have the advantage. Consideration of nature would then dictate that the latter was preferable. In this light, you would have to be fairly uncompromising if you continued to pursue the argument that it is cheating for athletes to spend time in a room in which the concentration of oxygen is artificially kept at the same low level as in a mountain hut, where they could reside without being accused of cheating. Nevertheless, this is what the athlete in question does. In order not to compromise clarity, he sticks *ad absurdum* to artificiality as a demarcation line: '*I have always thought that artificial manipulation in order to gain competitive advantage should be banned. Whether it is tablets, injections or something else is irrelevant. It must be banned.*' What about vitamin pills that are artificially manufactured? Should they also be banned? This was clearly taking the argument too far, but instead of giving up on artificiality, he chooses to sidestep the issue: '*But vitamins are a natural substance. They are not a chemical compound.*'

Here, however, he runs into another problem, namely that EPO is also a natural substance. '*Yes, but it is artificially, chemically produced, and that is banned.*' The athlete is, of course, well aware that vitamin C tablets are also artificially produced, and for that reason he adds in the next sentence: '*You can eat 10 kilos of vitamin C and that won't make you a better sportsman.*' This is doubtless correct. But his argument is no longer directed against artificiality, but against the effect the methods might (or might not) have, and this he immediately acknowledges: '*Yes, it is of course the effect that determines the doping list.*'

If an athlete can be permitted to spend time at high altitudes, then that is only fair if others are permitted to spend time in a hypobaric chamber or take EPO. If EPO is not acceptable, then nor is spending time at high altitudes. There is no way around it, if the requirement is that the rules have to have a consistent basis and are to be designed around the effect of a substance or a method. A similar difficulty would be encountered if we attempted to argue our way out of the problem of 'grey areas', as has already been suggested in the above discussion about hypobaric chambers.

In the discussion of products thought to lie in this 'grey area', we also found that athletes' views were influenced by their need to compete. Those who did not need 'grey area' products were typically critical. Replies to questions as to whether they had used them could, for example, be as follows:

> *Very little ... I believe that if I eat the correct food and have a good diet, then nutritional supplements are unnecessary. That is the view I have from my upbringing and from my own experience. I don't think tablets would have raised me any higher. But to take a multivitamin tablet and some fish oil to ensure the quality of your diet, that's OK. It means that you minimise the risk of getting ill.*

On the other hand, those who operated in branches of sports where 'grey area' products might give some advantage did not believe that the 'grey area' concept was of any use. As one of them says:

> *Grey areas and all that stuff, they don't exist in my world. Either it is on [the list] or it is not. If a pill came on the scene that meant that I progressed by 20 kg. and which wasn't a steroid and wasn't on the list, then I would take it. And if it then got banned the next day, then I wouldn't take it any more. That's how I feel. Unless it is something that makes you go crazy. Of course I'm not prepared to risk the rest of my life for that. But if it's not on the list, then it's legal. That's how it is. I don't even think it's open to debate.*

Asked whether he would use it if it was something that corresponded to hypobaric chambers, which could increase his muscle power, he replies without hesitating: 'Yes. *There are loads of things where I think they've gone right off the rails.*' He then goes on to elaborate by making a critique of the way elite sport is managed in his country. The organisation in charge has made it a declared aim to make the country the best place in the world to practise sport. At the same time it tries to score cheap points by distancing itself from 'grey area' products. This, in his view, is absurd. No athlete can eat at the same table as the top dogs, if he is subject to special restrictions. There is simply no room for latitude in sport at the highest level.

In his world, things are either black or white. He abides by the list that happens to be in force at the moment. Over and above that he takes anything he can that can provide a performance-enhancing effect and that is not directly damaging to his health. Waving a moralising finger at athletes who use 'grey area' products and setting restrictions for their use is in his eyes 'not on'. But even though there are things on the doping list that, in his opinion, ought not to be there, he still believes that the anti-doping campaign provides indispensable protection. It stands to reason. For his ambition is such that he will follow his fellow competitors to the very limits in risking his health. And he does not want competitive conditions of that kind. They would quite literally be destructive. He believes, therefore – just like the rider cited above – that sportspersons have a moral obligation towards their sport. It is all about not being caught, and the best way to prevent that is to stay on the right side of the line. His reasoning is as follows:

> *I think that sports people have a task ahead of them [for] doping ruins sport. No matter how little it is and no matter how stupid it is, if it is on the list, then don't take it. And if some kind of collective understanding of this doesn't emerge – and it won't because this is elite sport and people are egoists – then it is up to WADA and organisations like that to make sure that the rules are so strict that it cannot be done. That's the only way to do it ... otherwise these fantastic sports will die.*

The athletes who want to see an active anti-doping campaign are, then, not just those who are deeply uncompromising as regards performance-enhancing means. Disagreement arises as to how this campaign should be fought.

The difficult balancing act: too much or too little?

In our studies, the athletes who showed least sympathy for the use of doping were those who also advocated the harshest penalties. Even the most hardcore opponents of doping, however, were inclined to the view that the testing system had become a pain in the neck and wished that it could be reduced. Many comments ran, for example, as follows:

> *The worst time was in 1995, when I was tested 18 times here in [my home country] and 5 times abroad. Long distance runners were tested even more. But I think it ought to be possible to create statistical tools so that they wouldn't have to test that often. Then they could reduce the frequency of the tests and release a load of resources.*

This statement comes from an athlete who – even before the anti-doping campaign was intensified under WADA – thought that the frequency of the tests had become such a thorn in the side that he had begun to speculate about how it could be reduced. It bothers him that he, as a clean sportsman time and again has to provide proof of his clean bill of health. In his view it is a waste of resources to test athletes like him over and over again. These resources could be better employed in testing athletes who might be suspicious, those who show sudden, unexpected progress, for example. But even though he is dissatisfied with the way the fight against doping is tackled, he still sees testing as the only path open to sport and will not, therefore, say that recurrent tests are a problem. When asked directly whether he was frustrated at having to submit so many tests, he replied:

> *No. It is a necessary evil. I will do anything to make sport clean. And if that means that I have to pee in a cup 20 times a year, then that's a small price to pay. What is frustrating is that we do it, but it isn't done in other places.*

He does not have faith in athletes from other countries being monitored just as zealously by their anti-doping organisations, the so-called NADOs, as he is. And on the rare occasion when someone does get caught, he thinks that they get let off too easily. Two years is perhaps a harsh penalty in the Scandinavian countries, for here athletes end up being pilloried as well, stripped, he says, of all honour and glory.

> *But for an athlete from Italy or Russia, someone who comes from a culture in which cheating is not met with the same disapproval but is perhaps on the contrary more like the better you are at cheating the more of a popular hero you are – there two years suspension, why, that's just a new opportunity to load yourself up and return to the sport with a big comeback. In the final of the 100m. women's hurdles a few years ago, eight out of nine entrants had previously been done for doping. What's that supposed to be? If you've been done for doping, you shouldn't be allowed in any final.*

By extension, he feels that a lifelong quarantine should be introduced, even for first offenders. This is a view that we find again in a woman who has even been tested positive herself. This was, it is true, for a milder drug, and this colours her opinion.

> *I think that in many ways the list is stupid, because there are so many things on it. I don't know whether an eardrop is something that has any effect. But I know that if you have an ear-ache and can't bear it any longer, then the only thing you can get is something you aren't allowed to take. So you don't take it and go round with a pain in your ear – but why? I have difficulty imagining that it might have any performance-enhancing effect. I can't imagine that was the case. But there are some drugs that really are hard – EPO and anabolic steroids – and they've got to have tough penalties. But I can't see why there should be 400 drugs on the list, for there aren't that many.*

What she has in mind when she calls the list stupid is not her own case, but one about two girls who tested positive for ephedrine. One had taken slimming pills and the other eardrops that contained the drug. The interviewee is sure that they did not try to cheat. She believes, therefore, that penalties should be adjusted according to intention:

> *When someone starts out on a course, a body-builder in a fitness centre, when they are part of a treatment in a schedule … Things like that which are planned*

don't belong in sport and as far as I'm concerned they should be banned for life, because then it's not elite sport that they belong in.

The example is clear. The problem is just that it is not possible to determine in every case whether the drug that the athlete has tested positive for has been taken as part of a treatment with the aim of enhancing performance. If ephedrine is on the doping list, the reason is that the drug can have a performance-enhancing effect, and the test cannot tell whether the drug has been taken for a cough, or an ear-ache or with a view to improving performance. And working out which drugs are too trivial to be on the doping list is not as easy as she makes it sound when she adds with tautological conviction:

Everything that is not performance-enhancing – and now it's not ear-drops that make you better or pain-killers I'm talking about – that does not improve performance. Performance-enhancing is something which gives you a better performance. This is the sports world, you know, this is.

Tolerance generally towards doping is at an all-time low. This has made athletes all the more vulnerable, and that puts them under stress. Broadly speaking, athletes believe that the list includes too much and that monitoring is too intense, but they accept the regime because it does not appear that things can be otherwise. Desperation at the evident difficulties that exist in putting an end to the problem lead to yet further controls and yet more tests both during and outside competitions. WADA are fond of presenting themselves as the defenders of clean athletes, but as a result of their professional mistrust of athletes they end up coming across in practice as something quite different. The more the anti-doping campaign is intensified, the more sportspersons come to appear as criminals who have something to hide. This is tiresome. Like everyone else, athletes would like to be respected and to receive recognition for what they do. To rid themselves of suspicion, a number have, therefore, been talking about even more extensive control systems.

Paula Radcliffe, the women's world's marathon record-holder, was unable to attend the WADA conference in Copenhagen in 2003. She responded, therefore, to the invitation to attend by sending a statement, in which she supports WADA with a declaration that what is needed is to create a world-wide doping control system that the world can rely upon. Such a system, she goes on to explain, involves out-of-competition-controls and tests at all events and competitions in which elite sportspersons compete in order to avoid some of them keeping to minor, uncontrolled events and then setting spectacular records there. In addition she supports the idea of an 'athlete's passport', a system in which athletes regularly have their blood and urine tested. In that way it would be possible to keep an eye on the athletes' physiological parameters and – in the event of the organism showing abnormal biological irregularities that indicate doping – to treat these signs as a positive test.

To do this we need to have a worldwide scheme so that athletes can be tested regularly and reliably wherever they are based, and all athletes need to cooperate. Samples given could also be built up to help research to establish new tests.

(Radcliffe 2003: 10)

What she is suggesting is a wide-ranging surveillance system, and the crowning glory is a recommendation that doping tests should be frozen with a view to retrospective testing as new test methods evolve. When athletes come up with such a desperate proposal, they pressurise others into following their lead. Sceptical athletes have enormous difficulty in formulating any defence against yet more stringent restrictions of their personal freedoms. The gentlest questioning of the regime easily comes to give the impression that the athlete only supports the anti-doping campaign half-heartedly, and that in turn brings the risk of bringing suspicion on oneself.

It is, however, doubtful whether the wide-ranging system of control proposed by Radcliffe would benefit sport at all in the long term. There are grounds for supposing that many potential athletes will baulk at entering a field whose conditions demand that they submit to a regime that would be utterly unacceptable outside sport. Attempts to rescue the reputation of sport through further tightening of the anti-doping campaign focused on athletes would appear as a whole only to contribute to making something bad, worse. The use of doping does not seem to have decreased, and since the WADA initiative was launched, the image of sport has only deteriorated. It seems, therefore, as though the time is ripe to consider new strategies – both for the sake of sport and of the athletes involved. Hence the following and final chapter of the book attempts to outline an alternative approach to the doping problem.

10 The need for a fresh start

When Kelli White appeared at the Play the Game conference in 2005, and was asked about her views on the penalty for breaking the doping rules, she gave the following thought-provoking reply:

> I think they are harsh but that is the price that we pay for being athletes. I think that we give up a lot of our rights being athletes and we know this. Drug testing alone – standing there using the bathroom in front of someone at any given time, it is something you give up as a right being an athlete but I do believe that the consequences are a little harsh. If you just think about that: Four months in prison, four months house arrest versus two years of not being able to compete is hard. It is very hard.
>
> (White 2005)

As an elite athlete you have to urinate on demand under the watchful eyes of complete strangers. It is bizarre, but the process is unavoidable unless we wish to legalise doping in practice. Unfortunately, however, the urine test has not proved to be particularly effective. As mentioned, White tested negative 17 times in and out of competition while she was doped. This is not a unique occurrence and leads to the supposition that doping tests in competitions only work in cases of negligence, thoughtlessness or poor advice. And furthermore that out of competition tests only work in rare cases when they take athletes by surprise at an inopportune moment. This means that if athletes have expert advice and if their use of doping is carefully organised and timed, the risk of being caught is slight. For an initiative whose aim is to promote equal competitive conditions for all, it clearly presents a problem that those who can afford to work with the best doping doctors run less of a risk of testing positive than competitors with more modest means trying to find their own way to climb the last few rungs of the ladder. The proposal to have an athlete's passport has been made with a view to reducing opportunities to cheat. This is one way to catch more of those athletes who currently evade the net. The snag with this proposal is, however, that as long as it does not eliminate the opportunity, it only adds to the temptation. For the fewer athletes there are in a position to cheat, the greater will be the competitive advantage. Those doctors capable of getting round the system will continue to be highly sought after and highly paid.

White has a point, therefore, when she criticises the modest punishment given to those who assist athletes in doping themselves. The four months house arrest she mentions is, in fact, unusual. The doping raid against Fuentes, which had extreme consequences for some of his clients, ended the first time round with the charges being withdrawn. The case has since been taken up again, but since it failed the first time because Spain had no law prohibiting the doping of athletes, it is unlikely that this case – still in progress at the time of writing – will end in a particularly heavy punishment, or indeed in any punishment at all.

Hard-line action against athletes can, of course, be defended by saying that it is in the final analysis their own choice to set off down the doping road and that they therefore bear the responsibility. This is a valid argument. But it is not appropriate as a basis for an anti-doping campaign, because it ignores the complex system of incentives lapping around athletes and making them fall for the temptation. Once again we can learn from White's example. She explains:

> I did not set out in my career to cheat. That was never a thought in my mind. I was very naïve to the whole drug situation. I never thought it was as big as it was. I remember when I left our indoor nationals in 2003 not making that team, I felt that I was no longer a good athlete, and I think I fell into a black hole and I was desperate, but in making that decision I didn't consult anybody, because I knew what their answer would be. It would be: Don't do it. But in that desperation and in that moment, I didn't see any other way, and now I can see that I could have made a whole bunch of different choices and still be competing right now.
>
> (ibid.)

White was a victim of those very extreme sporting ambitions that are a precondition for reaching the top. This does not absolve her of her share of the responsibility, but on the other hand it does not seem to be reasonable to place total responsibility on her shoulders. If she had not been introduced to the doping doctor in the first place, there would have been less chance of her looking him up when she needed help. As one athlete pointed out in our interview study mentioned in the previous chapter:

> If I had wanted to dope myself, I would not have known what to do. If at one time I wanted to use EPO, I was not in an environment where I could get hold of it. There was no one I could ask ... It has to be done systematically. There has to be a support apparatus behind the athlete.

Such a system was at hand for White. She chose to make use of it. The trainer's liberal attitude to the use of performance-enhancing substances without a doubt made the decision easier. We do not imagine that those people we trust want to do us harm, and, when she re-established contact with Victor Conte, it was precisely because she was aware of the fact that Remi Korchemny had recommended him in the first place. As she says:

> I trusted the opinion of my coach and he led me to believe that everyone was doing it and that it was okay and that the only way to ever be good was to use drugs. I put my life in their hands and after reading many documents that were seized from the raid, I can see that they really took advantage of me and many, many other athletes.
>
> (ibid.)

The mental cocktail that provided the basis for her decision consisted of ambition, desperation and naivety. This was not the cynical risk assessment of a criminal consciousness looking for economic gain. To the question as to whether money was a motivating factor, she replies, 'the biggest thing wasn't money. It was to be healthy, it was to be able to compete' (ibid.). Her naivety would seem to be pronounced. But when she cites health as a motive for taking doping, the reason is that, like athletes in general, she has an offensive attitude to her health. Health is not something to be safeguarded. Health, for her, is the ability to perform. From that angle, performance-enhancing measures seem to be conducive to health. For anyone who focuses on their competitive skill, side-effects and long-term consequences fade into the background.

We can relate to this in two ways. We can, as has been said, choose the ultra-liberal position and argue that people are free and rational beings, and, in so far as athletes are responsible for their own actions, it is up to them themselves whether they want to take a gamble by staking their health. Being consistent thinkers, we would at the same time support the viewpoint that all drugs legislation is superfluous, that rules relating to the working environment should be agreed by employees and employers without interference from the authorities and so on (see Chapter 8). The alternative is that we are forced to accept intervention in some form or another. If a number of intellectuals have in recent years turned against intervention, the reason can be found in the way in which it manifests itself. A system that increasingly insists on the testing and surveillance of people who have done nothing to attract suspicion other than playing sport at the highest level should not be applauded. When those responsible for the doping list allow it to go to absurd lengths with the prohibition of restorative drips – in other words, of substances that promote health; when they add to the list drugs without providing proof that they are performance-enhancing (see Chapter 6), and, which is worse, remove a substance like caffeine with a proven performance-enhancing effect, some form of critique is called for. The same goes for *ad hominem* arguments levelled against athletes who, like Bode Miller, presume to air views about doping that are at variance from the accepted line (see

Chapter 6). Other examples could be mentioned. The fact that from time to time the anti-doping campaigners make overzealous decisions in their attempts to put an end to the problem does not make the proposal for a deregulation of doping any more rational. For, even though it would put an end to the absurdities that issue forth from both official and unofficial anti-doping initiatives, deregulation would only provide a superficial solution. The problem would be magicked away, but it would not have disappeared. There is no mention of any protection for the athletes. On the contrary, the proposal leaves them completely out in the cold.

The need for a new strategy

The absurdities of the anti-doping campaign cannot serve as an argument for giving up the campaign, but can be seen as symptomatic of the fact that it is not proceeding according to plan. Consequently they give grounds for taking a fresh look at how to combat doping. The Danish cyclist, Brian Holm, gives a vivid picture of the athletes' situation:

> In cycling they say that if you give a donkey and a racehorse the same to eat, they will still be a donkey and a racehorse. That's something I'd go along with. They also say that a donkey will never become a racehorse no matter what you give it to eat. That also sounds fair enough, though I am not sure that it also holds true. In fact I am sure that I have seen a couple of donkeys with no talent who became racehorses in almost record time.
>
> (Holm 2002: 107)

He gives the example of a small Italian rider who was not much good at anything but getting in the way of everyone else. As a professional, he came nowhere, but after five seasons it was as though he was possessed by the devil. He started to win prestigious cycling races and to Holm's great irritation stood up in front of the TV cameras and explained that the marked difference between Italians and other riders was that Italians simply had a more serious and professional attitude. Holm knew that the real explanation for the striking progress of the little Italian and many other riders during those years had something to do with them 'being attached to a new Italian high-tech physician' (ibid.: 108). The development he observed irritated him and many of the other riders who suddenly fell in the rankings due to an inexplicable turnaround. They knew that the price of increasing their performance by a mere 1 per cent was months of ruthless training and iron self-discipline. If they wanted to get back into the fray, training alone would not be enough. The way things were, 'if a rider who couldn't tell his arse from his elbow went to the right physician with the wrong morals and paid what it took, then he could in principle buy his way to victory and success' (ibid.: 108). Since the offer was on the table, the logic of sport ensured that it would be taken up. The fact that at the beginning it was middle-ranking riders who broke the hierarchy acted as a piece of brilliant marketing for the doping doctors behind their success and has undoubtedly contributed to the rocket-like expansion of their business. The blame for that development can scarcely be laid at the door of athletes, given that they live and breathe for their sport and that the least moderation or half-heartedness are promptly punished by decline and a dearth of results. Seen in this light,

> A quack would unfortunately be able to convince an ambitious but blue-eyed athlete in no time that a drug is completely harmless to the organism. Most people, of course, have a bit of respect for authority and cannot imagine that the nice doctor with his round glasses and white coat might have the morals of a used car dealer.
>
> (ibid.: 109)

A statement such as this seems to imply that athletes would, if it were possible to manage without, prefer a sport without doping; but also that they would prefer to compete on less than ideal conditions, if the alternative is to give up their career at the highest level. The problem is not primarily the athletes but the system that surrounds them. To direct efforts to counter doping primarily at athletes is to shoot wide of the mark. They can be fished out individually, or netted in shoals when they are discovered on the list of patients at the doping doctor's clinic. But no sooner would some athletes be removed than the gaps they left would be filled by others nurturing the same dream of success in the sporting arena.

The way in which the anti-doping campaign is conducted would correspond – without suggesting other parallels – to combating narcotics abuse by focusing solely on the drug user. We could fine them, imprison them or bring in the death penalty. It would make no difference. As long as the pushers go free, new clients will be lured into the trap as soon as others are forced to stop. The strategy just does not work. Instead the fight against narcotics goes to the root of the problem, focusing its efforts on producers, narcotics middlemen and pushers. Drug addicts, on the other hand, are regarded as victims and are left alone as long as they acquire the means to finance their habit legally. This is a strategy that the anti-doping campaign would do well to emulate. A point that was recently given fresh relevance when Alessandro Donati made public what is to date the most ambitious survey of the traffic in doping (Donati 2007). From it we can see that the doping market is organised in the same way as the narcotics trade and is to a large extent run by the same mafia families and other criminal bands, whose eyes have been opened to the lucrative business opportunities in doping.

The illegal world-wide trade in doping drugs was the topic for debate at the initiative of the US Drugs Enforcement Administration at a conference in Prague in 1993. Present were delegates from 19 of the world's most influential countries along with Interpol, the International Olympic Committee, the

International Narcotics Board, the World Health Organization, the US Department of State and the US Food and Drug Administration. The conference resulted in a request for all countries to increase their efforts to tackle the increasingly pervasive spread of steroids through legislation and public information initiatives. In addition, it was concluded that control of the drugs should be tightened through an intensification of customs efforts, and the registration of bulk producers, of quantities produced and of distribution nationally and internationally. Unfortunately these requests for action have not been carried out in practice to any great extent. Why this is so is hard to say. But Donati hints at an explanation by saying that, if we wish to discover why this is so:

> One would have to ask too many questions, which would remain unanswered or lead to frightening conclusions, about the role of pharmaceutical companies and those who should control them; the role of governments, which should protect public welfare; national legislations and international cooperation between prosecutors and police corps; and the historical, unrelenting development of drugs trafficking, which entails similar prospects for the traffic of doping substances.
>
> (ibid.: 15)

The implication of the questions Donati mentions is that the authorities may not find it worth their while to direct their spotlight on the murky financial interests that are at play, even though what is involved is far from small beer. He provides a number of examples of the way organised crime is behind the use of doping. In 1999 4,650,000 phials of EPO were stolen from the warehouse of a medical company in Nicosia. According to the Cypriot police, organised crime supplying the sports black market was behind it. The case was never investigated internationally and remains unsolved. This is somewhat surprising. As Donati points out, however, there are other and more curious aspects to the affair. The stolen EPO was sufficient to supply Europe's entire patient treatment needs for more than a year. Why is so much EPO stored in Cyprus, when it is known that the hormone has to be stored at low temperatures and even under optimal storage conditions does not have a very long shelf life? The phials have to be used within a few months, and this raises a number of additional questions. For which patients in which countries was the medicine originally intended (ibid.: 17)? How could it be that the warehouse facility was not guarded? How did the culprits dare to assume that no one would turn up during the substantial stretch of time it must have taken to empty the contents of the warehouse into the refrigerated lorries that must have been used to retain the quality of the product during transport? And equally curious, why does the medical industry overproduce EPO to the extent that, even though over 4 million EPO phials suddenly disappear, no problems arise in covering the requirements of patients?:

Clearly, if the Cyprus authorities were immediately in a position to declare that the stolen phials were destined for the black market of the sports milieu, they must have had some information or clues; did they advise Interpol of the theft and the fact that these phials were, probably, bound for a harbour in Europe? If the Cyprus authorities did not advise Interpol, surely at least they advised the World Health Organization, in view of the hypothetical damage to patients who needed the substance.

(ibid.: 17)

The case is a mystery, and all the more disquieting in that it was only one of a number of doping thefts during the 1990s. A considerable cache of EPO was also stolen in Australia immediately before the Games in Sydney in 2000; a large load of growth hormone was stolen in Phoenix, USA, a few weeks before the Winter Olympics in 2002, and in his homeland Donati mentions how the mafia in Naples, Comorra, has stolen doping drugs in large quantities (ibid.).

The way forward

The perception that doping has become a profitable market for an unholy alliance of medical firms, doctors and well-organised criminals paves the way for the realisation that the anti-doping campaign is doomed to failure as long as it focuses primarily on the testing and surveillance of athletes. The problem has to be tackled on a broad front. The urine test will continue to be the backbone of anti-doping work. Despite the fact that it can seem offensive, it is met with general acceptance from athletes, who see it as a lesser evil than the *de facto* deregulation of doping. Unfortunately it has proved to be inadequate in itself.

Doping drugs are difficult to trace, and medical experts using micro-dosages and camouflage substances can make detection still more difficult. The likelihood of improved methods of analysis being able in time to substantially alter this is slight. If the urine test is to be effective in earnest, then it is necessary to involve the medical industry in a binding collaboration. This might come about through an agreement or injunction paving the way for meticulous registration of the production and distribution of medication with a view to optimising the balance between the size of production and the registered requirements of patients. In addition, an agreement could be reached that substances such as EPO, which are difficult to trace, are provided with a biologically inactive marker – in other words, a substance that has no effect on the body but which is precipitated through urine over a longer period – which would make it traceable through the urine test. Furthermore, a rule could be introduced whereby new, potentially performance-enhancing medicines can only be certified once the producer has provided a sure-fire method for allowing the substance to be detected in a urine test. It might be a task for WADA to develop a proposal as to how this might be arranged in practice and how the far from insignificant costs involved in relation to the introduction of this system might be covered.

In addition, what has been demonstrated, not least by Operación Puerto, is that it is also necessary to take action in relation to the medical expertise available. It could be decided that athletes, who are already required to report their whereabouts, should also have their doctor (including private doctors) registered and certified by the national anti-doping agency, and furthermore should be confined to consulting only those physicians that are WADA-certified. This means the end of the current system with team physicians employed on a private basis. In so far as top professional sport requires doctors, these should be employed as independent practitioners within the structure of WADA and should be available in conjunction with matches and training as required and subject to a fee. Finally, a law should be introduced prohibiting doctors from assisting athletes with doping, and sanctions should be frighteningly severe and include fines, imprisonment and the removal from the medical register.

These proposals will doubtless be greeted by a range of objections. The professional teams will argue for the need to have their own physicians by referring to the fact that athletes are such valuable investments that it would be unreasonable to demand that their treatment be left in the hands of a body of free-floating doctors. Doping doctors will be able to defend their right to practise freely and oppose any extraordinary measures to monitor their work just because they happen to have something to do with elite athletes. And medical companies will be able to protect their interests by citing the fact that developing new drugs is a costly affair, and that it would add a serious extra expense if, in addition to combating illness, their products also have to live up to requirements in relation to anti-doping policies. Moreover, doubts might be raised as to whether making medicines more complex by adding trace substances with the sole aim of preventing their illegal use could be ethically justified to patients. Resistance might find additional grist to its mill by pointing out that it will be impossible to get every country to introduce legislation and get producers to commit themselves. To this could be added the final argument that the effort would at any rate be in vain, since doping drugs are often so easy to produce that they can be made in a home laboratory.

There is no doubt that such objections carry weight. And it will not be an easy matter to get the world to unite around an anti-doping regime such as the one outlined here. It is no easy matter to create a consensus between countries that doping is so great a problem that it can justify inconveniencing the powerful drugs industry. And even if WADA did manage to gain acceptance for the proposal and assemble nations to be signatories of an anti-doping code directed against the system that supports the use of doping, there is every reason to doubt whether this would have any significance in practice. What we have learned from the Code that was signed in Copenhagen in 2003 does not give much ground for optimism.

It is true that 202 national Olympic committees signed up to putting anti-doping initiatives into action, but in reality two years later less than half were testing their athletes. Since it has never been a good idea to let the fox guard the henhouse, Olympic committees were urged to establish independent anti-doping agencies. Some 40 of them – or less than half of those who were conducting tests – have done so. And only 20 lived up to the requirement regarding '[the] registered testing pool, whereabouts information, and out-of-competition' (Hanstad and Loland 2005: 4). Even though there are some who pull their weight, it does look as though commitment to anti-doping work on a global scale is only lukewarm. The explanation is probably to be found in the fact that other considerations weigh more heavily in many countries, and the likelihood is that this will apply to an even greater extent when larger financial interests are at stake. But even though the establishment of a global anti-doping effort directed towards the system that supports doping will meet opposition and substantial obstacles, it is nevertheless here that the anti-doping work of the future must place its energies if it is to make any progress. This is demonstrated by the increasing production of and trade in doping drugs that is taking place the world over. The case against Fuentes shows that efforts directed against doctors implicated in doping have a far larger impact than any amount of tests, however frequent, during or outside competitions.

Positive tests and subsequent doping penalties may indicate effective anti-doping work, but that is not what they really are. As long as anti-doping work places its main emphasis on monitoring the athletes, there are reasons to believe that the most important aim of the campaign is not protection of the athletes' health or of their chances to have a fair shot on a level playing field, but the protection of business interests through the continued cultivation of the illusion that sport is essentially a moral and healthy activity.

Appendix

Pro-Tour Teams' Code of Ethics

Preamble

The aim of UCI Pro Teams in writing and signing the current code of conduct is to send a clear signal of their wish at all times to abide by the ethical rules of the sport.

The establishment of UCI Pro-Tour aims to promote top performances and is therefore in this context an historic opportunity.

UCI Pro Teams stress that the introduction of the enclosed code of conduct must be seen in conjunction with their duty to ensure strict conformity with UCI's rules and, in particular, the regulations regarding the health of riders (paragraph XIII) and UCI's regulations regarding anti-doping (paragraph XIV).

UCI Pro Teams make the following undertaking:

I.   To place health and sporting ethics highest in the practice of their activities.

II.   To comply with the principles of fair play and conduct themselves properly towards the public, riders, organisers, teams as well as towards national and international authorities.

III. To make it possible for riders to carry out their activities under the best possible conditions.

IV.   To exclude any form of payment to sports or medical employees that is based on the riders' performance or results.

V.   To request every rider to submit in writing to his employer information about his personal trainer(s), doctor(s) and any other person outside the team who plays a part in the rider's physical, medical or psychological preparations.

VI.   To introduce a system of information and prevention for riders regarding the dangers of doping.

VII. To remind riders that they must give precise information as to their place of residence to any authority approved according to the

International Code of Anti-Doping who requests it, so that it is possible at any time to conduct a doping test without prior warning.

VIII. Subject to the right to terminate employment because of a serious offence, not to employ for races a licensed rider who is the subject of disciplinary action for infringement of UCI's regulations regarding anti-doping, carried out by any competent instance in accordance with the international code of anti-doping.

IX. Subject to the right to terminate employment because of a serious offence, not to employ a licensed rider for races who is the subject of an investigation or of criminal proceedings on the grounds of circumstances relating to the sporting activity, i.e. either an action that constitutes an infringement of UCI's regulations regarding anti-doping or some (other) intentionally criminal offence.

   1. after the start of the investigation or the case:
- if the person concerned has confessed to the charges, or
- if it can be seen from the information acquired by UCI Pro Team from an official source that the circumstances under discussion cannot reasonably be denied,

   2. in any other situation in which the case has been brought before an investigative judge or in the absence hereof is placed before a judge who handles the facts of the case.

X. If the circumstances described in paragraph XI are involved in a disciplinary action under paragraph VIII, then solely paragraph VIII shall apply. If, however, after the disciplinary hearing the person concerned comes before a judge, who hears and determines the reality of the case, the individual concerned shall not take part in any race for one month before conviction and shall remain excluded until sentence is passed. If the disciplinary case according to existing legislation is terminated because of a criminal case as described in paragraph IX, the individual concerned shall not take part in any race for one month prior to the hearing and until the case is concluded.

XI. Within the framework of existing national legislation to dismiss any rider or any other member of a team who has been found guilty by any sporting or judicial authority of infringement of the UCI's regulations on anti-doping, or in the instance of there having been pronounced sentence by a legal authority for intentional criminal action in relation to sporting activity. This condition shall not apply to the examples mentioned in subparagraph 2 of paragraph XII.

Reservation is made for the right of dismissal for any valid reason.

XII. For a period of four years after the passing of sentence not to appoint an individual to the team who has been sentenced for circumstances that constitute a conscious infringement of the UCI's anti-doping regulations.

The following circumstances are not regarded in the present context as conscious infringements:

a. infringements for which the individual has been sentenced pursuant to Article 262 of the UCI Regulations on anti-doping (special drugs),

b. infringements for which Article 264 or 265 of the UCI's anti-doping regulations has been applied (absence of fault or negligence or considerable fault or negligence),

c. infringements for which the individual has been sentenced pursuant to Article 266 of the UCI's anti-doping regulations, not including cases of sentencing for infringement in respect of Article 15.6.2 (linked to staffs' possession), 15.7 (trafficking) or 15.8 (handing over to a rider) (references to articles in the Anti-doping Regulations in the edition applicable in 2005),

d. any other infringement, for which the individual can establish to the Chairman of the Licensing Committee that it was not deliberate.

The present rule shall apply to judgements pronounced after 1 January 2005. No consideration is given to the following:

i. judgements that are the subject of an appeal case, if sentence has been passed in the court of the first instance before 1 January 2005,

ii. disciplinary sentences, if a judicial sentence was pronounced before 1 January 2005,

iii. judgements for which a disciplinary sentence has been passed before 1 January 2005.

XIII. Any ambiguity in the interpretation of Articles VIII–XII is to come before the Chairman of the Licensing Committee or a deputy appointed by him, whose decision will be final, enforceable and not subject to appeal.

(quoted from *Jyllands-Posten*, 25 March 2007, available at: /2005/10/25/ 204854.htm/2005/sep/16/cycling.cycling/2005/10/25/204854.htm)

Notes

1 What is doping?

1 As regards a chronic illness such as asthma, elite athletes are over-represented when compared with the remainder of the population. A Danish study of cyclists, swimmers and ice-hockey players showed that 44 per cent had respiratory symptoms as against 14 per cent of non-elite sportspeople. The highest incidence was found in swimmers, where 68 per cent had the symptoms under study (Backer *et al.* 2006).

2 This could, for example, follow the widely used Body Mass Index, which is calculated using the following formula:

Weight in kilos
(height in metres)^2

In other words, body weight in kilos divided by height in metres squared. Normal weight is defined as a BMI of between 20 and 25. Someone with a height of 184 cm is, therefore, reckoned to be underweight if they weigh less than 68 kg.

2 What is sport?

1 See Klaus Heinemann, *Einführung in die Soziologie des Sports* (1990).

2 A relevant objection would be that if activities take on two different forms, they cannot be said to be the same phenomenon but two qualitatively distinct phenomena. It should, therefore, be made clear that what is meant by the same activity is activities that can be identified using the same term such as football, badminton, swimming, etc.

3 In other words it lies within the category of *agon* in Roger Caillois' typology of play (see his *Les jeux et les hommes*, 1958). Caillois divides play into four types: (1) *agon* (competitive play); (2) *alea* (playing with chance); (3) *mimicry* (role play); and (4) *ilinx* (euphoric play). If I find it necessary to indicate that sport is *agonal* in a Cailloisian sense, I do so to rule out phenomena such as ludo, which occasionally appears as a competition but which in reality is an *alea* activity.

4 An anonymous reviewer objected to my definition, arguing that it could include pie-eating competitions. This objection, however, is rather a representation of a prejudiced perception of what sport can be, rather than a revelation of any inconsistency in the definition. So long as there is an International Federation of Competitive Eating (I.F.O.C.E.), which organise events that are governed by a written set of rules, record results, rank the eaters and ascribe significance to their performances, there is no reason to claim that eating competitions are not sport. That pie eating is taken seriously as a sport by organisers and participants is apparent at the homepage of I.F.O.C.E. http://www.ifoce.com/home.php. See also http://www.guardian.co.uk/uk/2006/nov/23/foodanddrink.

5 It is common knowledge in sports clubs everywhere that there are some players who have exceptional talents but who do not possess the correct attitude to exploit their talents to the full. The words 'He does not have the right attitude' is an expression commonly used typically by trainers or managers wanting to air their frustration at a talented player who resists going into harness to make a career in the club's first team but instead is satisfied to play further down the league.

6 For an in-depth analysis of internal and external motivators in sport, see McNamee (1995).

7 A soigneur is a servant in cycling teams. The soigneur takes care of sports directors' and riders' various needs. He is often very close to the riders, giving them support both mentally and physically.

8 The hollowness of the tributes accorded to the character-building qualities of sport is punctured by the psychologist, Thomas S. Tutko, who says, 'There are countless cases of dissatisfaction and disruption including violence in hockey, breaking of contract, suits involving accusations that there is a criminal element in sports, and so on … One wonders whether sports are building character or developing "characters"' (Tutko 1989: 115f).

9 An explanation of the complicated relations between sport, work and play is given in K. Blanchard, *The Anthropology of Sport* (1995). Put simply, Blanchard's point is that there are elements both of pleasurable play and of hard work in sport, but that it is not possible to make a consistent argument for sport either as work (like any other) or as play (like any other).

10 See Hoberman (1992), which retells among other things how Coubertin's compatriot, the highly respected doctor and sports enthusiast, Philippe Tissié, warned in 1896, the very year when the first Olympic Games were held, against intensive training and how later in 1919 he sharpened his tone, declaring that top sport was a life-threatening disease. See also Williams (1999), where we read of the howls of horror from Australia and England, when the captain of the English national test team, Douglas Jardine, starting using body-liners instead of bowling at the wicket in order to eliminate the dreaded 'homerunner', Donald Bradman, from the game. This was regarded as unsportsmanlike, and in newspaper articles it was presented as the death of the sport.

11 For important discussions of the ethical issues of boxing, see, for example, (Radford 1988; Parry 1998; Leclerc 1999).

3 Unchristian sport

1 For further exploration of the relationship between sport, risk and injury, see Howe (2003).
2 A clear example of this is Tony Schumacher's vicious tackle in the FIFA World Cup semi final in Spain 1982, that cost the French player Patrick Battiston three teeth, a damaged vertebrae, and a period in a coma. See http://www.youtube.com/watch?v = 3byTNRoxujo. And for those who might attempt to suggest that this is the one and only example, see an example from the German league from the previous year: http://www.youtube.com/watch?v = KIWWYOqG_9s. Quite a few players' biographies, in fact, admit that destructive violations are sometimes even calculated. See, for instance, Stafford Hildred and Tim Ewbank's (2000) biography of Roy Keane or the former Bolton player Stig Tøfting's (2005) biography, *No Regrets*.
3 For further exploration of violence in sport, see Bredemeier and Shields (1985).
4 For an alternative interpretation of the gender separation in sport, see Tännsjö (2000).
5 It may appear unfortunate to call bullying a natural phenomenon. For a convincing argument of the naturalness of violent behaviour, see Pinker (2002). However, it is important to stress that the claim that violent behaviour and bullying are natural is not to say that it is acceptable.
6 For an elaboration of this point, see Møller (2007).

4 Doping history – fact or fiction?

1 For a well-researched and detailed doping history, see Dimeo (2007).
2 See, for example, http://www.bikeraceinfo.com/classics/paris-roubaix/pr1896.html (accessed 1 August 2006).
3 For a full account of this case, see Møller (2005).
4 Domestiques are riders in the team who are supposed to help the team leader and other star riders in the race by bringing them water from the team car, provide wind protection, set the pace and so on.
5 In a thought-provoking paper, Angela Schneider suggests that if the Tour de France is to survive 'organizers and riders must come to really believe that if doping is the answer – we are asking the wrong question' (Schneider 2006: 223). In light of Skibby's admission and explanation for doping, it is difficult to see what the right question is and how it should be posed effectively.

5 The law of silence

1 His confession can be viewed at http://www.youtube.com/watch?v = 1oyWmXkc30o

2 For a critical review of the health argument, see Kayser (2007, 2009).
3 See *VeloNews* (2008), and the Ministerio de Educación Politica Social y Deporte (2006) 'Public General Act of 21 November on the Protection of Health and the Fight against Doping in Sport'.

6 When good intentions turn bad

1 The surveillance regime is described in the WADA Code 2007 article 14.3 where it states:

> *Athletes* who have been identified by their International Federation or *National Anti-Doping Organization* for inclusion in a *Registered Testing Pool* shall provide accurate, current location information. The International Federations and *National Anti-Doping Organizations* shall coordinate the identification of *Athletes* and the collecting of current location information and shall submit it to *WADA*. This information will be accessible, through *ADAMS* where reasonably feasible, to other *Anti-Doping Organizations* having jurisdiction to test the *Athlete* as provided in Article 15.

2 For a thorough analysis and documentation of the THG case, see Kristian Rasmussen (2005).
3 See 'Landis' Doctor: Test is False Positive', available at: http://abcnews. go.com/GMA/ESPNSports/story?id = 2251619& page = 1.
4 Jan Ullrich did, it is true, get a doping penalty of six months when he tested positive for amphetamine in 2002. The mildness of the penalty was due to the fact that the German cycling association accepted his explanation that he had taken the drug in conjunction with a visit to a discotheque. The episode took place while he was in the process of training himself up again after a prolonged knee injury.
5 See Abt (2006).
6 Since the code has so far only been published in Danish, the full text in English is attached as an appendix in this volume.
7 WADA's official statement on the Vrijman report can be read at: http://www.sportslaw.nl/documents/cms_sports.

8 Legalisation of doping

1 For further discussion of the ethical problems related to the use of hypoxic chambers, see, for instance, Spiggs (2005), Tamburrini (2005), and Schermer (2008).
2 In the Tour de France 2008, three athletes, Ricardo Ricco, Bernhard Kohl and Stefan Schumacher were tested positive for CERA, a third-generation EPO. This could be interpreted as evidence that the doping control now had caught up with the cheats. It is, however, more likely that the success

was only another half-battle won in a lost war. The 'catch' was a result of an unprecedented collaboration between WADA and the pharmaceutical company who made the drug. In secrecy they had joined forces to create a test for the drug so it was ready as soon as the product was introduced. Accordingly, the riders who may have thought the brand new drug was undetectable were caught by surprise. No less surprisingly – and rather dishearteningly for the anti-doping optimists – Ricco, was tested thirteen times during the period when he was using the drug and only two of his samples were detected as positive. Even so it is unlikely that top-level athletes will continue with their use of CERA. In many ways, it appears similar to the World Cup in cross-country skiing that was held in Finland in 2001. Here six Finnish skiers tested positive for plasma expander, a situation that has not recurred. One could also mention NESP, the second-generation EPO, which both Johan Mühlegg and Olga Danilova tested positive for during the Winter Olympic Games in 2004 at Salt Lake City. So long as there is no test for a doping product there is no reason to be cautious when using it. That is, there is no reason to use micro dosages. That may explain the few major test 'successes'.

Bibliography

Abt, S. (2006) 'Cycling: Above the Pack, But Not Suspicion', *International Herald Tribune*, 31 May.

Allison, L. (2004) 'Faster, Stronger, Higher', *The Guardian*, 9 August G2, pp. 2–3.

Andersen, O. S. and Jung, N. C. (1999) *Doping på landevejen* [Doping on the Road], Copenhagen: Møntergården.

Arneberg, G. A. (2001) 'Utidig med høydehus-debat VG nett'. Online. Available at: http://www.vg.no/pub/vgart.hbs?artid = 9661553 (accessed 13 May 2007).

Associated Press (2005) 'Worldstream', 19 October.

—— (2007) 'Guilty of Doping? Pay One Year's Salary, Optional Declaration Says', 19 June. Online available: http://blogcyclingnews.com/postdetail.cfm?postnum = 249 (accessed 26 November 2008).

Backer, V., Pedersen, L. and Lund, T.C. (2006) 'Får man astma af at dyrke topidræt?' ('Do You Get Asthma from Elite Sport?'), *Ugeskrift for læger* [Physicians Weekly], 168(51): 4532–4.

Banke, P. (2006) 'De er hyklere' [They Are Hypocrites], *B.T.*, 9 December.

Barthes, R. (1997) *The Eiffel Tower, and Other Mythologies*, Berkeley, CA: University of California Press.

Beamish, R. and Ritchie, I. (2006) *Fastest, Highest, Strongest: A Critique of High-Performance Sport*, London: Routledge.

Beck, U. (1986) *Risikogesellschaft: Auf dem Weg in eine andere Moderne*, Frankfurt am Main: Suhrkamp.

Becker, H. (1973) *Outsiders: Studies in the Sociology of Deviance*, New York: The Free Press.

Blanchard, K. (1995) *The Anthropology of Sport*, London: Bergin & Garvey.

Bøgeskov, L. (1998) 'Dopingsagen der ændrede verden' [The Doping Case that Changed the World], *Politiken*, 20 September.

—— (2001) 'Doping-mysteriet uden løsning' [The Doping Mystery Without a Solution], *Politiken*, 9 April.

Brandt, F. (2003) 'Saltin sår tvivl om THG-doping' [Saltin Calls in Question THG-Doping], *B.T.*, 23 October.

Brandt, H. H. (2003) 'Dopingmuren vakler igen' [The Doping Wall Totters Again], *Jyllands-Posten*, 24 October.

Bredemeier, B. J. and Shields, D. L. (1985) 'Values and Violence in Sports Today', *Psychology Today*, 19(10): 23–5, 28–32.

Brohm, J-M. (1978) *Sport: A Prison of Measured Time*, London: Ink Links.

Brunel, P. (1996) *An Intimate Portrait of the Tour de France: Masters and Slaves of the Road*, Colorado: Buonpane Publications.

B.T. (2005) 'Pernilla Wiberg skal sætte Bode Miller på plads' [Pernilla Wiberg Tells Bode Miller Where to Get Off], *B.T.*, 31 October.

Buffet, A. M. (1998) 'Ministerens dopingkorstog' [The Minister's Crusade], *Politiken*, 7 September.

—— (2001) 'Intet bevis i historisk dopingsag' [No Evidence in Historical Doping Case], *Politiken*, 9 April.

Burke, E. R. (1986) *Science of Cycling*, Champaign, IL: Human Kinetics Publishers, Inc.

Caillois, R. (1958) *Les jeux et les hommes*, Paris: Gallimard.

Cassell, E. J. (1992) 'The Body of the Future', in D. Leder (ed.) *The Body in Medical Thought and Practice*, London: Kluwer Academic Publishers.

Christiansen, A. V. (2005) *Ikke for pengenes skyld* [Money Is Not the Thing], Odense: University Press of Southern Denmark.

Coubertin, P. de (2000) *Olympism: Selected Writings. Pierre de Coubertin 1863–1937*, Lausanne: IOC.

Cranston, M. (1994) *The Romantic Movement*, Oxford: Blackwell Publishers.

Dekhuijzen, P. N. R., Machiels, H. A., Heunks, L. M., van der Heijden, H. F. and van Balkom, R. H. (1999) 'Athletes and Doping: Effects of Drugs on the Respiratory System', *Thorax*, 54: 1041–6.

Der Spiegel (2007) 'Fuentes sprach von Doping Wie vom Windelwechseln', 6 July.

Dimeo, P. (2007) *A History of Drug Use in Sport 1876–1976: Beyond Good and Evil*, London: Routledge.

Donahoe, T. and Johnson, N. (1986) *Foul Play: Drug Abuse in Sport*, New York: Basil Blackwell.

Donati, A. (2004) 'The Silent Drama of the Diffusion of Doping among Amateurs and Professionals', in J. Hoberman and V. Møller (eds) *Doping and Public Policy*, Odense: University Press of Southern Denmark.

—— (2007) *World Traffic in Doping Substances*. Online. Available at: http://www.wada-ama.org/rtecontent/document/Donati_Report_Trafficking_2007–03_06.pdf (accessed 1 November 2008).

DR.dk (2006) Report. Online. Available at: http://www.dr.dk/Sporten/Oevrig_sport, 17 January (accessed 7 April 2007).

Dubin, C. L. (1990) *Commission of Inquiry into the Use of Drugs and Banned Practices Intended to Increase Athletic Performance*, Ottawa: Canadian Government Publishing Centre.

Evald, J. (2007) Interview, *Jyllands-Posten*, 25 March.

Fjeldgaard, F. (2006) 'Mandags stævnemøde med Brian Holm' [Monday Date with Brian Holm], *Jyllands-Posten*, 11 December.

Fotheringham, W. (2004a) 'Millar is Pulled out of Tour', *The Guardian*, 29 June.

—— (2004b) 'Millar Admits to Years of Doping', *The Guardian*, 2 July.

—— (2004c) 'Sacked Millar to Lose World Title', *The Guardian*, 21 July.

—— (2004d) 'The Wrong Gear', *The Guardian*, 27 July.

Frederiksen, L. (1962) 'Correspondence', *Bulletin du Comité International Olympique*, May, No. 78, p. 47.

Glucksmann, A. (1997) *Verdens brist* [The World's Flaw], Copenhagen: Borgen.

Goksøyr, M. (1997) 'Toppidrettens indre rasjonalitet' [The Inner Rationality of Elite Sports], *Dagbladet*, 18 January.

Gray, J. (2002) *Straw Dogs: Thoughts on Humans and Other Animals*, London: Granta Books.

Gronen, W. and Lemke, W. (1987) *Geschichte des Radsports des Fahrrades*, Hausham: Fuchs-Druck und Verlag.

Grupe, O. (1975) *Grundlagen der Sportpädagogik*, Schorndorf: Hofmann.

Guttmann, A. (1978) *From Ritual to Record: The Nature of Modern Sport*, New York: Columbia University Press.

Hanstad, D. and Loland, S. (2005) 'What Is Efficient Doping Control?: A Study of Procedures and Their Justification in the Planning and Carrying Out of Doping Control in Sport'. Online. Available at: http://www.antidoping.no/files/%7BF022336E-40F0–49E5–95B1-B58AF4235BA9%7D.pdf (accessed 14 May 2007).

Heinemann, K. (1990) *Einführung in die Soziologie des Sports*, Schorndorf: Hofmann.

Hildred, S. and Ewbank, T. (2000) *Roy Keane: Captain Fantastic*, London: John Blake Publishing

Hoberman, J. M. (1992) *Mortal Engines: The Science of Performance and the Dehumanization of Sport*, New York: Free Press

—— (1995) 'Listening to Steroids', *The Wilson Quarterly*, Winter: 35–44.

—— (2005) *Testosterone Dreams: Rejuvenation, Aphrodisia, Doping*, Berkeley, CA: University of California Press.

Holm, B. (2002) *Smerten – Glæden. Erindringer fra et liv på cykel* [The Pain – The Pleasure: Memories of a Life on a Bike], Copenhagen: Hovedland.

Holt, R. (1981) *Sport and Society in Modern France*, London: Macmillan.

Houlihan, B. (1999) *Dying to Win: Doping in Sport and the Development of Anti-Doping Policy*, Strasbourg: Council of Europe Publishing.

Howe, D. (2003) *Sport, Professionalism and Pain: Ethnographies of Injury and Risk*, London: Routledge.

Idorn, J. (1996) *OL-Historie. Strejftog gennem myter, legender og danske medaljer* [History of the Olympic Games: A Raid through Myths, Legends and Danish Medals], Copenhagen: Gyldendal.

International Herald Tribune (2007) 'Top Cyclist Ivan Basso Admits Role in Blood-Doping Ring in Spain', 7 May.

Jakobsen, J. (2004) *Le Tour: Sejre, drømme og frygtelige nederlag i 100 år* [Le Tour: Victories, Dreams and Terrible Defeats in 100 Years], Copenhagen: Rosinante.

Jäger, R., Metzger, J., Lautmann, K., Shushakov, V., Purpura, M., Geiss, K-R. and Maassen, N. (2008) 'The Effects of Creatine Pyruvate and Creatine Citrate on Performance during High Intensity Exercise', *Journal of the International Society of Sports Nutrition*, 5: 4.

Jyllands-Poster (2007) 'Etik og morad på to hjul' [Ethics and Morality on Two Wheels], 25 March.

Kant, I. (1995) *Foundations of the Metaphysics of Morals and What is Enlightenment*, Englewood Hills, NJ: Prentice Hall.

Kayser, B. (2005) 'Viewpoint: Legalisation of Performance-Enhancing Drugs', *Lancet*, 366(1): 521.

Kayser, B. (2007) 'Current Anti-Doping Policy: A Critical Appraisal', *BMC Medical Ethics* 8:2.

—— (2009) 'Current Anti-Doping Policy: Harm Reduction or Harm Induction?', in V. Møller, P. Dimeo and M. McNamee M. (eds) *Elite Sport Doping and Public Health*, Odense: University of Southern Denmark Press.

Kimmage, P. (1998) *Rough Ride*, London: Yellow Jersey Press.

Krawzyk, B. (1977) 'The Social Origin and Ambivalent Character of the Ideology of Amateur Sport', *International Review of Sport Sociology*, 13(3): 35–49.

Kristensen, P. (ed.) (1996) *De Olympiske. Biografi af danske OL-deltagere, 1896–1996* [The Olympics: A Biography of the Danish Participants/Contestants of the Olympic Games, 1896–1996], Copenhagen: Danmarks Idrætsforbund.

Landis, F. (2007) *Positively False: The Real Story of How I Won the Tour de France*, New York: Simon Spotlight Entertainment.

Larsen, K. (1998) 'Bjarne Riis i raseri-hjørnet' [The Anger of Bjarne Riis], *Berlingske Tidende*, 27 July.

Leclerc, S. (1999) 'Sport Medicine and the Ethics of Boxing', *British Journal of Sports Medicine*, 33: 426–9.

Lenskyj, H. J. (2000) *Inside the Olympic Industry*, Albany, NY: State University of New York Press.

Levine, B. D. (2006) 'Should "Artificial" High Altitude Environments Be Considered Doping?', *Scandinavian Journal of Medicine and Science in Sports*, 16(5): 297–301.

Loland, S. (1997) '"Det kunstige" og toppidrett' [The Artificial and Top Sport]. Online. Available: http://www.dagbladet.no/kronikker/970318-kro-1.html.

Longmore, A. (1999) 'Time to Stop Cheating, Pleads Millar', *The Independent*, 27 June.

Lundby, C., Achman-Andersen, N. J., Thomsen, J. J., Norgaard, A. M. and Robach, P. (2008) 'Testing for Recombinant Human Erythropoietin in Urine: Problems Associated with Current Anti-Doping Testing', *Journal of Applied Physiology*, 105(2): 417–19.

Lundby, C., Thomsen, J. J., Boushel, R., Koskolou, M., Warberg, J., Calbet, J. A. and Robach, P. (2007) 'Erythropoietin Treatment Elevates Haemoglobin Concentration by Increasing Red Cell Volume and Depressing Plasma Volume', *Journal of Physiology*, January 1: 578.

Mackay, D. (2005) 'Pound Points the Finger for Armstrong Leak at Head of Cycling's Governing Body', *The Guardian*, 16 September. Online. Available at: http://www.guardian.co.uk/sport (accessed 13 January 2009).

Magney, J. (2003) 'Carl Lewis' Positive Test Covered up'. Online. Available at: http://www.smh.com.au/articles/2003/04/17/1050172709693.html (accessed 12 October 2008).

McNamee, M. (1995) 'Sporting Practises, Institutions and Virtues: A Critique and a Restatement', *Journal of the Philosophy of Sport*, XXII: 61–82.

Mignon, P. (2003) 'The Tour de France and the Doping Issue', *The International Journal of the History of Sport*, 20(2): 227–45.

Miller, S. G. (1991) *Arete: Greek Sports from Ancient Sources*, Berkeley, CA: University of California Press.

Ministerio de Educación Politica Social y Deporte (2006) 'Public General Act of 21 November on the Protection of Health and the Fight against Doping in Sport'. Online. Available at: http://www.csd.mec.es/csd/salud/03PrLeyDopaje (accessed 3 September).

Møldrup, C. (1999) *Den medicinerede normalitet* [Medically Reinforced Normality], Copenhagen: Gyldendal.

Møller, V. (1999) *Dopingdjævlen – analyse af en hed debat* [The Doping Devil], Copenhagen: Gyldendal.

—— (2005) 'Knud Enemark Jensen's Death during the 1960 Rome Olympics: A Search for Truth', in P. Dimeo (ed.) *Sport in History*, vol. 3, London: Routledge, pp. 452–71.

—— (2007) 'Walking on the Edge', in M. McNamee (ed.) *Philosophy, Risk and Adventure Sport*, London: Routledge.

Mottram, D. R. (ed.) (1996) *Drugs in Sport*, London: E & FN Spon.

Nietzsche, F. (1968) *The Twilight of the Idols of Anti-Christ*, Harmondsworth: Penguin Classics.

—— (1990) *The Birth of Tragedy and The Genealogy of Morals*, New York: Doubleday.

NRC *Handelsblad* (2007) 'English Version: The Rasmussen Scandal', 28 December. Online. Available at: http://www.nrc.nl/achtergrond/article874819.ece (accessed 12 October).

Paluska, S. A. (2003) 'Caffeine and Exercise', *Current Sports Medicine Reports*, 2: 213–19.

Parkinson, A. B. and Evans, N. A. (2006) 'Anabolic Androgenid Steroids: A Survey of 5000 Users', *Medicine & Science in Sports & Exercise*, 38(4): 644–51.

Parry, J. (1998) 'Violence and Aggression in Contemporary Sport', in M. McNamee and J. Parry (eds) *Ethics and Sport*, London: Taylor and Francis.

Pedersen, B. K. (2008) 'Skal den bedst dopede vinde' [Must the Best Doped Win?], *Berlingske Tidende*, 15 July.

Pedersen, P, (2008) Interview, *Jyllands-Posten*, 26 July.

Pinker, S. (2002) *The Blank Slate*, London: Penguin Books.

Porter, R. (1997) *The Greatest Benefit to Mankind: A Medical History of Humanity from Antiquity to the Present*, London: HarperCollins Publishers.

Pound, D. (2004) *Inside the Olympics: A Behind-the-Scenes Look at the Politics, the Scandals, and the Glory of the Games*, Chichester: John Wiley.

Povlsen, B. M. (2007) 'Etik og moral på to hjul' [Ethics and Morals on Two Wheels], *Jyllands-Posten*, 25 March.

Prokop, L. (1972) 'Zur Geschichte des Dopings', in H. Acker (ed.) *Rekorde aus der Retorte: Leistungssteigerung im modernen Hochleistungssport*, Stuttgart: Deutsche Verlags-Anstalt.

Rabenstein, R. (1991) *Radsport und Gesellschaft: Ihre sozialgeschichtlichen Zusammenhänge in der Zeit von 1867 bis 1914*, Hildesheim: Weidmann.

Radcliffe, P. (2003) 'An Athlete's View', in The World Anti-Doping Agency, *Play True*, issue 1.

Radford, C. (1988) 'Utilitarianism and the Noble Art', *Philosophy*, 63(243): 63–81.

Rasmussen, K. (2005) 'The Quest for the Imaginary Evil: A Critique of Anti-Doping', *Sport in History*, 25(3): 515–35.

Rigauer, B. (1969) *Sport und Arbeit, Sociologische Zusammenhänge und Ideologische Implikationen*, Frankfurt a.M.: Suhrkamp Verlag.

Riis, B. (1998a) Interview, TV2, 26 July.

—— (1998b) Interview, TV2, 4 August.

—— (2006) Interview, *Jyllands-Posten*, 21 November.

Ros, J. W., Pelders, M. G. and de Smet, P. A. (1999) 'A Case of Positive Doping Associated with a Botanical Food Supplement', *Pharmacy World & Science*, 21(1): 44–6.

Sahakian, B. and Morein-Zamir, S. (2007) 'Professor's Little Helper', *Nature*, 450: 1157–9.

Saltin, B. (2003) Interview, *Jyllands-Posten*, 24 October.

Sansone, D. (1988) *Greek Athletics and the Genesis of Sport*, Berkeley, CA: University of California Press.

Savulescu, J., Foddy, B. and Clayton, M. (2004) 'Why We Should Allow Performance Enhancing Drugs in Sport', *British Journal of Sports Medicine*, 38: 666–70.

Schänzer, W. (2005) 'Doping im Sport'. Online. Available at: http://www.dshs-koeln. de/biochemie/rubriken/07_info/info_02.pdf (accessed 19 August 2006).

Schänzer, W. and Thevis, M. (2007) 'Doping im Sport', *Medizinische Klinik*, 102(8): 631–46.

Schermer, M. (2008) 'On the Argument that Enhancement Is "Cheating"', *Journal of Medical Ethics*, 34: 85–8.

Schneider, A. J. (2006) 'Cultural Nuances: Doping, Cycling and the Tour de France', *Sport in Society*, 9: 212–26.

Simpson, V. and Jennings, A. (1992) *Dishonored Games: Corruption, Money and Greed at the Olympics*, New York: SPI Books.

Skibby, J. (2006) *Skibby:Forstå mig ret, fortalt til Brian Askvig* [Skibby: Don't Get Me Wrong], Copenhagen: Ekstra Bladets Forlag.

Sørensen, R. (2006) Interview, *B.T.*, 9 December.

Spiggs, M. (2005) 'Hypoxic Air Machines: Performance Enhancement Through Effective Training – or Cheating?', *Journal of Medical Ethics*, 31: 112–13.

Tamburrini, C. (2000) 'What's Wrong with Doping?', in T. Tännsjö and C. Tamburrini (eds) *Values in Sport: Elitism, Nationalism, Gender Equality and the Scientific Manufacturing of Winners*, London: Spon Press.

—— (2005) 'Hypoxic Air Machines', *Journal of Medical Ethics*, 31: 114.

Tännsjö, T. (2000) 'Against Sexual Discrimination in Sport', in T. Tännsjö and C. Tamburrini (eds) *Values in Sport: Elitism, Nationalism, Gender Equality and the Scientific Manufacturing of Winners*, London: Spon Press.

The New York Times (1960) 'Olympic Trainer Admits Giving Drug to Danish Cyclist Who Died', 29 August.

—— (2005) 'I.O.C. Stops Fighting Doping Laws in Turin', 29 October.

Tøfting, S. (2005) *No Regrets*, Copenhagen: People's Press.

Tutko, T. S. (1989) 'Personality Change in the American Sport Scene', in J. H. Goldstein (ed.) *Sports, Games, and Play: Social and Psychological Viewpoints*, London: Lawrence Erlbaum Associates.

Umminger, W. (1963) *Supermen, Heroes and Gods: The Story of Sport through the Ages*, London: Thames and Hudson.

VeloNews (2008) 'Puerto Inquiry Dropped, Spanish Papers Report'. Online. Available at: http://velonews.com/print.php?article = 11867 (accessed 26 November 2008).

Verroken, M. (1996) 'Drug Use and Abuse in Sport', in D. R. Mottram (ed.) *Drugs in Sport*, London: E & FN Spon.

Vinnai, G. (1970) *Fußballsport als Ideologie*, Frankfurt a.M.: Europäische Verlagsanstalt.

Vinton, P. (2005) 'Bode Miller's Take on Doping in Alpine Skiing: Legalize It?', *Ski Racing*, 38(2), October.

Voet, W. (2001) *Breaking the Chain: Drugs and Cycling, the True Story*, London: Yellow Jersey Press.

Voy, R. (1991) *Sports, Drugs and Politics*, Champaign, IL: Leisure Press.

Vrijman, E. J. (2006) *Independent Investigation Analysis Samples from the 1999 Tour de France*. Online. Available at: http://www.velonews.com/media/report1999.pdf (accessed 12 May 2007).

WADA (2003) *World Anti-Doping Code*, Montreal: WADA.

—— (2004) Press release, 26 March.

—— (2006) *Minutes of the WADA Executive Committee Meeting 16 September 2006*, Montreal: WADA.

WADA's Ethical Issues Review Panel (2006) 'The Safety & Ethics of Hypoxic Altitude Systems', Online. Available at: http://www.gbshaun.com/altitudeforall//wada_statement.html (accessed 3 March 2007).

Waddington, I. (2000) *Sport, Health, and Drugs: A Critical Sociological Perspective*, London: E & FN Spon.

Weber, M. ([1904–5] 1985) *The Protestant Ethic and the Spirit of Capitalism*, New York: Scribner's Press.

Werge, L. (2006) 'Løgnens mester' [Master of Lies], *Ekstra Bladet*, 1 July.

White, K. (2005) 'Why I Became a Part of the BALCO Affair (+ Questions and Answers)'. Online. Available at: http://www.playthegame.org/Knowledge%20Bank/Articles/Why_I_became_part_of_the_BALCO_affair.aspx (accessed 14 August 2006).

WHO ([1946] 1948) 'Preamble to the Constitution of the World Health Organization as Adopted by the International Health Conference, New York, 19–22 June, 1946'. (Signed on 22 July 1946 by the Representatives of 61 States (Official Records of the World Health Organization, no. 2, p. 100) and Entered into Force on 7 April 1948).

Williams, J. (1999) *Cricket and England: A Cultural and Social History of the Inter-War Years*: London: Frank Cass.

Woodforde, J. (1970) *The Story of the Bicycle*, London: Routledge & Kegan Paul.

Woodland, L. (1980) *Dope: The Use of Drugs in Sport*, London: David and Charles.

—— (2003) *The Crooked Path to Victory: Drugs and Cheating in Professional Bicycle Racing (Cycling Resources)*, San Francisco: Cycle Publishing, copyright Les Woodland.

Zetterberg, H., Hietala, M. A., Wallin, A. and Blennow, K. (2007) 'Guidelines for Brain Concussion in Sports: How Are They to Be Applied in Boxing?' *Lakartidningen*, 104(22): 1715.

Websites

http://www.bikeraceinfo.com/classics/paris-roubaix/pr1896.html (accessed 1 August 2006).

http://www.cyclingnews.com/news.php?id = news/2006/jun06/jun29news (accessed 7 March 2007).

http://www.cyclingnews.com/news.php?id = news/2005/sep05/sep09news3 (accessed 8 January 2007).

http://www.cyclingnews.com/news.php?id = news/2005/sep05/sep16news (accessed 8 January 2007).

http://www.cyclingnews.com/news.php?id = news/2006/jun06/jun03news (accessed 12 January 2007).

http://www.cyclingnews.com/news.php?id = news/2006/jun06/armstrongstatement (accessed 12 January 2007).

http://www.dr.dk/Sporten/Oevrig_sport; (accessed 17 January 2006).

http://www.guardian.co.uk/uk/2006/nov/23/foodanddrink (accessed 20 August 2008).

http://www.ifoce.com/home.php (accessed 20 August 2008).

http://216.46.1.34/wada/wada_ang.mpg. (accessed 6 January 2007)

Index

adrenalin 42
Aimar, Lucien 43
alcohol 32
Allison, Lincoln 73, 74
amateurism 93, 104–5
Amaury Sport Organisation (ASO) 81
American Cycling Association 102
American Medical Association 36
Amineptine 46
amphetamines 36–37, 43, 99
anabolic steroids 116–17, 133
anaerobic oxygen depletion 74
anaesthetic, local 99
analogues 78
Andersen, Olav Skaaning 49–50, 52, 64–65
Anderson-Schiess, Gabriela 9
anger 27
anorexia 10
Anquetil, Jacques 42, 111
Anti-Doping Denmark 66, 82
Armstrong, Lance 71, 84–85
Association of Summer Olympic
  International Federations 88
Astana team 66
Astana/Würth 81
asthma 7, 148 n
athletes: attitudes to doping 128–32;
  deification of 105; legal position of
  83–84; mistrusted by WADA 134;
  pleasure as motivation 20; pressure to
  perform 125–26; right to self-
  determination 9, 111, 115, 138;
  salaries 19–20; trust in WADA 89;
  views on doping tests 132–35
athlete's passport 134–35, 136–37
Ayotte, Christiane 87, 88

Bangsborg, Vagn 38, 41
Barthes, Roland 27

Basso, Ivan 65–66, 80–81
Battiston, Patrick 150 n
Baunsøe, Niels 38, 41–42
Beamish, Rob 120–22
Betablockers 1
Blanchard, K. 149 n
blood doping 79–80, 81, 82, 116, 123–24
body-building 116–17
Body Mass Index 148 n
body, the: culture of 94; and health 28–30; mechanistic view of 98–99, 101–2;
  view of, in Middle Ages 29, 30; will
  to power 28, 30
Bøgeskov, Lars 38, 40–41
Bordeaux–Paris cycle race 96, 97
boxing 8, 9, 22, 27, 33, 94, 95
Bradman, Donald 149 n
British Association of Sports Medicine 5
British Athletic Federation 71
Brochard, Laurent 45
Brohm, Jean-Marie 18, 19–20, 102
Bubka, Sergej 75
Buffet, Marie-George 19
bullying 150 n
Burke, Edmund R. 102

caffeine 6, 46, 99, 124, 138
Caillois, Roger 148 n
Calvin, Jean 103
Calvinism 103
canal swimmers 32
capitalism 93, 103–4
Casoni, Ilario 50
CERA 151 n
chloroform 36
cholesterol 78, 84
Christianity: nurture of weakness 26–28

Christiansen, Ask Vest 92, 124–27, 128
Christie, Linford 70–71
cocaine 32, 36, 98
Cofidis team 53
Comorra 142
competition 15; equality 107
Conconi, Francesco 121, 123
conscience, bad 30
contact lenses 113
Conte, Victor 127–28, 138
cortisone 46, 150 n
Coubertin, Pierre de 13, 17, 20, 28–29
Council of Europe: definition of doping 5
Court of Arbitration for Sport (CAS)
    81, 83, 87
creatine 6, 109
cycle races 96–98
cycling 32, 35–36, 37, 111; Derailleur
    gears 105; doping controls 42;
    freewheeling hub 105; origins of 95–
    97; stars as exploited workers 19; and
    weakness 27

Dæhlie, Bjørn 109
Damoxenos, the boxer 33
Damsgaard, Rasmus 66
Danilova, Olga 152 n
Denmark Cycling Union (DCU) 60
Desgranges, Henri 105
dispensation 7
DNA sampling 1
doctors: registration of 143
domestiques 45, 150 n
Donahoe, Tom 37
Donati, Alessandro 123–24, 140–42
dop 32
doping: arguments for limiting 108–15;
    athletes attitudes to 128–32; ban as
    paternalistic 118–22; blood doping
    79–80, 81, 82, 116, 123–24;
    criminalisation of 76; deregulation of
    64, 89, 106, 115–18, 128, 139, 142; as
    destructive 91; detection 142;
    detrimental effects of 116; and drug
    addiction 18; enforced medication
    101; as evil 105; incitements to 124–
    27; linked to narcotics trade 140–42;
    tolerance towards 134; users seen as
    corrupt 126–27; WADA definition of
    4–5, 6, 11, 78, 107, 108, 130
doping controls: cycling 42; faith in 70–
    72; inadequate 75–76
doping list 116, 131–32, 133, 134, 138;
    criteria 11–12, 84, 130

doping tests 37, 79, 89, 138, 142;
    Anquetil 111; athletes views on 132–
    35; equality in 133; ethics of 84–89;
    integrity of 85; IOC 42; retrospective
    testing 135; urine testing 85–89, 117
Dressel, Birgit 91, 104
drips, intravenous 59, 63, 66, 107, 116,
    138
Dubin, Charles 5, 6

eardrops 133
East Germany: sports system 120–22
endurance sports 10
energy bars 4
Enlightenment 93, 100, 101, 111; and
    freedom ideal 102; humanism 106, 111
envy 28
ephedrine 8, 133, 134
equality 130; in competition 107; in
    testing 133
erythropoietin (EPO) 6, 8, 11, 43–44,
    47, 50, 51–52, 53, 55, 56, 61, 66, 74–
    75, 84, 92, 99, 113, 127, 129, 133, 137;
    CERA 151 n; inactive marker 142; a
    natural substance 130–31; NESP 152
    n; theft of 141–42; urine test for 117;
    WADA testing for 71–72
ether 32
Evald, Jens 83–84; 'The Press and
    Doping' 82
exercise 15

fair play 14, 18, 25, 107
fatigue 99
Fédération Internationale de Football
    Association (FIFA) 72
Ferrari Institute 50
Festina scandal 43–44, 45, 49, 51–52,
    60–61
financial motivation 16–17, 55, 90–92,
    92–93, 104, 138
Fischer, Josef 97–98
Fjeldgaard, F. 68
football 25, 36, 112
Fotheringham, William 54–56
foul play 14, 22, 25
freedom 102
Fuentes, Eufemiano 57, 65, 78, 80, 81,
    83, 137, 144

Galen 33–34
General Association of Summer
    Olympic Federation 87
Gewiss-Ballan team 50

ginseng 124
Giro d'Italia 43, 47–48, 80
gladiators 32
Glucksmann, André 28
Goksøyr, Matti 109–10
governments 75, 76
Gray, John 106
greed 27
Greeks, ancient 32, 33
grey area products 109–10, 129–30, 131
Griffith-Joyner, Florence 71
growth hormones 46, 142
guilt, feelings of 128

haematocrit values 43, 60, 113; limits
    to 44–45, 47, 50; Riis 64–65, 66;
    testing 9
Hamburger, Bo 45
Hayes, John 35
health 47, 63–64; argument in doping
    89, 107, 116, 138; and the body 28–
    30; doping as damaging to 8
health checks 8
health risks 7–8, 20, 149 n
hero–villain template 52–56
Hicks, Thomas 35
hierarchy in sport 15, 25, 28, 30, 90
high altitude training 129, 131
Hippocrates 33–34
Hoberman, John 91–92, 104, 149 n
Holm, Brian 10, 67–68, 139–40
Houlihan, B. 5; Jensen case 37–38, 38
humanism 106, 111
Huret, Constant 96–97
hypobaric chambers 6, 107–8, 109, 113,
    114, 116, 129, 130–31, 151 n
hypoxic devices *see* hypobaric chambers

immune system 91
interiorization 30
International Association of Athletics
    Federations (IAAF) 71
International Cycling Union (UCI) 8,
    72, 81, 84, 88, 96
International Federation of Competitive
    Eating (I.F.O.C.E.) 149 n
International Narcotics Board 141
International Olympic Committee
    (IOC) 7, 37, 72, 73, 76, 77, 120, 140;
    Athletes Commission 87, 88; doping
    tests 42; misconduct of officials 89
Interpol 140, 142
intervention 138
Italian Olympic Committee 121

Jack & Jones 65
Jaksche, Jörg 57
Jardine, Douglas 149 n
Jensen, Knud Enemark 37–42, 48
Jensen, Preben Z. 39, 41
Johnson, Ben 5, 17, 70, 73
Johnson, Neil 37
Jørgensen, Jørgen B. 38, 41
Jorgensen, Oluf 39
jousting 32
Jung, Niels Christian 49–50, 52, 64

Kant, Immanuel 111
Kemp, Michael 95
Kimmage, Paul 67; *Rough Ride* 57, 69
Klümper, Armin 91
knights 32
Kohl, Bernhard 151 n
Korchemny, Remi 127
Kreugas, the boxer 33

*Laboratoire Nationale de Dépistage du
    Dopage* (LNDD) 86–87, 89
Landis, Floyd 79–80
laser treatment 113
law of silence 57–59, 67, 68
Leblanc, Jean-Marie 51
Lewis, Carl 70
Liberty Seguros/Würth 81
Linton, Arthur 34–35, 36, 48
Ljungquist, Arne 73
Loland, Sigmund 110–11, 111–12, 113–15
long-distance running 35
Longmore, A. 53
Lundby, C. 117
lust 27
Luther, Martin 103

Marxism 18, 26, 92–93
McEnroe, John 94
medicine: attitudes to 36; enforced
    medication 101; registration of 142;
    scepticism towards 99; and trace
    substances 143; work of the devil 105
Meier, Armin 62
Messi, Lionel 112
Mikkelsen, Brian 87, 88
Millar, David 53–56, 56–57, 76, 126
Millar, Stephen G. 33
Miller, Bode 74–75, 138
Mills, George Pilkington 1, 96
mimetics 78
minerals 59, 63, 66, 107, 116
modafinil 127

modernity 29, 93–94, 100–101, 111
Monarch bicycles 99
moral standards 72, 73, 89, 132
Mottram, David R.: *Drugs in Sport* 38
Mount Ventoux 27
Mühlegg, Johan 152 n

Nandrolone 70, 71
nanny state 102
naturalness 109–10
Nebiolo, Primo 123
Nemean Games 33
NESP 152 n
nicotine acid 38
Nietzsche, F. 30; *The Twilight of the Idols
of Anti-Christ* 26–27
noradrenalin 42

Olympic committees 143–44
Olympic Games 15; 1908 13; 1996 109;
ancient 32; linked to World
Exhibition 94; London (1908) 35; Los
Angeles (1932) 36; motto 94, 105;
Rome (1960) 37; spirit of 108; St
Louis (1904) 35
Operación Puerto 65–66, 79, 81, 143
opposition: core element in sport 15–16
oxygen, pure 32, 36, 116

pacemakers 96, 97
Paris–Brest cycle race 96
Pausania 33
Pedersen, Bente Klarlund 79–80
Pedersen, Peder 60
Pélissier, Francis 36
Pélissier, Henri 36
penalties 1, 82–83, 133–34, 136, 137
performance enhancement: non-doping
methods 11; *see also* doping
pie eating 148 n
Pietri, Dorando 35
plasma expander 152 n
Play the Game 52, 127, 136
Porritt, Arthur 5
Pound, Dick 37, 48, 70, 72, 74, 76, 84,
85–89
predestination 103
pride 27–28
Pro-Tour Teams 81; Code of Ethics
145–47; ethical code of conduct
82–84
professionalism: emergence of 93–94
Protestantism 106; the 'calling' 103–4;
doping as evil 105

Rabobank 84
Radcliffe, Paula 134–35
Rasmussen, Michael 84
records 97–98, 105
recreation 148 n; sport as 15, 70
research 85, 116–17
Ricco, Ricardo 151 n
Richie, Ian 120–22
Riis, Bjarne 10, 44, 45, 50, 52, 60–65;
heamatocrit values 64–65, 66; as
sports director 65–67
rituals 25
Rodal, Vebjørn 109
Rogge, Jacques 87
Romantic movement 94
Ronaldo, Cristiano 112
Roniacol 39, 41–42
Rouen–Paris cycle race 96
Rousseau, Jean-Jacques 94, 110
Roussel, Bruno 51
rugby 20
Ryckaert, Eric 51

Saiz, Manolo 81
Saltin, Bengt 77–78
salts 63, 66, 107, 116
Saunier Duval-Prodir team 56
Schneider, Angela 150 n
Schumacher, Stefan 151 n
Schumacher, Tony 150 n
science: as progress 121–22
sedatives 99
self-administration 125
self-sacrifice 15–16, 30–31
Sevilla, Oscar 66
Simoni, Gilberto 80–81
Simpson, Tom 42, 43
Skibby, Jesper 45–47, 49, 58–60, 63, 64,
67–68
skiers 19–20
skiing 74, 114; waxing skis 109–10;
World Cup cross country 152 n
slimming pills 133
social class 93
soigneurs 17, 149 n
Sørensen, Rolf 45, 67–68
spectacles 113
speed 97–98
spirit of sport 107, 108
Spitz, Mark 18
sport: aristocratic nature of 28–29;
capitalist societies 93; character-
building 17–18, 20–21, 93, 105, 148 n;
definition of 14–17; democratic

approach 28; developmental
tendencies of 18–19; as evil 24–26; and
general society 22–24, 31; hierarchy of
15, 25, 28, 30, 90; ideals of 129; image
of 76–77; and industrial revolution 94;
inequality of 29; Marxist critique of
18, 92–93; a narcotic 18; opposition as
core element 15–16; pedagogical
function 13, 18, 21, 24–25; as
recreation 15, 70; spirit of 6, 12, 13–14,
107, 108; stage-managed 93; as
unnatural 109–10; as work 18, 149 n
sporting behaviour 20–21, 25–26
sportspersons: deadly sins 27–28; as
helpless victims 19
squash 24, 36
Starhemberg, Graf Wilhelm 98
Stéphane 97, 98
steroids 1, 73, 78, 120, 141
stimulants 1
strychnine 32, 35, 36, 98
sugar 59, 63, 107, 116
superficial treatments 9
support systems 112
surgery: replacement 101
surveillance 75, 102, 135, 138, 142
Svatkovsky, Dmitry 31
swimming 36

Talbot, Bishop 13
talent, natural 108, 110–11, 111–13
Tamburrini, Claudio 116–18, 117, 121;
on doping ban 118–19
Tavshedens Pris (The Price of Silence) 49–
51, 52, 64
Team CSC 65
technology: abuse of 121
Telekom team 51–52, 65–66, 67
tennis 94, 95
testosterone 4, 79, 107, 113, 117
tetrahydrogestrinone (THG) 77–78, 84,
127
thalidomide 105
Therapeutic Use Exemption (TUE) 7
throwing disciplines 23
Tissié, Philippe 97, 98, 149 n
Torres, Fernando 112
Tour de France 17, 27, 59, 105, 150 n;
1923 36; 1998 13, 19, 43, 60, 76; 2006
79; 2008 151 n; code of conduct 81–
82; *see also* Festina scandal
Tour of Denmark: 1995 50, 52
transfusion technique *see* blood doping
transplantations 101

Tutko, Thomas S. 149 n

Ugens Profil (Profile of the Week) 66
Ullrich, Jan 66, 80, 151 n
Umminger, Walter: *Supermen, Heroes
and Gods* 99
Union Cycliste Internationale (UCI) 8,
72, 81, 84, 88, 96
United States Anti-Doping Agency 77
United States Department of State 141
United States Drug Enforcement
Administration 140
United States Olympic Committee
(USOC) 70
urine testing 85–89, 117, 136, 142

Verbruggen, Hein 86
Verroken, Michele 38
Vienna–Berlin cycle race 98
Vinokourov, Alexander 66, 80, 81–82
Vinton, P. 74
violence 22–24, 150 n
Virenque, Richard 51
vitamins 11, 59, 99, 107, 109, 124, 128, 130
Voet, Willy 43–44, 45, 51
Voy, Robert 32, 35, 38
Vrijman, Emile J. 86–87, 88

Waddington, Ivan 43, 49, 117
Walsh, David 52–53
Warburton, 'Choppy' 34
weak, the 26–28
Weber, Max: *The Protestant Ethic and
the Spirit of Capitalism* 103–6
Weckamin 99
weight reduction 10, 61, 109
Wesley, John 104
whereabouts rules 84, 89, 143
White, Kelli 127–28, 136, 137–38
Wiberg, Pernilla 75
will to power 28, 30
will to purity: and will to win 1–2
will to suffer 23
will to win 16–17, 28, 44, 47, 57, 90, 90–
92; and evil 25; and will to purity 1–2
Williams, J. 149 n
Wimbledon 94
Winter Olympics: Grenoble (1968) 37;
Salt Lake City (2004) 152 n; Turin
(2006) 76, 84
women 29
Woodland, Les 34–35, 36–37
World Anti-Doping Agency (WADA)
7, 64, 76, 82, 84, 120, 132, 135, 142;

athletes trust in 89; Code of Ethics
75, 77; Congress 2006 6; definition of
doping 4–5, 6, 11, 78, 107, 108, 130;
doctors certified by 143;
establishment of 72–75, 76; Ethical
Issues Review Panel 6, 108; ethics 84–
89; mistrust of athletes 134; spirit of
sport 13–14; testing for EPO 71–72;
and weight reduction 10

World Health Organisation (WHO) 5,
141, 142
worldwide doping control system 134–
35, 143

youth, culture of 30

Zatopek, Emil 18
Zülle, Alex 57, 62